Exceptional Me

Exceptional Me

*How Donald Trump Exploited the
Discourse of American Exceptionalism*

Jason Gilmore and Charles Rowling

I.B.TAURIS

LONDON • NEW YORK • OXFORD • NEW DELHI • SYDNEY

I.B. TAURIS
Bloomsbury Publishing Plc
50 Bedford Square, London, WC1B 3DP, UK
1385 Broadway, New York, NY 10018, USA
29 Earlsfort Terrace, Dublin 2, Ireland

BLOOMSBURY, I.B. TAURIS, and the I.B. Tauris logo
are trademarks of Bloomsbury Publishing Plc

First published in Great Britain 2021

Cover design by Alice Marwick
Cover image: © Bloomberg/Getty Images

A catalogue record for this book is available from the British Library.

A catalog record for this book is available from the Library of Congress.

ISBN:	HB:	978-0-7556-2695-3
	PB:	978-0-7556-2694-6
	ePDF:	978-0-7556-2697-7
	eBook:	978-0-7556-2696-0

Typeset by Integra Software Services Pvt. Ltd
Printed and bound in Great Britain

To find out more about our authors and books visit www.bloomsbury.com
and sign up for our newsletters

Contents

List of Figures

Acknowledgments

Completing a book like this is an endeavor that requires effort and sacrifice from more than just the authors who write it. We can say without any doubt that we would not have been able to research and write this book without all of the incredible support that we received from so many different sources all along the way.

To David Domke, you have been a guiding light for both of us over the years and we want to thank you sincerely for coaching us through more than just the writing of this book. You have been so incredibly generous to us with your time, your counsel, and your inspiration. We share with you some of the best memories of our lives: from crazy road trips and powering through our dissertations to floating face-up under the stars in the Gulf of Mexico and so many more memorable moments. You continue to inspire us in so many different ways.

We also want to thank our incredibly supportive colleagues at Utah State University (USU) and the University of Nebraska at Kearney (UNK) for all of their encouragement and guidance through this process. To Brad Hall, Jen Peeples, Matt Sanders, and John Seiter at USU and William Aviles, Joan Blauwkamp, Diane Duffin, Peter Longo, Claude Louishomme, and Satoshi Machida at UNK, we thank you for all of your generous support. Each of you provided a different north star to us at critical times as we navigated the sometimes-tumultuous waters of researching and writing this book. We would also like to thank Nicole Allen and Jason Edwards for their work on a related project which helped us to further hone and shape the ideas presented in this book.

To our research assistants Tomoya Averett, Ryan Ball, Donnie Corwin, and Garrett Rasband, thank you for all the hard work you put into collecting speeches, tweets, academic works, and news articles. Your willingness to match our level of dedication and intensity during this process made our lives easier as we were plowing ahead with the manuscript. Your efforts were invaluable to this project. We cannot thank you enough.

We would also like to thank the team at I.B.Tauris/Bloosmbury for all of their hard work and support on this book. A special thanks to Tomasz Hoskins for helping us to see the larger significance of this work and to Viswasirasini

Govindarajan, Giles Herman, and Nayiri Kendir for guiding us through the publication process. It has been a true pleasure working with you all.

Jason Gilmore

I regularly reflect on the fact that my cup is overflowing with amazing people who boost me up and cheer me on. And sure enough, there they were, ready to have my back yet again as I embarked on this crazy project. To my mom and my brother Roger, you have been my biggest cheerleaders for so long. I love you both so much. To my good friend Robert Drucker, there is no way I can thank you enough for everything you have done for me. You are a true friend. To Dan Sterns and Justin Clark, thank you for talking through the ideas with me and for your feedback along the way. Thanks also to François Dengah and Joshua Thoms for prying me away for some much-needed reprieves during the most intense writing moments. Finally, to Chuck, I would not have wanted to write this without you. I count it as one of the blessings of my life that I get to work with you, my friend.

And most importantly, to my lovely wife, Zaira, you are the bedrock of all of my efforts. Your endless belief in me and patience have made all of this possible. You should also know that the most important lesson I learned from this process, I learned from you: sometimes it's just plumb necessary to put down the damned horcrux *y disfrutar de la pinche vida*. I love you so, so much. Finally, to my little Sprout, I love you more than I knew I was capable of loving. This is all for you.

Charles Rowling

This experience would not have been possible without the love and support I have received over the years from my family and friends. To my mom and dad, you encouraged, facilitated, and supported such a positive and intellectually stimulating environment for me throughout my upbringing. Surrounded by books and meaningful conversations about history, politics, and the world, which continue to this day, you not only shaped what career I wanted to pursue, but also the kind of person I wanted to be. I am so lucky to have you as my parents. I love you. To Jim Scott, who saw promise in me as an undergraduate student and has provided invaluable guidance, encouragement, and support for me over the years. I am so grateful for your mentorship and our friendship. Lastly, to Jason, your vision for this project and passion to see it through were simply incredible. Thank you for allowing me to come along for the ride. I truly cherish our friendship and what we have accomplished together.

To my wife and best friend, Jennifer, upon whom I rely for so much support and advice on just about everything. You understood the demands of this project from the outset and provided me with the patience and encouragement that I so needed. I could not have written this without your love and support. Love you, babe. And to my wonderful kids, Evelyn, Charlie, and Sam, it is the absolute best thing in the world to be your dad. You inspire me every day and I love you so much.

Introduction: The Exceptional Me Strategy

In late April of 2015, not long before officially declaring his candidacy for president, Donald Trump attended a Texas Patriots PAC—a local Tea Party group—event titled "Celebrating the American Dream" to talk about his vision for the future of the country. The moderator asked Trump to discuss an idea that had been at the forefront of conservative thought in America for a long time: "Define American exceptionalism. Does American exceptionalism still exist? And what can we do to grow American exceptionalism?" Such a line of questioning should have come as no surprise. Republicans had long claimed to be the true guardians of American exceptionalism in American politics, often portraying Democrats as nonbelievers or even apologists for American influence and power in the world.[1] This was perhaps most evident during the presidency of Barack Obama, when Republicans relentlessly challenged Obama's belief in American exceptionalism (as well as his citizenship and patriotism).[2] In turn, as Republicans prepared to take the presidency in 2016, their official party platform clearly and unequivocally embraced American exceptionalism. Indeed, the first sentence of the platform preamble read: "We believe in American exceptionalism [full stop]." It then emphasized that the Republican Party "embraces American exceptionalism and rejects false prophets of decline and diminution."[3]

It was, therefore, likely surprising to many conservatives at the Texas Patriot PAC and around the country when Trump responded to these questions by dismissing American exceptionalism, stating bluntly: "I don't like the term. I'll be honest with you... I never liked the term." Trump argued that American exceptionalism is a fleeting concept, given that the United States was losing out to its global competitors at an alarming rate. He noted, for example, "Germany is eating our lunch. So they say, 'Why are you exceptional? We're doing a lot better than you.'" To Trump, America is only exceptional when it is winning on the global stage, which, in his view, it clearly was not. For too long, he argued, America has sacrificed its interests and well-being for the benefit of others, allowing other nations to take advantage of the United States and weaken it in the process. Within this context, Trump then quickly pivoted, stating: "*I'd* like to make us exceptional."[4]

Just under two months later, on June 16, 2015, Trump descended the escalator at Trump Tower to officially announce his candidacy for the presidency. Neil Young's *Keep on Rockin' in the Free World* blared on the loud speakers to welcome him on stage. He joined his daughter Ivanka, who had introduced him just moments before. Perhaps not surprisingly—in retrospect at least—Trump began by acknowledging his crowd size: "Wow. Whoa. That is some group of people. Thousands... This is beyond anybody's expectations. *There's been no crowd like this.*" After lobbing some attacks on his competitors, talking about how their candidacy announcements paled in comparison to his, Trump got down to business: "Our country is in serious trouble. We don't have victories anymore. We used to have victories, but we don't have them." The United States, according to Trump, was losing to everyone. China? "They kill us." Japan? "They beat us all the time." Mexico? "They're laughing at us, at our stupidity. And now they are beating us economically. They are not our friend, believe me. But they're killing us economically." He noted: "The U.S. has become a dumping ground for everybody else's problems" and is "becoming a Third-World country." In his vision, the United States was in ruins, other countries were taking advantage of it, and, most importantly, the United States was no longer Number 1 in anything. These proclamations of peril and doom rang louder still considering the fact that in the entire speech Donald Trump had not made a single reference to American exceptionalism—a stalwart in any traditional candidate's campaign launch speech. There simply was no space for it. The country, according to Trump, was no longer the beacon of hope so many had talked about. It was not an example for the world to emulate. And it was not leading the world in any respect. Put succinctly in his aptly titled campaign book, *Crippled America: How to Make America Great Again*: "The idea of American Greatness, of our country as the leader of the free and unfree world, has vanished."[5] American exceptionalism was no longer, and the United States of America, in Trump's view, had become a laughing stock.

Trump then pivoted to address the cause of these problems. In his classic combative style, he pulled no punches and placed blame at the feet of politicians in Washington. Unlike the majority of his predecessors, Trump did not focus his attacks solely on his opponents—the Obama administration and the Democratic Party. He saw no problem, in fact, with spreading the blame around and taking aim directly at Republicans as well. Sure, Obama and the Democrats shouldered part of the blame, but Republicans were just as guilty. Trump targeted the George W. Bush administration, for example, for the disastrous policies that led to the Iraq War. The problem, therefore, wasn't a single party. It was the whole Washington establishment, Republicans and Democrats alike. Being politicians was what made them the culprits. He went on: "Well, you need somebody, because politicians are all talk, no action. Nothing's gonna get done. They will not bring us—believe me—to the promised land. They will not... They will never make America great again. They don't even have a chance." Attacking both parties was a sly tactic, as it set up Trump's next move. If politicians were the problem, then it was incumbent upon the American people to elect someone who wasn't a politician. They needed to elect someone different. And Trump was different.

In her introduction, Ivanka Trump had already set up Trump's punchline. "Most people strive their entire lives to achieve great success in a single field," she said, "My father has succeeded in many at the highest level and on a global scale. He's enjoyed success in a vast diversity of industries because the common denominator is *him*." Trump echoed these sentiments. According to the newly announced candidate, he was unique because he was not a politician. And even though the country was no longer exceptional, Trump painted a grand picture of himself as being exceptional, which was why he argued that he alone could solve the problems of Washington and make the country "great again." Everything Trump touched, according to him, was exceptional. He talked about his golf courses as being "the *best courses* in the world." Again, on the crowd gathered at the event, he offered: "There's been *no crowd like this*." On the wall he proposed to construct on the US-Mexico border: "*nobody builds walls better than me*, believe me." On ISIS: "*Nobody would be tougher on ISIS* than Donald Trump." On rebuilding the country's infrastructure: "*Nobody can do that like me*. Believe me." In fact, if it had anything to do with Trump, it was exceptional: "I know *the smartest negotiators in the world*." To drive it all home, Trump stated: "I will be *the greatest jobs president* God ever created. I tell you that."[6] The picture was clear. The United States of America was no longer exceptional. In fact, it was in ruins and no longer Number 1 in any sense. But there was one person, and one person alone, who could restore American exceptionalism.

The proclamations about the "crippled" state of the United States, coupled with Trump's self-promoted "exceptional" ability to address the problems facing it, were the seedlings of what would become Trump's rhetorical strategy for his 2016 bid for the presidency, one loosely based in the language of the historic concept of American exceptionalism but spruced up with Trump's signature self-focused branding and promotion techniques. These tactics were the beginnings of what we call Donald Trump's *exceptional me strategy*, and it is the focus of this book. We will detail how Trump's exceptional me strategy has developed and evolved over two stages of his political life: (1) the 2016 "Make America Great Again" presidential campaign and (2) the Trump presidency.

The exceptional me strategy, version 1.0, details Trump's strategic communications during the 2016 presidential campaign, and it has four parts. The first part of the campaign version of Trump's exceptional me strategy was to actively downplay and generally avoid the idea that the country was exceptional. Where other candidates tend to wax philosophical about the exceptional qualities inherent in the nation as a way of inspiring the American people to envision a better America, especially in the general election campaign, Donald Trump all but avoided the concept in his campaign speeches. His strategy was to promise an American exceptionalism in the future, one that he would bring to fruition once he was in office. It would defeat his purposes, therefore, to make the case for an America that was already exceptional. This was a clear departure from how presidential candidates traditionally crafted their campaign messaging.

The second part of the strategy was directly related to the purposes of the first. Specifically, Trump actively and overtly disparaged American exceptionalism, strategically painting a picture of an America that was explicitly *unexceptional* in comparison with the rest of the world. Not only was the United States no longer exceptional, according to Trump, it was losing to everyone and routinely coming in last place. This was a pivotal piece of Trump's strategy, as it allowed him to make the argument that the country needed someone different to restore American exceptionalism. This laid the foundation for the third step in this strategy, which was to actively place blame for America's decline not only on the party in power but on his own party as well. Again, instead of focusing all of his criticism on his Democratic rivals, Trump openly and willingly took on his own Republican Party, often putting the party's standard bearers—George W. Bush, John McCain, Mitt Romney, among others—in his crosshairs. In Trump's vision, politicians from both parties were to blame for America's decline. America, therefore, needed someone unique, someone who was, in a word, exceptional.

The final part of the exceptional me strategy version 1.0 was a new one to presidential campaigns. After making the case that American exceptionalism was in shambles and placing blame for this condition on Washington politicians of both parties, Trump then sought to portray himself as the lone antidote to this mess. This was embedded in his "Make America Great Again" slogan, which many read to mean "Make America *Exceptional* Again." Instead of relying on his party's platform, however, to make the case for how the country could restore American exceptionalism, Trump offered himself as the one, uniquely qualified person in all of politics to bring America back, again contrasting himself to a field of not only Democratic presidents but Republicans ones as well. This was perhaps best illustrated in his acceptance speech at the 2016 Republican National Convention when he said: *"Nobody knows the system like me,* which is why *I alone can fix it."*[7] Throughout the 2016 Make America Great Again campaign, Trump made one thing perfectly clear: if anything was exceptional, it was Trump.

Once in the presidency, the exceptional me strategy needed to be updated. An incumbent president could not continue to sidestep American exceptionalism while actively disparaging the nation as Trump had done during the campaign and expect to have any chance at reelection. He was finally in the driver's seat, and at least some of the buck was going to have to stop at his desk, whether he liked it or not. Trump's inaugural address was the perfect opportunity to start morphing the exceptional me strategy from a campaign strategy to a presidential one. The speech carried some of the same campaign tropes. For instance, Trump gave little attention to celebrating American exceptionalism but spoke more directly about the decrepit state of the country and how it had fallen from its exceptional standing. He placed blame at the feet of politicians on both sides of the isle: "For too long, a small group in our nation's Capital has reaped the rewards of government while the people have borne the cost… the establishment protected itself, but not the citizens of our country." He then pivoted. In a move that seemed to signal a symbolic shift, Trump offered: "But that is the past. And now we are looking only to the future." According to Trump, "January 20th, 2017, will be remembered as the day the people became the rulers of this nation again." He then promised, "America will start winning again, winning like never before."[8] In short, a Trump presidency would be like none other, and the people of the United States would be the beneficiaries. The exceptional me strategy version 2.0 was starting to take hold.

By June 18, 2019, Trump had made the full transition to the updated version of the exceptional me strategy as he announced his 2020 candidacy before a crowd in Orlando, Florida. In Vice President Mike Pence's introduction, the message was clear: "[Trump] said we'd make America great again, and that is exactly what we've done in just two-and-a-half short years." Trump then picked up where Pence had left off, fully embracing American exceptionalism, but with one caveat—his administration was the reason for its return:

> Our economy is the envy of the world. Perhaps the greatest economy we've had in the history of our country. And, as long as you keep this team in place, we've a tremendous way to go. Our future has never ever looked brighter or sharper. The fact is, the American dream is back, it's bigger and better and stronger than ever before.

Put simply, America was exceptional again and clearly his administration was to thank for it. Trump then shifted to make his case for his reelection in 2020, describing the exceptional qualities of his presidency:

> We accomplished more than any other President has in the first two and a half years of a presidency and under circumstances that no President has had to deal with before, because we did in the middle of a great and illegal witch-hunt, things that nobody has been able to accomplish. Not even close. Nobody's done what we've done in two and a half years. We went through the greatest witch-hunt in political history.

Indeed, what he was trying to make clear here was that "your favorite President, Donald Trump,"[9] was above and beyond any president before him. He alone had restored American exceptionalism, and the only way to maintain it was to elect him again. This was at the core of his new campaign slogan, "Keep America Great."[10]

This version of the exceptional me strategy evolved from its campaign version to fit the narrative of a sitting president who has to prove in deeds that he can deliver while in office, not just talk about promises of greatness. Version 2.0 of the exceptional me strategy has five parts. Because Trump was now responsible for the country, the first step was to make the gradual case that the United States was yet again becoming exceptional. Whereas other presidents had come into office trumpeting American exceptionalism to garner national unity and excitement around their presidencies, Trump strategically waited to make the case for American exceptionalism. This was perhaps best reflected in this statement during the first year of his presidency: "We're now in the process of rebuilding America, and there's a new optimism sweeping across our country like people have not seen."[11] Nonetheless, Trump offered minimal support for the idea of American exceptionalism early on. Indeed, the time was not quite ripe for American exceptionalism. The "American carnage," as he put it, was still raw.[12] The country was still in the unexceptional state that his predecessors—both Democrat and Republican—had left for him. "I inherited a mess" was his excuse.[13] Again, Trump waited. He needed to have some policy wins and signs of some observable change in the country itself. Only then did he begin to paint a picture of a new and emerging American exceptionalism. As this strategy played out, and Trump began to the make the case for American exceptionalism, his references to American *un*exceptionalism decreased precipitously.

The second part of this strategy is born out of the first. As Trump began to paint an emerging picture of American exceptionalism, he actively made sure to include language directly crediting himself and his administration for its emergence. In this way, Trump defined American exceptionalism not as something inherent in the nation itself but as something that can be gained or lost, something that Trump alone was able to restore. In other words, unlike other presidents who understood American exceptionalism to be something outside of themselves, something embedded in the character of the nation and its people, Trump saw it as being directly tied to his unique abilities and accomplishments while in office. He needed to make sure the American public knew who to thank for making America exceptional again.

The third step was to portray both himself as president and his presidency as exceptional, respectively. This tactic is similar to the one used in his campaign, as he continued to laud himself as exceptional. Trump expanded this technique as he made the case that his time in office was *the* exceptional presidency. In this light, everything about Trump's presidency was exceptional. His election was "the *greatest defeat* in the modern history of American politics."[14] His policies were "historic" and greater than anything the country had ever seen. Even when it came to negatives and critiques, they were exceptional because they were related to Trump. The Mueller investigation was part of "the *greatest witch hunt* in political history,"[15] and on the subject of impeachment, he said: "you can't impeach somebody for doing *the best job of any president, in the history of our country.*"[16] Overall, this was the rhetorical tactic that Trump favored most during his presidency, much more so than proclaiming American exceptionalism. In essence, no one outshines Trump, not even the United States of America.

The fourth step was to make the argument that America was exceptional only because Trump was president and that reelecting him was the only way the American people could "Keep America Great," or, in other words, "Keep America Exceptional." An important part of this tactic was to warn the American people that although American exceptionalism had been restored, its sustainability hung by a thread. From this perspective, the only way to maintain American exceptionalism and the country's renewed greatness was to keep Donald J. Trump in the presidency. Trump routinely warned that if he were not reelected, the country would fall apart, the stock market would crash, and the swamp would fill back up. This allowed Trump to, yet again, make the case that he, and he alone, was the master of American exceptionalism.

The final step in the 2.0 version of the exceptional me strategy was to equate himself and his political base as being the true representative of the country as a whole. We refer to this as Trump's "*Me* the People" tactic. Trump employed this populist tactic in three central ways. First, Trump went to great lengths to make the argument that he was the one true embodiment of the American people. Put simply in that same 2020 campaign announcement speech, Trump offered: "Together, we stared down a corrupt and broken political establishment and we restored government of, by, and for the people." Trump was, in effect, saying that his will was the same as the will of the entire American people, while overtly disregarding the fact that there were more Americans who opposed his presidency than those who supported it. Second, Trump regularly cast his supporters as being the "true" Americans and "real" American patriots. They were loyal to him and he was loyal right back. Time and again, when Trump referred to "the American people," it was clear he was speaking to them directly. Finally, Trump portrayed his critics—from Democrats and journalists to Never-Trumpers—as being "the enemies of the people" who were trying to subvert American democracy by challenging his power. As Trump saw it, anyone who dared criticize him was, in fact, criticizing the country itself, as well as the American people. For Trump, he and the nation were one and the same.

This book focuses on detailing the various facets of this unique rhetorical approach to American exceptionalism. In order to better understand the origins of American exceptionalism as a rhetorical tactic, we begin by setting the stage with a discussion of the historical foundations of this idea and how it has evolved into a point of immense partisan contention in the modern political era. Then, to achieve a robust understanding of the exceptional me strategy, we conduct a thorough analysis of Trump's campaign and presidential communications since before he announced his candidacy for the presidency in 2015. We keep a keen eye focused on the political contexts within which his exceptional me strategy has been employed to provide a more complete understanding of why it has been successful within such a large swath of the American public. To illustrate how Trump deviated from his predecessors, we also provide comparative evidence on how other presidential candidates and presidents traditionally employed the language of American exceptionalism in their public communications. We then document the life of the exceptional me strategy in the American body politic since Trump took office. Specifically, we examine how conservative voices in Congress and in right-leaning news organizations actively amplified his strategy and how Democrats sought to counter it—perhaps best encapsulated in Bernie Sanders' slogan, "Not Me. Us."[17] We then discuss the unique characteristics of this rhetorical strategy and the potential implications it will have on the future of American politics, the presidency, and American exceptionalism itself. Finally, in the epilogue, we reflect on the implications of the exceptional me strategy in light of the COVID-19 pandemic, the protests in response to the killing of George Floyd and others, and the 2020 presidential election.

Throughout the ensuing chapters we will detail the development and relative success of the exceptional me strategy in Trump's political life. Overall, one thing will become clear from our analysis: Donald J. Trump is fundamentally unlike any of his political contemporaries when it comes to communicating American exceptionalism. Whereas traditional politicians on both sides of the political divide have tended to celebrate the various tenets of American exceptionalism in a multifaceted fashion—the country's unique and exemplar institutions and democracy, its people who many presidents categorized as "the hardest working people on earth,"[18] its shining example for the rest of the world to follow, its superiority of ideas and ideals, its status as the leader of the free world and beyond—Trump took a fundamentally different path. In Trump's vision, the country's ideals, institutions, and people are not what make America exceptional. According to Donald Trump, Donald Trump, and Donald Trump alone, is what makes America exceptional. This is the crux of the exceptional me strategy.

American Exceptionalism and Presidential Discourse: A Framework

Today, by the grace of God, we stand a free and prosperous nation with greater possibilities for the future than any people ever had before in the history of the world.

—Harry Truman[1]

In modern American politics, there are few concepts more stirring and so capable of inspiring large swaths of the American people as the idea of American exceptionalism. This notion that the United States of America is an exceptional nation, one that was placed on earth to guide the world out of darkness and one that is so distinct from any other country in human history that it should stand as the gold standard for the rest of the world to emulate, is an idea that predates the birth of the United States as a nation. From the beginning, this idea served to build national cohesion and social order among Americans, and, for many around the world, it meant that the United States was a beacon of hope and a nation that all others should aspire to be like. Indeed, as Deborah Madsen has suggested, those who left Great Britain did so with hopes of building a "redeemer nation" on the American continent, one that would "save the rest of the world from itself."[2] Puritan settlers further believed that because they had established a society that shed the perceived structural flaws of the European styles of government and society, it would stand as a model for the rest of the world to follow. This idea was captured in the widely cited words of John Winthrop, then governor of the Massachusetts Bay Colony, who told his followers, "For we must consider that we shall be as a City upon a hill. The eyes of all people are upon us."[3] These early settlers were likely unaware of the life that this idea would take on in America after their passing. American exceptionalism was only just beginning to gain steam. Over time, it would become deeply embedded in the American psyche.

It should come as no surprise, then, that politicians have long celebrated American exceptionalism in their communications to the American people. Indeed, as the nation was being established, the Founding Fathers seemed to inherently understand the power that weaving a narrative about America's special, exemplary, or even God-favored status could have on instilling a sense of unity and cohesion throughout the country during its early years. This was perhaps most evident in Thomas Jefferson's first inaugural address, during which he proclaimed that America was the "world's best hope."[4] Invocations of American exceptionalism since that time have been omnipresent in American politics, wielded by politicians, journalists, and community leaders from all walks of life to convey a sense of greatness and hope, adventure and individual opportunity, and, most of all, an unwavering, even divine, national spirit.[5] Retelling, over and over, the mythical story of American exceptionalism has become a prominent and essential feature in American political discourse, often employed to appeal to voters,[6] to garner public support for policies,[7] and to inspire foreign populations to follow the United States' lead on any given issue.[8]

The idea has been so pervasive in American politics that scholars, pundits, and politicians alike have routinely sought to assess the validity of American exceptionalism, wondering aloud whether this idea is verifiable in some measurable way.[9] Some argue that there are some distinguishable characteristics that make the United States exceptional, such as its unique system of government,[10] its unprecedented political power,[11] its dominant economic influence,[12] and its far-reaching international cultural impact.[13] According to former vice president, Dick Cheney, and his daughter, Liz Cheney, there is no doubt:

> Yes, we are exceptional… We have guaranteed freedom, security, and peace for a larger share of humanity than has any other nation in all of history. There is no other like us. There never has been. We are, as a matter of empirical fact and undeniable history, the greatest force for good the world has ever known.[14]

Others have taken a more nuanced position on the subject, suggesting that the United States is exceptional, but in both positive and negative ways.[15] Still others have questioned whether the country is actually different—in any meaningful way—from other nations.[16] More recently, some have gone as far as to argue that the "American Century"[17] has passed and that the rise of other powers in the world—China, for example—has contributed to what political scientist and CNN analyst Fareed Zakaria has deemed "The Post-American World."[18] The true power of American exceptionalism, however, is found outside of these debates. What these arguments do not fully account for is that it matters little whether the facts empirically prove the United States to be exceptional or not—the idea of American exceptionalism resonates among the American public nonetheless.[19] To them, the United States is exceptional not because it can be proven by some test or systematic comparison but because large swaths of the American people believe it to be true. This makes American exceptionalism a particularly potent rhetorical tool for politicians when speaking to the American people.[20] Politicians ignore this reality at their own peril.

The power and importance of this idea among Americans run deep and transcend ideological perspectives. For example, the Gallup polling firm found that a full 80 percent of U.S. adults agreed with the statement that the United States "has a unique character that makes it the greatest country in the world." Furthermore, believing in America's unique grandeur was tied to international attitudes. Specifically, 66 percent said that because of its exceptional status, the United States has "a special responsibility to be the leading nation in world affairs."[21] Similarly, the Public Religion Research Institute found strong support for a religion-based form of exceptionalism: almost 60 percent of Americans agreed with the statement "God has granted America a special role in human history."[22] More recently, a 2017 poll by Rasmussen found that 69 percent of likely voters believe that the "United States is more exceptional than other nations."[23] In short, the idea of American exceptionalism is widely held among large portions of the American public. This sentiment is perhaps captured best in Stephen Colbert's 2011 book *America Again: Re-Becoming the Greatness We Never Weren't* when he said, "America is the greatest, freest, bestest nation that God ever gave man on the face of this earth."[24]

Presidents have historically been seen by the American public as the foremost champions of American exceptionalism and, therefore, those who should most adamantly defend it on behalf of the American people.[25] This idea—that the United States is a singular, superior, or even God-favored nation—is one that US presidents have long depended on to garner national support for policies, to unify the nation, and to forge its dominant path in global affairs. Scholars suggest that US presidents are highly strategic when and how they communicate powerful ideas like American exceptionalism.[26] For instance, presidents tend to invoke this idea in major addresses to the nation when they are attempting to rally the American people around a specific cause or issue.[27] Furthermore, research has shown that presidents tend to invoke American exceptionalism more frequently and prominently in times of national uncertainty—war and economic recession.[28] This occurs as presidents seek to reassure the American public and instill confidence that the nation will overcome its hardship. Presidents, therefore, tend to be quite creative when they speak of American exceptionalism, celebrating everything from its unique institutions and "hardest working" people, to its symbolic status as global leader and a beacon of hope for the rest of the world. As a result, many Americans have come to expect—even demand—that presidents not only invoke this idea but fully embrace and celebrate it in their public communications. Indeed, it is often seen as a measure of their patriotism.[29] The story of American exceptionalism in modern presidential politics, however, is one that has evolved over time and in relation to the changing world order. While all US presidents have put forth their own vision of American exceptionalism, their purposes and reasons have changed.

American Exceptionalism Catches Fire

On September 1, 1945, the nation gathered around their radios to hear President Harry Truman report on the events at Tokyo Bay, where the United States was securing the surrender of the Japanese government, which served as the official end to the Second World War. President Truman's speech to the nation sought to put the country on a new footing, one that would help the country move forward from the turmoil of the Second World War and reaffirm its renewed consecration "to the principles which have made us the *strongest nation on earth.*" He emphasized: "This is a victory of more than arms alone. This is a victory of liberty over tyranny." He went on: "It was the spirit of liberty which gave us our armed strength and which made our men invincible in battle. We now know that that spirit of liberty, the freedom of the individual, and the personal dignity of man, are *the strongest* and *toughest* and *most enduring* forces in all the world."[30] America's position in the world had fundamentally changed and Truman was eager to announce it to the world. America, in his mind, had finally proven itself to be truly exceptional.

The end of the Second World War instigated a marked change in how presidents talked about American exceptionalism. Before the Second World War, presidents primarily understood and spoke about American exceptionalism in two principle ways. First, the United States was portrayed as a *singular* nation in that its form of government was unique or fundamentally different from that of any other nation on earth. Second, the United States was characterized as a beacon of hope for the rest of the world, serving as a *model* for others to emulate. Such sentiment, for example, was evident in the words of Abraham Lincoln; that is, the United States was the "last best hope of earth."[31] Franklin Roosevelt too echoed this idea: "The Almighty God has blessed our land in many ways. He has given our people stout hearts and strong arms with which to strike mighty blows for freedom and truth. He has given to our country a faith which has become the hope of all peoples in an anguished world."[32] Nonetheless, with regard to on-the-ground proof of America's exceptional status in world affairs, the proverbial rubber had not quite met the road. Before the Second World War, the United States did, indeed, stand as a symbol of something different in the world, but it was not yet tested or proven. As a result, presidents tended to quietly speak of it. That, of course, would change.

American exceptionalism caught fire within the American imagination after the end of the Second World War. By not only emerging from the Second World War victorious but also less decimated by the war than the other world powers, the United States had begun to solidify its "exceptional" status on the world stage.[33] And there was now reason to believe that this had happened not by chance, but because of the unique principles and hope that America represented. US presidents, after the war, quickly expanded their rhetorical repertoire when talking about American exceptionalism. As before, they saw the country as unique and as a beacon of hope and inspiration for the rest of the world, but now presidents could speak confidently about the country's relative global *superiority* and about how—because of its exceptionalism—it should stand as the world's political and moral *leader*.[34] And within this context, American exceptionalism was becoming firmly entrenched within the collective consciousness of the American people.

America's case for exceptional status, however, still had one competitor— the Soviet Union. And so, throughout the Cold War, it was incumbent upon US presidents to make repeated arguments about the legitimacy of American exceptionalism as a way of further differentiating the United States from its global rival. As the two countries battled for the hearts and minds of people throughout the world, US presidents leaned heavily on the appeal of American exceptionalism. In the words of John F. Kennedy:

> [P]eople everywhere, in spite of occasional disappointments, look to us—not to our wealth or power, but to the splendor of our ideals. For our Nation is commissioned by history to be either an observer of freedom's failure or the cause of its success. Our overriding obligation in the months ahead is to fulfill the world's hopes by fulfilling our own faith.[35]

Richard Nixon took this idea a step further:

> Two hundred years ago this nation was weak and poor. But even then, America
> was the hope of millions in the world. Today we have become the strongest
> and richest nation in the world. And the wheel of destiny has turned so that
> any hope the world has for the survival of peace and freedom will be determined
> by whether the American people have the moral stamina and the courage to
> meet the challenge of free world leadership. Let historians not record that when
> America was the most powerful nation in the world we passed on the other
> side of the road and allowed the last hopes for peace and freedom of millions of
> people to be suffocated by the forces of totalitarianism.[36]

For Ronald Reagan—a self-proclaimed champion of American exceptionalism—
there was, without a doubt, something unique about the United States that set
it apart from the Soviet Union. Notably, Reagan consistently referred to the
country as the "shining city on a hill," emphasizing time and again that the
United States—due to its unwavering commitment to freedom and dignity—
would outlast the Soviet threat. Indeed, in his first inaugural speech, Reagan was
uncompromising:

> If we look to the answer as to why for so many years we achieved so much,
> prospered as no other people on earth, it was because here in this land we
> unleashed the energy and individual genius of man to a greater extent than has
> ever been done before. Freedom and the dignity of the individual have been
> more available and assured here than in any other place on earth. The price for
> this freedom at times has been high, but we have never been unwilling to pay
> that price.[37]

US presidents, therefore, had something to prove about American
exceptionalism during the Cold War. For them and for their American
audience, the United States was not only special but its history, principles, and
contributions to the rest of the world were undeniably superior to those of the
Soviet Union.

With the fall of the Soviet Union and the end of the Cold War, a new age of
American exceptionalism had emerged. Notably, the country's newfound status
as the world's sole superpower meant to many that American exceptionalism had
finally been fully confirmed. The United States now stood atop the existing world
order, prompting conservative journalist and pundit Charles Krauthammer
to call it America's "unipolar moment."[38] Similarly, neoconservative scholar
Francis Fukuyama called it "The End of History,"[39] proclaiming that American
democracy had, as expected, triumphed over all other forms of government.

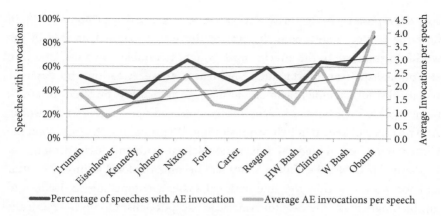

Figure 1.1 Invocations of American exceptionalism in major speeches to the nation by US presidents, September 1, 1945, to January 19, 2017.[43]

US presidents throughout this time period were consistently strong champions of American exceptionalism (see Figure 1.1), but once the Cold War ended, they further honed their definition of American exceptionalism and then turned up the volume.[40] It was Democratic president Bill Clinton who probably best summarized the post–Cold War vision for American exceptionalism in a campaign speech on foreign policy in 1996:

> The fact is America remains *the indispensable nation*. There are times when America and only America can make a difference between war and peace, between freedom and repression, between hope and fear. Of course, we can't take on all the world's burden. We cannot become its policemen. But where our interests and values demand it and where we can make a difference, America must act and lead.[41]

It was a political winner for Clinton, who again called the United States "the world's indispensable nation" in his acceptance speech at the 1996 Democratic Convention in Chicago and employed the phrase over twenty more times during in his second term in office. It was even echoed by Clinton's secretary of state, Madeline Albright, who stated, "[w]e are the indispensable nation. We stand tall and we see further than other countries into the future."[42] To refer to the United States not only as unique but indispensable was succinct and powerful, and it set the stage for how other post–Cold War presidents would talk about America's role as the world's sole superpower.

The presidency of George W. Bush, however, was characterized by a different world order. Although the United States continued to be the world's sole superpower, the terrorist attacks on 9/11 created a profound shift in how the United States—and the rest of the world—viewed its role in the world. In response to the attacks, Bush sought to double down on American exceptionalism in an effort to lift up and reassure a weary nation. One day after the attacks, for example, Bush emphasized: "America was targeted for attack because we're the brightest beacon for freedom and opportunity in the world. And no one will keep that light from shining."[44] Throughout the Cold War, the United States had shared the international stage with the Soviet Union, but in a unipolar world, the United States had become the focal point—for better and for worse—within the international system, compelling its leaders to unflinchingly make the case for American exceptionalism to both Americans and to the rest of the world.[45]

Without question, the idea of American exceptionalism in American politics reached its historic peak under the presidency of Barack Obama.[46] It was a natural fit for a president who had essentially launched his national political career on a platform of American exceptionalism. During his national debut as the keynote speaker at the 2004 Democratic National Convention in Boston, Obama offered: "I stand here knowing that my story is part of larger American story, that I owe a debt to all of those who came before me, and that, in no other country on earth is my story even possible."[47] As president, Obama made his embrace of American exceptionalism unmistakable, going so far as to even say: "I believe in American exceptionalism with every fiber of my being."[48] Obama also distinguished himself from his predecessors by being the first president to ever explicitly utter the term "American exceptionalism" in a speech. As Figure 1.1 illustrates, Obama invoked the idea of American exceptionalism in more speeches and significantly more often than any of his predecessors in both the post–Second World War and post–Cold War eras. What was clear by the end of the Obama presidency was that American exceptionalism had taken center stage in American politics. As these examples illustrate, presidents, regardless of political party, have tended to employ a multidimensional rhetorical approach to American exceptionalism as a rallying cry for a US-led world order, as a way to inspire and reassure a weary public in response to threats faced during the Cold War and post–9/11 eras, and as a way to win over the support of the American people. American exceptionalism, therefore, was historically employed by politicians of both parties to unite people, not divide them. This, however, would profoundly change. Some were beginning to recognize its potential as a political weapon.

Patriotism as a Bludgeon

On January 11, 1989, as President Ronald Reagan prepared to hand over the government to his successor, George H.W. Bush, he sat down before the nation to deliver a sentimental farewell address. The speech exuded American exceptionalism as Reagan reflected on one of his favorite themes, America's status as a "shining city upon a hill." He said:

> I've spoken of the shining city all my political life, but I don't know if I ever quite communicated what I saw when I said it. But in my mind it was a tall, proud city built on rocks stronger than oceans, windswept, God-blessed, and teeming with people of all kinds living in harmony and peace; a city with free ports that hummed with commerce and creativity. And if there had to be city walls, the walls had doors and the doors were open to anyone with the will and the heart to get here. That's how I saw it, and see it still.

To Reagan, a belief in American exceptionalism was fundamental to the American experience and to making sure the country keeps moving in the right direction. Reagan then pivoted to what he called "the great tradition of warnings in presidential farewells." He started by saying that he was proud of the "resurgence of national pride" that he claimed happened as a result of his presidency, calling it "the new patriotism." But, he warned, many Americans are straying from the unrestrained belief in American exceptionalism that was common in his upbringing. He warned that those people "aren't sure that an unambivalent appreciation of America is the right thing to teach modern children. And as for those who create the popular culture, well-grounded patriotism is no longer the style."[49] These warnings reflected a growing sentiment on the political right. Patriotism and American exceptionalism had lost steam in American culture because of the turmoil and dissension of the 1960s and 1970s, and Republicans saw it as their party's charge to bring it back.[50] At the same time, there were those on the right who saw their counterparts on the left as having all but abandoned patriotism and a belief in American exceptionalism. According to many Republicans, Democrats spent too much time protesting and challenging the country, and not enough time praising it unabashedly. This, they were beginning to realize, could be very useful when wielded as a political bludgeon.

Not five months before Reagan's farewell speech, Vice President Bush's presidential campaign had already begun wielding patriotism as a political weapon. Specifically, the Bush campaign sought to characterize their

Democratic opponent, Michael Dukakis, as insufficiently patriotic and, therefore, weak on foreign policy. In effect, the strategy was based on the notion that a president—or political party—who does not adequately embrace or exhibit patriotism could not be expected to effectively promote or advance America's interests abroad. In particular, the campaign alleged that Dukakis did not fully support the Pledge of Allegiance, referring to a bill he vetoed when governor of Massachusetts. Bush even included this accusation in his acceptance speech at the Republican National Convention: "[S]hould public school teachers be required to lead our children in the Pledge of Allegiance? My opponent says no, and I say yes."[51] Bush then accentuated this critique by leading the entire New Orleans convention hall in the Pledge of Allegiance to cap off his address. On September 21, 1988, *The Christian Science Monitor* chimed in with the following description: "George Bush is wrapping himself in the American flag, and Michael Dukakis is seeing red. The Stars and Stripes, long a popular political backdrop, now has become the most potent and emotional symbol of the 1988 campaign."[52] Although Bush denied the strategy, saying, "I'm not questioning his patriotism,"[53] the underlining message was clear: the Republican standard bearer was laying partisan claim to patriotism. Even Reagan's Education Secretary, William Bennett, said Dukakis had "disdain for the simple and basic patriotism of most Americans."[54] In response to these attacks, Dukakis orchestrated a now infamous photo-op with him riding around in an M1 Abrams tank in an attempt to prove his patriotic chops and his toughness on foreign policy. The stunt was an attempt at grand political theater, but it backfired. Most saw it as a gimmicky. Almost everyone saw it as contrived. The Bush campaign saw it as opportunity. Immediately after the stunt, they released attack ads using the footage to show just how inauthentic and artificial Dukakis' claims to patriotism really were.

Four years later, Bush was back with more. This time, his focus was on his new challenger, Bill Clinton, the folksy governor from the state of Arkansas. Throughout the campaign, the Bush camp repeatedly shone a spotlight on Bill Clinton's vacation to Moscow in 1969 and his opposition to the Vietnam War as signs of Clinton's weak sense of patriotism and disloyalty to the country. Again, Bush did not outright claim that Clinton did not love his country, but the challenges were palpable enough to elicit a strong response from Bill Clinton early in the campaign. At the first presidential debate on October 11, 1992, in St. Louis Missouri, Clinton, never breaking eye contact, addressed Bush directly:

> [W]hen Joe McCarthy went around this country attacking people's patriotism,
> he was wrong. He was wrong. And a Senator from Connecticut stood up to

him, named Prescott Bush. Your father was right to stand up to Joe McCarthy. You were wrong to attack my patriotism. I was opposed to the war, but I love my country. [Turning to the camera] And we need a President who will bring this country together, not divide it. We've had enough division. I want to lead a unified country.[55]

The audience erupted with applause. Unlike Dukakis, Clinton made it clear that questioning his patriotism was a nonstarter. He was willing to hit back. Clinton ultimately emerged the victor of the overall exchange, winning the presidency by a landslide. But the door remained open, and Republicans began to look for new ways to paint themselves as the party of patriotism and portray their counterparts as patriotic naysayers. Indeed, Republican Speaker of the House Newt Gingrich was so confident about his party's advantage that he once jokingly commented, "it is time to stop challenging or seeming to challenge the patriotism of Democrats and liberals. Enough historical evidence exists"[56] to support the notion. Republicans in Washington sensed a weakness in their Democratic counterparts, a weakness that could be wielded for political advantage. And so, Republicans have brought the issue front and center, time and again.

On September 2, 2003, Massachusetts Senator and Vietnam Veteran John Kerry strategically and symbolically chose Patriot's Point, South Carolina to announce his candidacy for the presidency. Standing in front of a backdrop of the aircraft carrier U.S.S. Yorktown, Kerry leaned heavily on his patriotism and service to the country. Kerry began by reflecting on his service both during and after the Vietnam war:

[W]hen we came home, we had a simple saying: Every day is extra. I used my extra days to join other veterans to end a war I believed was wrong. I saw courage both in the Vietnam War and in the struggle to stop it. I learned that patriotism includes protest, not just military service. But you don't have to go half way around the world or march on Washington to learn about bravery or love of country. Again and again, in the causes that define our nation, we have seen the uncommon courage that is common to the American people.[57]

Given that George W. Bush had, according to the *New York Times*, "steeped himself in the imagery and oratory of patriotism, military service and national strength"[58] in the aftermath of the 9/11 terrorist attacks, it only made sense that the Democratic Party would seek out a candidate who it could legitimately characterize as a symbol of patriotism and strength. John Kerry was just that symbol. Kerry's history as a decorated Vietnam veteran who had dedicated his professional life to public service had placed him in the top tier of candidates as soon as he announced his intention to run for the presidency. After a surprise win in the Iowa caucuses, he took a lead he would not relinquish, winning the nomination handily, dominating in all but five contests and effectively wrapping up his nomination by Super Tuesday on March 2, 2004. Who better to challenge George W. Bush in the post–9/11 era—conventional wisdom suggested—than a decorated Vietnam War veteran who had served his country on more than just the battlefield? Former Clinton aid and Democratic activist Sydney Blumenthal was so confident about Kerry's patriotic armor that he penned an op-ed for the *Guardian* titled, "Kerry will win the patriot game."[59] Surely, Kerry could withstand any potential challenges to his patriotism from a president who had avoided seeing the battlefield in Vietnam by volunteering for the Air National Guard. Would the Republicans even dare?

What came next would go down as one of the most unexpected and effective attacks on a presidential candidate in modern history. And it came on all fronts. The Republican Party and its surrogates employed a three-pronged strategy to chip away at Kerry's seemingly impenetrable patriotic armor. First, taking a page from his father's presidential campaign strategies from over a decade earlier, the George W. Bush campaign engaged in a whisper campaign, spreading false rumors and innuendo about Kerry's lack of patriotism while denying any responsibility for having spread the rumors. As Bush spokesman, Steve Schmidt, stated in an interview with the *Washington Post*: "Nobody has ever questioned his patriotism. What's in question is John Kerry's judgment."[60] In response, Kerry sought to reframe the issue: "[W]e know that they [Republicans] don't own the flag: they don't own patriotism; they don't own strength. All of these values belong to all of America."[61] Second, the conservative media directly sought out storylines that would question Kerry's patriotism and loyalty to the nation. For instance, in an interview with Sean Hannity on his radio show, then Fox News host Oliver North stated: "John Kerry's whole history is one of anti-American positions." He then admitted to challenging his patriotism: "I will do that. I've done that."[62] Several Fox News hosts also rolled out a campaign in which they questioned Kerry's loyalty to the nation, often posing the question of whether he was more French than American.[63]

The fatal blow for Kerry, however, was landed when the Swift Boat Veterans for Truth, a 527 political advocacy group, attacked Kerry's Vietnam War record. The campaign included a multifaceted ad blitz of television commercials featuring Vietnam War veterans—few who had actually served with Kerry—accusing him of exaggerating his war record, disrespecting the country, and dishonoring his fellow veterans. In one of the ads, veterans spoke to the camera questioning the merits of Kerry's Bronze Star and Purple Hearts. Another ad claimed that Kerry had "renounced his country's symbols" by throwing his military medals and ribbons over the fence at the Capitol building in Washington, D.C., in protest of what he saw as an unjust war. A final ad featured snippets of John Kerry's testimony before the Senate Foreign Relations Committee on April 22, 1971, in which he criticized the Vietnam War and gave an account of some of the atrocities committed by other American soldiers during the war. In the ad, one veteran addresses Kerry directly: "How could you accuse us of being war criminals?"[64] Even former Republican presidential nominee and fellow veteran Bob Dole weighed in on the debate on CNN's *Late Edition*, saying:

> One day he's saying that we were shooting civilians, cutting off their ears, cutting off their heads, throwing away his medals or his ribbons. The next day he's standing there, "I want to be president because I'm a Vietnam veteran." Maybe he should apologize to all the other 2.5 million veterans who served. He wasn't the only one in Vietnam.[65]

Throughout this episode, the Bush campaign remained on the sidelines, only officially condemning the group or their misleading attacks after the damage was done. In response, Kerry went on the offensive, questioning the draft records of top Bush officials. At a rally at the University of Pittsburgh, for example, Kerry stated:

> I'm tired of these Republicans who spend so much time denigrating Democrats and other people's commitment to the defense of our nation. I'm tired of Karl Rove and Dick Cheney and a bunch of people who went out of their way to avoid their chance to serve when they had the chance. I went [to Vietnam]. I'm not going to listen to them talk to me about patriotism and how asking questions about the direction of our country somehow challenges patriotism. Because asking questions about the direction of our country is patriotism.[66]

It was too little, too late. The Republican Party, conservative media, and various surrogates had effectively sowed seeds of doubt about Kerry's patriotism in the minds of much of the American electorate. In the aftermath of the 2004 election, scholars, journalists, and pundits pointed to Kerry's lackluster defense of his military record as what sank his campaign. According to Newsweek, "The Kerry high command failed to see the potential for damage [of the Swift Boat Veterans attack] until it was too late."[67] In the end, the damage was done. The Democratic war hero had been dressed down, and many Americans had fully embraced the narrative that Kerry was unpatriotic and un-American. This was a watershed moment. It signaled to future

Democratic presidential candidates that they would no doubt need to defuse these attacks and, in effect, work hard to "prove" their patriotism if they were to ever win the presidency.

Scholars suggest that Democrats have such a hard time proving their patriotism because it is an issue that the Republican Party has worked diligently to "own" in the minds of the American public.[68] Americans, therefore, tend to think of the Republican Party as being more patriotic in general than their Democratic counterparts.[69] This means that Republican candidates often benefit from citizens almost instinctively or reflexively assuming them to be patriotic, regardless of whether they emphasize patriotism or not in their communications. In other words, they do not need to prove their patriotism because people already believe it to be the case. The opposite, however, is true of Democrats. Regardless of how much they talk about their own patriotism, they still fight an uphill battle to "prove" it to the American public.[70] The American people have come to expect their politicians, especially those seeking the presidency, to be full-throated champions of patriotism and American exceptionalism. It follows that being perceived as the party that is weak on patriotism—or love of their country—is a serious deficit to overcome.

Public opinion polling since the Reagan era seems to support this notion that the Republican Party has become the party of patriotism. The Roper Center for Public Opinion Research at Cornell University has collected public opinion polling data on perceptions of partisan patriotism over the past four decades. Notably, the data support the notion that Republicans tend to "own" patriotism within the minds of the American public. Two national polls conducted in 2001 and 2010, for example, focused on determining which party Americans perceived to be more "patriotic." In both polls, respondents viewed the Republican Party as substantially more patriotic (41 percent and 43 percent, respectively) than the Democratic Party (24 percent and 29 percent, respectively). In addition, polls asking more specific questions about the perceived patriotism of presidential candidates have shown similar results. In fact, since 1984, Americans have consistently expressed the view that Republican presidential candidates are more patriotic than their Democratic opponents: Ronald Reagan (87 percent) versus Walter Mondale (81 percent), George H.W. Bush (68 percent) versus Michael Dukakis (55 percent), Bob Dole (38 percent) versus Bill Clinton (18 percent), and George W. Bush (49 percent) versus John Kerry (34 percent).[71] What has become increasingly clear: in the modern political era, when it comes to patriotism and the belief in American exceptionalism, Democrats work at a deficit and Republicans often get a pass.

American Exceptionalism Weaponized

The 2008 presidential election brought an unprecedented wave of challenges to patriotism against the Democratic Party. Democratic hopeful, Senator Barack Obama from Illinois, had already undergone challenges to his religion in his 2004 bid for the Senate, as conservative personalities had sought to portray him as a secret Muslim, which doubled as a way of suggesting that he was not American enough. Those attacks remained in the presidential campaign cycle, but the effects were compounded by the fact that a journalist had noticed in 2007 that Obama was not wearing an American flag lapel pin. Conservative media seized upon it, calling into question Obama's patriotism. Soon after that, conservative media sites began circulating the rumor that Obama was actually born in Kenya, a fact that if true would disqualify him from the presidency. Although the rumor was false, it began to gain traction among conservative pundits. On June 9, 2008, only two days after Hillary Clinton had conceded the Democratic primary to Obama, the conservative website *The National Review Online* called for Obama to release his birth certificate. Obama obliged just three days after.[72] He then scheduled a speech for June 30th in Independence, Missouri, to speak directly on the subject of patriotism:

> [I]t is worth considering the meaning of patriotism because the question of who is—or is not—a patriot all too often poisons our political debates, in ways that divide us rather than bringing us together. I have come to know this from my own experience on the campaign trail. Throughout my life, I have always taken my deep and abiding love for this country as a given. It was how I was raised; it is what propelled me into public service; it is why I am running for President. And yet, at certain times over the last sixteen months, I have found, for the first time, my patriotism challenged – at times as a result of my own carelessness, more often as a result of the desire by some to score political points and raise fears about who I am and what I stand for. So let me say this at outset of my remarks. I will never question the patriotism of others in this campaign. And I will not stand idly by when I hear others question mine.

The crowd erupted in applause. Not only would Obama not concede patriotism to the other party, he sought to redefine it as the territory of no party. He went on:

> None of us expects that arguments about patriotism will, or should, vanish entirely; after all, when we argue about patriotism, we are arguing about who we are as a country, and more importantly, who we should be. But surely we can agree that no party or political philosophy has a monopoly on patriotism.[73]

The public, however, was unmoved. Just 15 days after the speech, a *CBS News/New York Times* poll found that the American public continued to see patriotism as in the wheelhouse of the Republicans, with 73 percent saying that they believed John McCain was "very patriotic," whereas only 37 percent thought the same of Obama.[74] Throughout the general campaign, however, Obama's Republican challenger John McCain stayed mostly above the fray, never challenging Obama's patriotism directly. In fact, he famously came to Obama's defense during town hall forum in Lakeville, Minnesota, on October 11, 2008. One voter expressed that he was "scared" of Obama, to which McCain responded: "I have to tell you, he is a decent person, and a person who you do not have to be scared of as president of the United States. Now look, if I didn't think that I'd be one heck of a lot better president, I wouldn't be running. And that's the point." He was met with jeers and shouts from the crowd that Obama was a "liar" and a "terrorist." Later McCain extended a microphone to a woman who said, "I can't trust Obama. I have read about him, and he's not, um, he's an Arab." McCain immediately grabbed the microphone and stated, "No ma'am. No ma'am. He's a decent family man, a citizen that I just happen to have disagreements with on fundamental issues and that's what this campaign is about." This time, the crowd gave a mix of cheers and applause. One thing was clear: McCain was not going to resort to the same tricks that many in his party had employed before him. "I want to fight, and I will fight," he said, "But I will be respectful. I admire Senator Obama and his accomplishments, and I will respect him."[75] Ultimately, John McCain lost the election for far more reasons than not going for the jugular by attacking Obama's patriotism. McCain's principled approach, however, was not well received within much of the Republican base. Indeed, the campaign unearthed the reality that there was a growing swath of Republicans who were more energized by the more aggressive populist and demagogic campaigning of his vice presidential pick, Sarah Palin, than McCain's classic, "man of integrity" approach.

Soon after President Obama took office, the attacks escalated. The catalyst came on April 4, 2009, when Obama was addressing a NATO summit in Strasbourg, France. British journalist Edward Luce from the *Financial Times* asked Obama, "Could I ask you whether you subscribe, as many of your predecessors have, to the school of American exceptionalism, that sees America as uniquely qualified to lead the world?" Obama, sensing the international audience around him, struck a diplomatic tone, saying:

I believe in American exceptionalism, just as I suspect that the Brits believe in British exceptionalism and the Greeks believe in Greek exceptionalism. I am enormously proud of my country and its role and history in the world. If you think about the site of this summit and what it means, I don't think America should be embarrassed to see evidence of the sacrifices of our troops, the enormous amount of resources that were put into Europe postwar, and our leadership in crafting an alliance that ultimately led to the unification of Europe. We should take great pride in that.[76]

The critiques from the right were fierce and immediate. Sean Hannity suggested that Obama had "marginalized his own country by saying our sense of exceptionalism is no different than that of the British and the Greeks."[77] James Kirchick, former assistant editor of *The New Republic*, called Obama a "Squanderer in Chief" and offered a full rebuttal to Obama's statement:

This is impossible. If all countries are "exceptional," then none are, and to claim otherwise robs the word, and the idea of American exceptionalism, of any meaning. Besides, American exceptionalism is demonstrable—Cuban journalists, Chinese political dissidents, Eastern Europeans once again living in the shadow of a belligerent Russia and, yes, even some Brits and Greeks look toward the U.S. and nowhere else to defend freedom.[78]

In his book *A Nation Like No Other: Why American Exceptionalism Matters*, Newt Gingrich echoed these sentiments: "[I]t is worthwhile to consider the perspective of the larger group of people who have forgotten or just don't really understand what American exceptionalism actually means. President Obama, for example, simply does not understand this concept."[79]

What opponents on the right conveniently overlooked was that Obama immediately followed up his comments with:

And if you think of our current situation, the United States remains the largest economy in the world. We have unmatched military capability. And I think that we have a core set of values that are enshrined in our Constitution, in our body of law, in our democratic practices, in our belief in free speech and equality that, though imperfect, are exceptional.

Regardless, the Republicans no doubt saw an opportunity. Not only could they continue to claim ownership of patriotism, they could now lay claim to patriotism's highest form—the belief in American exceptionalism. And just a year and a half after that ill-fated comment, Gallup found that many Americans had become skeptical of Obama's belief in American exceptionalism. Specifically, the poll found that 37 percent of those surveyed doubted that President Obama "believes the U.S. had a unique character that makes it the greatest country in the world."[80] And even though the sentiment likely cut along partisan lines, it revealed a rift that could be exploited.

Around the same time as the Gallup poll, celebrity billionaire Donald J. Trump was starting to explore the possibility of challenging Obama in the 2012 presidential election. At the time, he launched the website ShouldTrumpRun.com to gauge public interest in his potential candidacy. Three months later, in an effort to bring attention to his potential presidential run, Trump decided to make a splash on the national scene by reviving an old attack on Obama. Appearing on a string of television shows between March 23 and April 7 of 2011, Trump went on the offensive, making an array of unfounded claims that Obama was trying to conceal something on his birth certificate. On one occasion, he stated: "I'm starting to wonder myself whether or not he was born in this country." The attacks included suggestions that the birth certificate Obama released in 2008 was a fake, that he was born in Kenya, and that he was a secret Muslim. Put succinctly, "Why doesn't he show his birth certificate? There's something on that birth certificate that he doesn't like."[81] As sinister as it may have been, it was effective political theater. It tapped into the underlying sentiment on the right that Obama was not nearly American enough, if American at all. Obama answered by releasing his long form birth certificate a few weeks later. He then addressed Trump's claims during his White House Correspondents Dinner speech—with Trump sitting in the crowd:

> [N]o one is happier, no one is prouder to put this birth certificate matter to rest than the Donald. And that's because he can get back to focusing on the issues that really matter, like, did we fake the moon landing? What really happened in Roswell? And, where are Biggie and Tupac?[82]

Trump's tactic, however, was at least somewhat effective. In fact, a *USA Today/ Gallup* poll conducted after the allegations found that 24 percent of Americans surveyed indicated that they believe Obama was either "definitely" or "probably" not born in America. Another 18 percent expressed that they believed that he was only "probably" born in the country.[83] In the end, while Obama's release of the long form birth certificate, as well as his public mocking of the allegations, may have quieted these attacks for the moment, for Trump, it was a political winner. And so, he would revive these same attacks time and again throughout the Obama presidency.

By the time the 2012 campaign came around, many Republicans were no longer constrained by the coy tactics of the past when challenging the patriotism of Democratic presidential candidates. The proverbial gloves had come off. Republicans took the issue head-on and they were working at an advantage. According to a 2011 *Fox News* poll, former Massachusetts governor Mitt Romney, who would become the Republican presidential nominee, was viewed as significantly more "patriotic" among Americans compared to Obama. Specifically, 75 percent of registered voters believed Romney to be "patriotic," whereas only 60 percent saw the same in Obama.[84] Upon launching his candidacy in Stratham, New Hampshire, Romney was quick to the attack. Perhaps sensing an opening, he fully embraced American exceptionalism, proclaiming that the United States is "richest, greatest country on earth" and emphasizing how the United States had always been a beacon of hope for the rest of the world. He went on:

> I believe in that America. I know you believe in that America. It is an America of freedom and opportunity. A nation where innovation and hard work propel the most powerful economy in the world. A land that is secured by the greatest military the world has ever seen, and by friends and allies across the globe. President Obama sees a different America and has taken us in a different direction.[85]

During the Republican primary, Romney ratcheted up his attacks on Obama's insufficient embrace of American exceptionalism:

> I believe we are an exceptional country with a unique destiny and role in the world. Not exceptional, as the President has derisively said, in the way that the British think Great Britain is exceptional or the Greeks think Greece is exceptional. In Barack Obama's profoundly mistaken view, there is nothing unique about the United States.[86]

Perhaps Romney's most poignant attack on Obama came in March of 2012, as he was beginning to pull ahead of his Republican competitors. He offered: "Our president doesn't have the same feelings about American exceptionalism as we do. And I think over the last three or four years, some people around the world have begun to question [it]."[87] Again, this was not unfamiliar territory for Obama, who, a few days later, responded with a laugh, saying:

> It's worth noting that I first arrived on the national stage with a speech at the Democratic Convention that was entirely about American exceptionalism,

and that my entire career has been a testimony to American exceptionalism. But I will cut folks some slack for now because they're still trying to get their nomination.[88]

What was clear was that Romney and the Republicans saw Obama as weak on American exceptionalism and were going for the jugular. While patriotism and the belief in American exceptionalism do not alone win elections, they do move voters. And the Republican Party knew they had the advantage.

The attacks did not let up during Obama's second term. In fact, they increased significantly. The Republicans were now laser-focused on claiming American exceptionalism as their own and continuing to hit on Obama's perceived weakness on the issue. The peak came in 2015 as the Republican Party and some of their presidential hopefuls were hashing out their 2016 electoral strategy and party platform. The first shot was fired by Louisiana governor and presidential hopeful Bobby Jindal, who in February of 2015 stated: "This is a president who won't proudly proclaim American exceptionalism, maybe the first president ever who truly doesn't believe in that."[89] Former New York City mayor Rudolph Giuliani also emphasized in 2015: "I do not believe, and I know this is a horrible thing to say, but I do not believe that the president loves America." He continued, "with all our flaws we're the most exceptional country in the world. I'm looking for a presidential candidate who can express that, do that and carry it out."[90] The next day, Giuliani defended his comments: "I don't hear from him [Obama] what I heard from Harry Truman, what I heard from Bill Clinton, what I heard from Jimmy Carter… about what a great country we are, what an exceptional country we are."[91] This was interesting, considering that Obama had invoked the idea of American exceptionalism far more than any other president before him in the modern era (see Figure 1.1). Regardless, many Republicans were looking to make American exceptionalism the central issue of the 2016 election.

During an interview in 2015 for his book *Exceptional: Why the World Needs a Powerful America*, for example, former vice president Dick Cheney offered:

> If you go back 70 years… you'll find presidents of both parties from FDR and Harry Truman and Jack Kennedy to Nixon and Reagan and the Bushes and forward… shared a basic fundamental proposition… that the U.S. did have a role to play in the world as the exceptional nation. Barack Obama clearly doesn't believe that.[92]

The book, written with his daughter Liz Cheney, focused specifically on highlighting the deficiencies of Obama and the Democrats on the issue of

American exceptionalism. According to the Cheneys: "President Obama had departed from the bipartisan tradition going back seventy-five years of maintaining America's global supremacy and leadership." Nonetheless, Americans need not despair—they argued:

> Just as one president has left a path of destruction in his wake, one president can rescue us. The right person in the Oval Office can restore America's strength and our alliances, renew our power and leadership, defeat our enemies, and keep us safe... We are living in another hinge point in history and require a president equal to this moment. We must choose wisely.

They urged Americans to choose a president who will:

> [E]nsure that our children know the truth about who we are, what we've done, and why it is uniquely America's duty to be freedom's defender... [O]ur children need to know that they are the citizens of the most powerful, good, and honorable nation in the history of mankind, *the* exceptional nation.[93]

It should have come as no surprise, then, that a year later, when the Republican Party released their official 2016 party platform just before the National Convention, it was steeped in the language of American exceptionalism. It proclaimed in the first two lines of the preamble: "We believe in American exceptionalism [Full stop]. We believe the United States of America is unlike any other nation on earth [Full stop]." Furthermore, the platform stated: "We believe that American exceptionalism—the notion that our ideas and principles as a nation give us a unique place of moral leadership in the world—requires the United States to retake its natural position as leader of the free world."[94] The Republican Party was laying the foundation for its nominee to overwhelm the Democratic competition with a full-throated embrace of American exceptionalism. Indeed, at least on the surface, the party's exceptionalistic vision seemed to correspond with Donald Trump's campaign slogan "Make America Great Again," which, again, many read to mean "Make America Exceptional Again." As the following chapters will show, however, Trump had a very different vision for American exceptionalism. It was the exceptional me strategy.

Act One

The Exceptional Me Strategy Version 1.0 and the 2016 Presidential Elections

*Un*exceptional We: Setting the Foundation

We affirm our party's tradition of world leadership established by President Eisenhower and followed by every Republican president since. It stands for enormous power — and the prudence to use it sparingly, precisely, and only in grave necessity. It stands for involvement, not intervention. It requires consultation, not permission to act. It leads from the front — and ensures all others do their parts as well. It embraces American exceptionalism and rejects the false prophets of decline and diminution.

—2016 Republican Platform[1]

On November 3, 2015, Donald Trump released his campaign book, *Crippled America: How to Make America Great Again.*[2] Before addressing anything else in the book, Trump dove immediately into explaining why he chose a photograph of himself that was "so angry and so mean looking" for the cover. "In this book we are talking about Crippled America"—he explained—"Unfortunately, there's very little that is nice about it." He went on:

> So, I wanted a picture where I wasn't happy, a picture that reflected the anger and unhappiness that I feel, rather than joy. Because we are not in a joyous situation right now. We are in a situation where we have to go back to work to make America great again. All of us. That's why I have written this book.

According to Trump, then, the situation in America was bleak. The self-proclaimed branding expert was, in effect, branding the United States as "Crippled" and in utter disarray, a line of argument that would become a central tenet of his overall campaign strategy and appeal to the American electorate. Trump continued: "Nobody likes a loser and nobody likes to be bullied. Yet, here we stand today, the greatest superpower on Earth, and everyone is eating our lunch. That's not winning." The country, he argued, had never been in such dire straits. And what of American exceptionalism? According to Trump: "This is America today, the shining city on a hill, which other countries used to admire and try to be like." Trump then turned it up a notch: "The idea of American Greatness, of our country as the leader of the free and unfree world, has vanished." The picture was clear. It was not just that the country had problems. It was that the United States had lost its way and had fallen from grace. "They used to fear us. They used to want to be us. We were respected"—he wrote—"Now they're laughing at us."

Just seven days after the book was released, Trump took center stage for the fourth GOP debate of the primary season in Milwaukee, Wisconsin. It was the first debate in the GOP primary season where fewer than ten candidates took the stage, and Trump was the frontrunner. As such, Trump got the first question of the night. Neil Cavuto of Fox News asked him if he supported raising the minimum wage to $15 an hour. Trump wasted no time in taking up the same line of argument he had laid out in his book. He responded: "I can't be [supportive of raising the minimum wage] Neil. And the reason I can't be is that we are a country that is being beaten on every front economically, militarily. There is nothing that we do now to win. We don't win anymore." Throughout the night, Trump referred to a variety of "messes" that the country was in. For example, on foreign trade, Trump said: "China and India and almost everybody takes advantage of the United States—China in particular, because they're so good. It's the number-one abuser of this country." Trump offered a similar evaluation of the country's infrastructure: "We are $19 trillion dollars, we have a country that's going to hell, we have an infrastructure that's falling apart. Our roads, our bridges, our schools, our airports."[3] To Trump, there was little to praise about the state of the country. This was the foundation of the exceptional me strategy.

Many within the US media picked up on Trump's negative tone and warned of its potential pitfalls as a campaign strategy. In a July 21, 2016, article in the *Washington Post*, for example, journalist Jenna Johnson warned that Trump's vision of the country, "sounds like a terrible, terrible place."[4] According to Johnson:

> In Trump's eyes, the United States is practically a Third World country, with crumbling roads, aging bridges and decrepit airports. It's led by "stupid people" — even Mexico has smarter leaders, he says — and the entire world is laughing at America and its "depleted military." Cities have "exploded" with violence; Islamic State fighters posing as refugees might attack at any moment; and the economy is "doing lousy," with a real unemployment rate that could be eight times as high as the official one.

She went on to warn that "staying negative could turn off many general-election voters, and it risks clashing with their personal experience, because life has improved for many Americans in recent years." Rarely, if ever, had a presidential candidate painted such a bleak picture of the United States. Where were the full-throated proclamations of America as the "shining city on a hill" that American voters had become so accustomed to from other presidential candidates? Journalist Marc Fisher argued:

> The premise behind "Make America Great Again" is that the country is no longer great. It can be great again, and the campaign has a certain can-do billionaire in mind as the guy to make that happen, but at the moment, the leading contender for the nomination of the party that regularly touts the notion of American exceptionalism is arguing that the country ain't what it used to be.[5]

Similarly, British strategist Simon Anholt offered: "A large problem with Trump is he doesn't view America as a world leader, working hard to tackle to common challenges facing the whole of humanity."[6] Trump's supporters, however, seemed to be giving him a pass on American exceptionalism. To the surprise of his critics—including Democrats, journalists, and Republicans alike—Trump's proclamations of American doom and decline were not only not hurting his candidacy, they seemed to be boosting it. Trump's "Crippled" branding of the United States seemed to be resonating with voters from all walks of life. In effect, they were responding favorably to the exceptional me strategy.

In this chapter we examine how Trump sought to modify the modern American jeremiad—a rhetorical approach traditionally used by presidential candidates to challenge the opposition party in power—to fit his unique candidacy and advance his broader political objectives. First, we establish that Trump was an anomaly in his treatment of American exceptionalism during his campaign. Whereas previous oppositional presidential candidates had reliably embraced and celebrated American exceptionalism, consistently invoking the concept throughout their public communications, Trump was more reluctant to invoke American exceptionalism during his campaign. In particular, our analysis will show how Trump invoked the idea significantly less often than the last three presidential nominees who had opposed the party in power (Kerry 2004, Obama 2008, Romney 2012). Second, our analysis will show that Trump also profoundly deviated from these predecessors by the manner and extent to which he sought to portray America as explicitly *un*exceptional. Notably, such references by Trump were far more frequent than his invocations of American exceptionalism. Indeed, Trump routinely disparaged America, stating, for example: "We lose all the time" and the rest of the world is "eating our lunch."[7] We contend that this rhetorical strategy was designed to tear down the nation in such a way as to set himself up to be seen as the only savior who would be able to "Make America Great Again."

The Modern Jeremiad: Foundations of the Exceptional Me Strategy

Presidential candidates, like Trump, who seek to take office from—or after—a sitting president of the opposing party traditionally set up their campaign communication strategies to follow the principles of a rhetorical framework called the modern jeremiad.[8] The history of the modern jeremiad is inextricably intertwined with the history of American exceptionalism.[9] In its original form, the jeremiad was a sermon preached by Puritan ministers to the settlers of the Massachusetts Bay Colony in the 1600s. The idea that this new colony was to be a "city upon a hill," one that had a special covenant with God and would shine for the rest of the world, served as the foundation for the jeremiad.[10] The Puritan jeremiad had three parts. Ministers would first remind parishioners of their special responsibility to serve as an example for the rest of the world. This reminded parishioners of their duty to act in ways that reflected positively on the colony. Then, ministers would reprimand the community for the sins that they had committed and inform them that because of this, they had broken their covenant with God.[11] In a final move, they would call upon their followers to repent for their sins and comport their behavior in order to restore the sacred covenant. Ministers would use the jeremiad to keep their followers anxious and vigilant about their behavior as a way of maintaining order, moral standards, and unity within the colony.

Over time, the Puritan jeremiad became a mainstay in the broader American culture, familiar to virtually all of its citizens, as Americans became "conditioned to its style and ready to listen to those who use it."[12] The Puritan form of the jeremiad, however, slowly gave way to a more popular form used in American politics. The idea that the colony had a special covenant with God morphed into the broader idea that the entire country had a special relationship with God. As such, America had been placed on earth to stand above all nations as the model of morality and democratic ideals. The Puritan jeremiad changed further as it became absorbed into the process of building national identity and mainstream politicking. Political scientist Mark Jendrysik refers to this new version as the *modern* political jeremiad. Although the modern jeremiad differs in substance from its Puritan form, it generally retained its format. The model is fairly straightforward. First, it portrays the United States as an exceptional nation, one that is different from—and even superior to—all others, and as the shining example for other countries to emulate. It then portrays the United States as being in danger of losing its exceptional status in the world because it has lost touch with its special covenant. Finally, it assures the American people that the covenant can be restored if they would only move to change the direction of the nation, primarily through removing the opposing party from power. In this way, the modern jeremiad is a rhetorical tactic best suited for candidates, like Trump, who seek to unseat or replace a president of the opposing party because it allows them to directly blame their political opponents for having squandered American exceptionalism under their watch.[13] Such a move seeks to effectively persuade voters that their own candidacy—and the various policy positions that they have embraced—is the only effective solution to stop the country's descent and address its pressing problems.

This rhetorical trifecta has been used by opposition presidential candidates throughout the modern political era. Each of the three steps of the modern jeremiad—as used in oppositional campaigns—strategically builds upon the previous. First, presidential candidates lay a foundation for their campaign by telling a complex and rich story about the various ways in which the country is exceptional. In this way, they show supporters that they are deeply invested in American exceptionalism and have extensive knowledge of the country's unique history and role to play in international affairs. The 2012 Republican presidential nominee Mitt Romney, for example, put it succinctly: "I believe we are an exceptional country with a unique destiny and role in the world."[14] In essence, given that opposition presidential candidates are seeking the highest office in the land and aspiring to become the recognized leader of the country, it is no doubt strategically beneficial to them that they be perceived by the American public as unapologetic champions of American exceptionalism. In particular, such an embrace of American exceptionalism often enables candidates to inspire and motivate potential supporters to partake in the political process and join their cause. Indeed, such an unabashed embrace of American exceptionalism tends to resonate widely during presidential campaigns because the stakes for the country are so high and voters are looking for a leader to champion their collective cause.

Once the foundation is established, and a convincing case for American exceptionalism has been made, opposition presidential candidates tend to then turn toward warning the American people that the exceptional status of the country is in danger because of the other party in power. This involves explicitly portraying the policies and actions of the sitting president and members of their party as threats to the country's ability to stand as the shining "city on a hill" for the rest of the world. Typically, this is done by laying out a laundry list of national problems as the cause of America's perceived decline and then placing blame for these problems squarely on the backs of those in power. But candidates, at times, might take the additional—albeit risky—step of portraying the United States as explicitly unexceptional in comparison to the rest of the world. In other words, candidates might emphasize policy areas in which the country is not performing at the same level as other countries or they might claim that the United States is no longer the beacon or leader in the world. For example, during his 2016 campaign, Trump stated: "In Hillary Clinton's America, we have surrendered our status as the world's great economy, and we have surrendered our middle class to the whims of foreign countries."[15] Presidential candidates, however, tend to rarely and only selectively employ this tactic. Should they focus too much on portraying the country as unexceptional, they run the risk of being perceived by voters as skeptics—or even worse, nonbelievers—of American exceptionalism. Selectively focusing on a specific area in which the country has fallen behind other countries—and blaming the other party for it—allows opposition presidential candidates to then highlight how voting for them would help fix those specific problems.

Portraying the other party as the culprits who are undermining or threatening American exceptionalism sets candidates up nicely for the final step of the modern jeremiad—to offer voters a solution. Traditionally, presidential candidates offer their own candidacy, their policy positions, and their party platform as the way to restore American exceptionalism. Barack Obama, for example, offered this during his 2008 campaign:

> [N]ot only will our schools out-educate the world and our workers outcompete the world; not only will our companies innovate more and our economy grow more, but at this defining moment, we will do what previous generations of Americans have done—and unleash the promise of our people, unlock the promise of our country, and make sure that America remains a beacon of opportunity and prosperity for all the world.[16]

It is unclear whether presidential candidates in the modern era are familiar with the rich history of the modern jeremiad that is so intrinsically embedded in the American story or whether they consciously know that they are employing it during their campaigns. Although the modern jeremiad has informed or shaped American politics since the founding of the nation, it is not as though this is a concept that is openly discussed among politicians, campaign strategists, journalists, or citizens. Nonetheless, the benefits of the modern jeremiad are so self-evident, and the model of the jeremiad so easy to plug-and-play, that all modern opposition candidates—save Trump, as we will detail—have employed it time and again when seeking the presidency. In the next two chapters, we will detail the various ways that Trump's exceptional me strategy deviated from the structure of the modern jeremiad in his 2016 campaign.

American Exceptionalism in Communication

We begin our analysis of the exceptional me strategy, version 1.0, with a focus on comparing the campaign speeches of Trump to those of other modern presidential candidates who were seeking to replace a president of the opposing party. We analyzed more than 330 speeches in total. We focus our analysis on two related, albeit conflicting, concepts related to American exceptionalism and the modern jeremiad that presidential candidates can communicate in their campaign speeches: American exceptionalism and American *un*exceptionalism.[17] We begin by examining how candidates invoke American exceptionalism. To invoke American exceptionalism is to explicitly refer to the United States using exceptional language. Whereas American exceptionalism is implied in much of presidential campaign discourse—as virtually all references to the United States can elicit American exceptionalism sentiment in most voters—our analysis focuses on those occasions when candidates invoke the idea with clear language that portrays the nation as explicitly exceptional in some concrete way. By unequivocally invoking this culturally resonant idea, candidates signal to voters that they fully understand its meaning, value, and importance and that they embrace it unequivocally.

There are four different ways in which presidents and presidential candidates can invoke American exceptionalism.[18] The first thematic category is the basis of all American exceptionalism references: American singularity. Politicians since the inception of the nation have spoken abundantly of America's singular, or unique, status among nations. Examples of these invocations include references to the United States as different, unique, special, one-of-a-kind, or the only country to do something. Such references get at the core of the idea of American exceptionalism because they explicitly distill the different qualities that make the country *the* exception to the international community. The second thematic category focuses more on depicting the United States as a country that is superior to other countries in a number of ways. As discussed in the previous chapter, these types of references became much more commonplace after the United States emerged from the Second World War as one of two global superpowers. Since that time, examples of these themes have been pervasive in presidential discourse. For instance, American superiority is regularly communicated through references to the United States as the greatest nation on earth or as having the most powerful military, the largest economy, the hardest working people, or the greatest democracy. The list goes on and on. In essence, these references tend to highlight some aspect of the United States as being better than what you would find in other countries.

The next two thematic categories have more to do with the specific roles that the United States must take when engaging with the international community as the world's exceptional nation.[19] The first one focuses on portraying the United States as a model for the rest of the world to follow. Politicians throughout American history have leaned heavily on this type of invocation as they have made the case that the United States has certain special qualities that other countries should seek to emulate. Examples of these invocations include references to the United States as a whole, or specific qualities of the country, as exemplary, as the model of global excellence, and as a standard by which other countries should be measured. Invoking such an idea in political speeches can further convince American citizens their country is, indeed, exceptional.

The other type of American exceptionalism related to the role of the United States in the world references the country's sole position as the world's leader. This type of invocation is also tied to the emergence of the United States as a global superpower after the end of the Second World War when presidents and politicians alike actively sought to make the case that the United States, and not the Soviet Union, should lead the world in a sensible and moral direction. Examples of these invocations include references to the United States as *the* global leader or as leading the world in some category. Taken together, these four themes of American exceptionalism portray the United States as a truly exceptional nation that sets the standards of the international community, and they provide a solid strategic foundation upon which candidates can then employ the modern jeremiad. There is nothing implied in these references. Each explicitly refers to the country as exceptional in some clear, unambivalent way. Together, they represent the pillars of traditional presidential campaign discourse.

Invoking American Exceptionalism

We begin with an examination of the manner and extent to which recent opposition presidential candidates (John Kerry in 2004, Barack Obama in 2008, Mitt Romney in 2012, and Donald Trump in 2016) invoked any theme of American exceptionalism—singular, superior, model, or leader—in their official campaign speeches.[20] This is an important starting point, we argue, because it establishes how Trump, as a presidential candidate, compared to his predecessors in how he drew upon the modern jeremiad and approached American exceptionalism throughout the course of his campaign. Figure 2.1 shows the percentage of speeches in which these candidates invoked the idea of American exceptionalism at least once and their average rate of invocation per speech. What was clear and evident in our reading of every word of these speeches was that each presidential candidate from John Kerry to Donald Trump invoked American exceptionalism at least in some form in their speeches. This makes sense, given that no candidate would be so foolish as to completely ignore this foundational idea and still expect to have a fighting chance to win the presidency. Donald Trump's approach to American exceptionalism, however, was significantly different—both in the manner and extent to which he referenced it—from his contemporaries. In fact, Trump invoked American exceptionalism in fewer than half as many speeches (23 percent) as John Kerry (61 percent) and Barack Obama (59 percent) and less than a third as many speeches as his fellow Republican, Mitt Romney (91 percent). Whereas all three of his predecessors were deliberate—brazen even—in their embrace of the idea, Trump no doubt sought to tell a different story.[21]

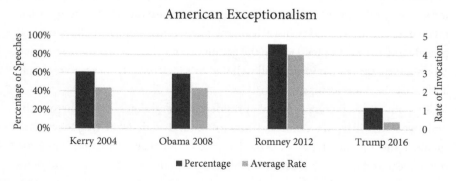

Figure 2.1 Percentage and rate of all types of American exceptionalism language across all speeches from 2004 to 2016.

The difference between Trump and the others is even more stark when we consider the average rate of American exceptionalism invocations that each presidential candidate employed in their campaign speeches. John Kerry and Barack Obama, for example, invoked American exceptionalism over five times as often as Trump. Even more remarkable, fellow Republican Mitt Romney invoked American exceptionalism over ten times as frequently as Trump.[22] Moreover, while each of the other candidates invoked American exceptionalism on average more than two times per speech, Trump only invoked it around once every three speeches. These findings are revealing. They indicate that, unlike his predecessors who strategically sought to build their campaigns upon the foundation of American exceptionalism, Trump was reluctant, if not outright opposed, to portraying the nation as already exceptional. He was straying from the modern jeremiad toward a strategy more suited for his unique style and vision.

Redefining American Exceptionalism

As a next step, we explored the distinct ways in which presidential candidates invoked American exceptionalism in their campaign speeches. Again, it is traditional for a presidential candidate to wax philosophical about the various aspects of American exceptionalism as they make their case for the presidency. Often, candidates even become sentimental when they speak of unique or special aspects of the nation, such as its origins, principles, or institutions, compared to the rest of the world. They regularly dig deep into recounting the various ways that the country is superior to other countries, citing various reasons or examples. They speak of the nation as being a model or the shining beacon for the rest of the world to follow. And they often praise the way the country has taken over sole moral and political leadership in world affairs. Broadly speaking, presidential candidates tend to run the gamut of American exceptionalism when on the campaign trail, knowing full well that this idea reliably serves to motivate and unify the American people.

To gain clear picture of how presidential candidates have rhetorically employed this idea, we examined how often and with what frequency they invoked the distinct types of American exceptionalism—singular, superior, model, leader. Figure 2.2 illustrates obvious distinctions in how the candidates sought to portray the idea of American exceptionalism to the American electorate. Indeed, what is remarkably clear here is the difference between

Trump and his predecessors. Notably, all of Trump's predecessors—John Kerry, Barack Obama, and Mitt Romney—sought to paint a multifaceted picture of America as an exceptional nation, each touching extensively on every facet of the idea. For them, it seemed, these ideas were deeply embedded in the DNA of the American experience. Thus, it was neither difficult nor forced when they spoke of American exceptionalism. Donald Trump's conception of American exceptionalism, by contrast, was a different story entirely. Notably, Trump lagged significantly behind all three of his predecessors in his invocations of each facet of American exceptionalism. In addition, Trump's portrayal of American exceptionalism was incredibly narrow compared to his predecessors. He focused almost entirely on one single facet of American exceptionalism—superiority—throughout his campaign. This was a profound departure from how candidates have traditionally employed the modern jeremiad in their speeches. After all, American exceptionalism, in all of its glory, establishes the foundation of the jeremiad.

These differences between Trump and the others become even more glaring when we look at some examples from the campaign trail. It is important first to note some similarities. As displayed in Figure 2.2, Trump invoked American exceptionalism significantly less often than his predecessors, but his laser focus on American global superiority echoed traditional campaign language. Trump stated, for example, "We will promote our America values, our American way of life, and our American system of government which are all the best in the world."[23] Similarly, Kerry offered this: "America is more than a piece of geography-more than a name of a country; it is the most powerful idea in human history, freedom and equal opportunity for all."[24] And Obama argued that "America cannot meet the threats of this new century alone, but the world cannot meet them without America. It's time for America to show the world that we're still the last, best hope of Earth. It's time for America to lead again."[25] According to Trump, Kerry, and Obama, American superiority in the world was something that must be recognized and celebrated. Elsewhere, Trump argued that "we have to promote the exceptional virtues of our own way of life. We have an exceptional country, an exceptional way of life."[26] This was comparable to what Romney proclaimed: "This is key to the success of the American experiment. America does not just exist for the people, it has been made exceptional by the people."[27] Most notably, what these examples illustrate is that Trump was not entirely unfamiliar with the value and importance of invoking American exceptionalism on the campaign trail, even if those references were relatively few comparatively.

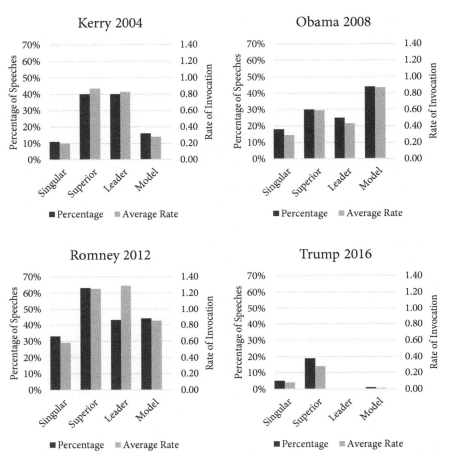

Figure 2.2 Percentage and rate of different types of invocations of American exceptionalism across all speeches from 2004 to 2016.

The similarities between Trump and the other candidates, however, end there. What was noticeably absent from Trump's overall campaign were references to America's special role as a leader in the world. This was, of course, consistent with Trump's America First approach to American foreign policy, which promised to pull the United States back from its traditional self-proclaimed role as moral and political leader in the world.[28] But Trump's almost complete omission of these ideas in campaign communications was peculiar to say the least. Indeed, these ideas were highly visible in how Kerry, Obama, and Romney portrayed the nation to the American public. Kerry, for example, said: "America wasn't put here to dominate the world. We have a higher calling: to lead it." He also offered: "It symbolizes the spirit of America—that there are men and women who are ready to do what it takes to live and lead by our values."[29] Obama, similarly, offered this:

> We are America. We are the nation that liberated a continent from a madman, that lifted ourselves from the depths of depression, that won civil rights, and women's rights, and voting rights for all our people. We are the beacon that has led generations of weary travelers to find opportunity, and liberty, and hope on our doorstep. That's who we are.[30]

Romney, who can perhaps be best described as someone who embraced all facets of American exceptionalism at full volume all the time, was no different. In a speech addressing US foreign policy, Romney emphasized:

> God did not create this country to be a nation of followers. America is not destined to be one of several equally balanced global powers. America must lead the world, or someone else will. Without American leadership, without clarity of American purpose and resolve, the world becomes a far more dangerous place, and liberty and prosperity would surely be among the first casualties.[31]

Such language, in fact, had been a mainstay in presidential politics throughout the twentieth and early twenty-first centuries, which made Trump's decision to outright avoid it in his campaign communications even more meaningful. Trump's portrayal of American exceptionalism, therefore, was likely constrained by his own understanding of competition. In essence, American exceptionalism was about winning or losing, and, according to Trump, America was losing more than it was winning.

It is important to note that it was relatively rare for Trump to invoke American exceptionalism in a purely positive manner. Unlike his predecessors, who invoked the idea to inspire voters with a grand vision of what America is and what it stands for, Trump focused much of his time on the negative. We can see this play out, for example, when Trump discussed the US military. Trump was unequivocal about the military's superiority in comparison with the rest of the world, but he tended to simultaneously refer to it as being in total disrepair. Take, for example, this statement from Trump: "We will eliminate the Obama-Clinton defense sequester and rebuild our badly depleted military. When did we ever need it more? Greatest people on Earth in our military, but it's badly depleted."[32] In a similar vein, Trump said:

> It's like, if I were the enemy, I would say, I can't believe they're that stupid. They're taking my people and they're putting them all over the place, because you have great military right here. And our military... *Our military cannot be beaten.*

But you know what could happen? When we don't know where they are, where they're coming, you've them all over the place [emphasis added].[33]

To refer to the United States and its military leaders as "stupid" was a bold move—one most politicians would likely avoid at all costs—but it fit Trump's overall message that voters should be very worried about the status of their country. For many, it was an unfathomable move. For Trump, it was foundational to his exceptional me strategy.

America as *Unexceptional*

To provide a more robust picture of how Trump further deviated from his contemporaries in his conception of American exceptionalism and the modern jeremiad, we examined how common it was for these presidential candidates to compare the United States with the rest of the world in an unfavorable light. Specifically, we examined each candidate's usage of the language of American exceptionalism to speak of the country as being explicitly *un*exceptional.[34] Invocations of American *un*exceptionalism can manifest in many different forms. First, candidates can refer to the United States as no different or any more special than other nations. This might include the statement that "the United States is no different from the rest of the world." Second, candidates may refer to the country as being inferior to other countries. For instance, a candidate may say: "China's economy is far superior to our own." Third, candidates may refer to the United States as no longer a model for the rest of the world to follow. They might say, for example, that "countries now look to other countries such as Germany as a model to follow instead of the United States." Finally, candidates might invoke American unexceptionalism by stating that the country is no longer the global leader that it once was. For instance, they may say, "America's time as the leader of the free world has ended."[35] Any way you slice it, invocations of American unexceptionalism explicitly portray the United States as fallen from its special status.

Our next step, therefore, was to examine how presidential candidates have invoked these different types of American *un*exceptionalism. Specifically, we compared the frequency and consistency with which presidential candidates referred to the United States as unexceptional in some way. Figure 2.3 shows the full comparison between the four candidates. Again, at first glance it is clear that Trump engaged in this tactic in a significantly different manner than did his predecessors. A closer look at the findings reveals that Trump invoked

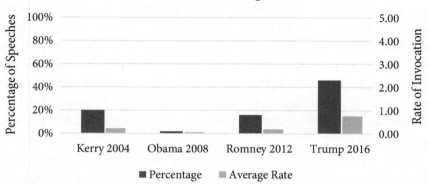

Figure 2.3 Percentage and rate of invocations of American unexceptionalism across all speeches from 2004 to 2016.

American unexceptionalism in more than twice as many speeches as John Kerry, close to three times as many as Mitt Romney, and twenty-three times as many as his immediate predecessor, Barack Obama.[36] If we consider the average rate at which the candidates invoked the idea, the differences become even more clear. For instance, Kerry averaged less than one invocation in every four speeches. Similarly, Romney averaged one in every five speeches. Obama, strikingly, only averaged American unexceptionalism invocations once every fifty speeches. Trump, by contrast, averaged just under one invocation per speech.[37] As would be expected, traditional presidential candidates were cautious about invoking this provocative form of American exceptionalism. Trump clearly was not.

Trump's unique relationship with this type of discourse can be seen more clearly when comparing him in real terms with his predecessors. Although, Kerry, Obama, and Romney did, at times, invoke American unexceptionalism, such critiques were much more narrowly focused than those expressed by Trump. In fact, all three focused the vast majority of their critiques on how the education system or health care within the United States had fallen behind the rest of the world. Barack Obama, for example, focused one of his three total American unexceptionalism invocations—by far the least of any of the four candidates—on how the United States was behind other countries in offering broadband and the other two arguing: "By 12th grade, our children score lower on their math and science tests than most other kids in the developed world."[38] For John Kerry, seventeen of his twenty critiques of American exceptionalism targeted the US health care system. Specifically, it was a mainstay of his stump speeches to say that the United States was the "only industrialized nation on the planet which doesn't understand that healthcare is a right and not a privilege."[39] Mitt Romney was no different. He regularly argued: "It is unacceptable, in my view, for the nation that invented public education to have kids performing now in the bottom third or bottom quartile in the world."[40] What is clear is that each of Trump's predecessors targeted specific issues—primarily education and health care—in their relatively sparse number of references to American unexceptionalism.

Trump, by contrast, was much more willing to cast a variety of aspects of the country in an unexceptional light, and to do so frequently. On the economy, for example, Trump stated: "[W]e have surrendered our status as the world's great economy, and we have surrendered our middle class to the whims of foreign countries."[41] On trade, he said: "We have the most incompetently worked trade deals ever negotiated probably in the history of the world."[42] Trump, like his predecessors, also targeted the country's educational system. In his campaign launch speech, for example, he said: "And they're [the American people] tired of spending more money on education than any nation in the world per capita, than any nation in the world, and we are 26th in the world, 25 countries are better than us in education."[43] Perhaps more strikingly, Trump referred to education in America's inner cities as "worldwide bad."[44] On the country's infrastructure, Trump chided: "[W]e're becoming a third world country, because of our infrastructure, our airports, our roads, everything."[45] In fact, referring to the United States as a third world country was a common refrain for Trump. In his words: "We're running like they run right now a third world country folks, OK? You saw what happened, it's running like a third world country, we're being talked about all over the world, nobody can believe it."[46] Similarly, he offered: "Our country looks bad to the world, especially when we are supposed to be the leader."[47] To Trump, therefore, not only was the United States like a third world country but because of it, the "shining city on the hill" was no longer the beacon it once was.

Another important way that Trump invoked American unexceptionalism was to speak of the United States in terms of how it fares in competition with the rest of the world. Specifically, Trump regularly spoke of the United States in terms of winning and losing. In Trump's words:

> [O]ur country doesn't win anymore. We don't win with trade, we don't win with
> our great military, we don't allow them to win, we don't win with ISIS. The world

is laughing at us. We don't win at the borders. We don't win with taking care of our vets. We don't win with anything. We don't win anymore.[48]

In Trump's competitive conception of the world, other countries are "eating our lunch." According to Trump, Japan "beat us all the time," Mexico is "beating us economically," and China is "killing us." In fact, China was a common focus for Trump. For instance, he said:

> No, I love them. But their leaders are much smarter than our leaders, and we can't sustain ourself with that. There's too much—it's like—it's like take the New England Patriots and Tom Brady and have them play your high school football team. That's the difference between China's leaders and our leaders. They are ripping us. We are rebuilding China. We're rebuilding many countries. China, you go there now, roads, bridges, schools, you never saw anything like it. They have bridges that make the George Washington Bridge look like small potatoes. And they're all over the place.[49]

Casting America's competitive relationship with the rest of the world in terms of winning or losing aligned well with Trump's conception of American exceptionalism as being about American superiority. More importantly, it enabled him to portray the United States as a nation in ruins that was no longer exceptional.

Perhaps the most telling finding in our analysis comes in Figure 2.4, where we compared Trump to the others in his invocations of American exceptionalism versus American unexceptionalism. Not only did he invoke the idea significantly less frequently than any of his predecessors, but he was the only one to favor disparaging American exceptionalism over championing it—and, it should be

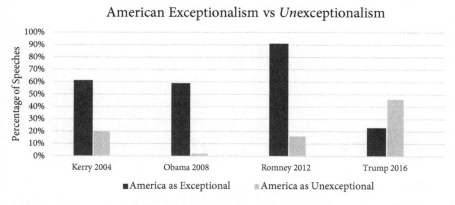

American Exceptionalism vs *Un*exceptionalism

Figure 2.4 Comparing the percentage of invocations of American exceptionalism and American unexceptionalism across all speeches from 2004 to 2016.

noted, he did so by a wide margin. More broadly, what these results indicate is that Trump possessed a profoundly different conception of American exceptionalism than Kerry, Obama, and Romney. Traditionally, candidates who employ the modern jeremiad aspire to be seen as carrying the torch of American exceptionalism, an idea that was born at the inception of the nation and has thrived throughout the history of the country. To be sure, jeremiads have been known to identify problems within the nation and, at times, portray the nation as having lost its way. Such critiques, however, are usually couched within much louder proclamations of American exceptionalism. Put another way, the country may be facing problems, but the nation—its history, its government, its people— remains inherently exceptional at its core. These aspects of the nation, in effect, are static and cannot be changed. This was not, however, how Trump spoke of the nation. Indeed, his conception of American exceptionalism throughout the 2016 election was that of a competition, a zero-sum game. And, according to him, the United States was losing. The country was in a decrepit state, American exceptionalism was in serious danger, if not totally lost, and the world had turned against an America that was once a beacon of hope for the world. For Trump it was simple. "The world hates us"—he explained—"The world hates us."[50]

3

Exceptional Me: From "Yes We Can" to "I Alone Can Fix It"

I will be the greatest jobs president that God ever created, believe me.
—Donald J. Trump[1]

The convention floor of the 2016 Republican National Convention in Cleveland, Ohio, was teeming with energy and anticipation as the crowd excitedly waited for Donald Trump to emerge and give his nomination acceptance speech. The arena was crowded with fervent Trump supporters holding red and blue signs with a number of slogans like, "Make America One Again," "Latinos Para Trump," and "Make America Work Again." Trump was preceded on stage by his daughter, Ivanka, who again would introduce her father. As she emerged on stage, *Here Comes the Sun* by the Beatles rang out and a massive furled American flag set the digital backdrop. She began by saying: "One year ago, I introduced my father when he declared his candidacy. In his own way, and through his own sheer force of will, he sacrificed greatly to enter the political arena as an outsider."[2] She went on: "Real change, the kind we have not seen in decades is only going to come from outside the system. And it's only going to come from a man who's spent his entire life doing what others said could not be done. My father is a fighter." She continued, calling her father an "extraordinary man" and setting up his punchline, yet again:

> He is the single most qualified person to serve as chief executive of an $18 trillion economy. My father will call upon the best and brightest people from all spheres of industry and both sides of the aisle. A new set of thinkers, to face our country's existing and future problems with fresh perspective and brand-new solutions. Come January 17, all things will be possible again. We can hope and dream and think big again. No one has more faith in the American people than my father. He will be your greatest, your truest, and your most loyal champion.

The crowd erupted and people rose to their feet. The underlying message in Ivanka's speech was almost identical to the one she had given over a year earlier when Trump had launched his 2016 presidential campaign. Her father, according to her, was an exceptional man who had run an exceptional business and would no doubt bring exceptional things to the country. She was, in effect, setting up the exceptional me strategy.

When Trump emerged on stage, the place exploded with wild applause, whistles, and screams. The backdrop had changed to a row of over thirty standing American flags on poles and a massive "TRUMP" spelled out in white letters laced with gold on a gold background above the flags. Jerry Goldsmith's *The Parachutes*, from the movie *Air Force One*, played loudly throughout the hall as Trump waved at the crowd and mouthed "thank you." After soaking in the applause for a moment, Trump got down to business. His first order of business was to caution Americans about the degrading state of the country:

> Our convention occurs at a moment of crisis for our nation. The attacks on our police, and the terrorism in our cities, threaten our very way of life. Any politician who does not grasp this danger is not fit to lead our country... Our roads and bridges are falling apart, our airports are Third World condition, and forty-three million Americans are on food stamps... the symbol of American prestige around the globe was brought down in flames. America is far less safe—and the world is far less stable—than when Obama made the decision to put Hillary Clinton in charge of America's foreign policy. Let's defeat her in November, OK.[3]

He went on, speaking extensively of how the country had fallen into disrepair. Almost immediately after the speech, journalists began to comment on the overall tone of doom and gloom in the speech. The negativity was palpable. The next day, the *Washington Post's* Jenna Johnson called the speech: "Donald Trump's Vision of Doom and Despair in America."[4] Trump's message that the country was in shambles was coming through loud and clear.

Once he had set the scene of doom, Trump then turned to argue that the troubles the country faced came at the hands of politicians in Washington who had put their own interests before those of the nation. Furthermore, he argued that it was clearly those same politicians who were responsible for the country's decline: "The problems we face now—poverty and violence at home, war and destruction abroad—will last only as long as we continue relying on the same politicians who created them in the first place. A change in leadership is required to produce a change in outcomes." As Ivanka had said in her introduction, the answer was to elect someone who came from outside of the Washington establishment, someone different, someone like Trump. Trump then got to the central message of his campaign: "I have joined the political arena so that the powerful can no longer beat up on people that cannot defend themselves. Nobody knows the system better than me, which is why I alone can fix it." If one were searching for the slogan of Trump's exceptional me strategy, this was clearly it. And he was unveiling it for the very first time before the American public.

Thus far, we have shown how Trump's exceptional me strategy strayed from how traditional opposition candidates for the presidency have employed the first step of the modern jeremiad in their presidential campaigns. Specifically, instead of building a robust argument detailing the various ways that the United States is an exceptional nation, Trump focused his campaign messaging on crafting a picture of an America that had lost its way and was no longer exceptional. In this chapter, we extend our discussion and analysis of how Trump's exceptional me strategy strayed from the basic tenets of the modern jeremiad in the context of the 2016 presidential campaign. We begin by detailing how Trump parted ways, yet again, from the approach taken by his predecessors. Specifically, we detail how he sought to blame America's decline on politicians, not just from the opposing party in power but from all sides of the political aisle. This was perhaps most evident in Trump's frequent references to "draining the swamp" and his repeated claims that "politicians in Washington" and "the Washington establishment" were the culprits of America's decline. Such statements, it should be noted, were rarely qualified as references to Democrats alone. Instead, they were meant to apply all politicians, Democrats and Republicans alike. This, in effect, allowed Trump, a political outsider untainted by the dysfunctionality of Washington, to position himself as the savior who could lead America back.

We then turn to illustrate how Trump branded himself as *the* exceptional candidate, emphasizing the qualities and characteristics that made him— rather than the nation—exceptional. In particular, we provide data to illustrate how Trump engaged in what we refer to as "self-exceptionalism" throughout the campaign, which was significantly at odds with what his contemporary predecessors (Kerry, Obama, and Romney) had done. Whereas these other presidential nominees had tended to encompass their own identities within the larger story of American exceptionalism, Trump made it all about himself. If something was exceptional, it was Trump—something particularly noteworthy considering he rarely offered this same type of praise for the nation during the campaign. In the end, Trump's promise of "I alone can fix it" resonated with many voters across the political spectrum, we argue, because many Americans were disenchanted with politics as usual in Washington and they were seeking a political outsider whose unique approach (or exceptional, as Trump would describe it) to politics might finally solve the many problems that had long plagued politics in Washington.

Enough Blame to Go Around

Presidential candidates seeking to unseat the incumbent party in the White House devote a significant portion of their campaign speeches to delineating all of the various ways that the opposing party and their president have done damage to the country. Blaming the other party is what allows candidates to make a convincing argument that their own policies will fix the problems that the sitting president has caused. It sets them apart. This part of the modern jeremiad is a campaign staple, one that has been deployed by candidates from both sides of the political aisle throughout the modern political era. John Kerry, for example, referenced George W. Bush—the sitting president and his Republican opponent—over 500 times in his campaign, routinely calling out his failed policies and lack of effective leadership. When Kerry announced his candidacy, he made it clear:

> I reject George Bush's radical new vision of a government that comforts the comfortable at the expense of ordinary Americans, that lets corporations do as they please, that turns its back on the very alliances we helped create and the very principles that have made our nation a model to the world for over two centuries. An economic policy of lost opportunity and lost hopes is wrong for America. An international policy where we stand almost alone is wrong for America. George Bush's vision does not live up to the America I enlisted in the Navy to defend, the America I have fought for in the Senate—and the America that I hope to lead as President.[5]

Barack Obama, by contrast, built a case for why a vote for his Republican opponent, John McCain, was really a vote for the flawed policies of the outgoing Bush administration. During his campaign, Obama brought up the Bush administration and its flawed policies over 200 times, emphasizing that McCain's platform was filled with "the same old Bush-McCain policies."[6] He went on:

> John McCain has served his country with honor, and I respect that service. But for two decades, he has supported policies that have shifted the burden on to working people. And his only answer to the problems created by George Bush's

policies is to give them another four years to fail. Just look at where he stands and you'll see that a vote for John McCain is a vote for George Bush's third term.

Mitt Romney was even more aggressive, referring to Obama over 700 times in his speeches and attacking him on issues ranging from Obamacare to his policies in Iraq and Afghanistan. The target was squarely on Obama's back and the picture, according to Romney, wasn't pretty. Simply put: "Barack Obama has failed America."[7] These types of attacks have virtually no political downside, and they come easily to candidates who are making an argument that their own policies and vision for the country are far superior to those of the opposing party in power.

In this way, Trump was no different from his predecessors. Throughout the 2016 campaign, for example, Trump attacked the Democratic Party, his opponent Hillary Clinton, and the Obama administration unreservedly, labeling their policies as outright detrimental to the nation and demanding their expulsion from power. Trump focused most of his attention on Hillary Clinton, speaking her name over 900 times in his speeches and attacking her on everything from her record in the Senate to her support of the "disastrous" policies of the Clinton and Obama presidencies. Trump, for example, accused Clinton of supporting trade plans in both administrations that "gave China millions of our best jobs, and effectively let China rebuild itself."[8] In return, he said, "Hillary Clinton got rich." Similarly, he offered this:

> Arm in arm, we will rescue the nation from the Obama-Clinton disaster, which is exactly what it is, that has bled our country dry and spread terrorism unabated across the world, that's what's happening. You saw it just now, maps came out yesterday, they said ISIS far bigger, it's all over the place. It's all over the place. We're going to get rid of it, folks.[9]

Put succinctly, Clinton, the Obama administration, and the Democrats were "destroying our country."[10] Nonetheless, while Trump's language was certainly more jagged than the language his predecessors had chosen to use, the tactic was still the same—paint a picture of how the opposing party was failing the country and offer your own vision for how to fix it.

At the same time that presidential candidates apply this no-holds-barred approach to attacking the opposing party, they also tend to be very careful not to do the same to their own party. Doing so carries with it the risk of disrupting unity within the party ranks and undercutting the foundation of their campaign heading into the general election. Indeed, it is traditionally seen as detrimental to tear down one's own party in any way during a presidential campaign because of the potential damage it might do to down-ballot candidates. Instead, presidential candidates tend to celebrate—not denigrate—their party and its standard-bearers, enlisting their support on the campaign trail and citing their successes and accomplishments both past and present. This decorum of respecting and paying homage to leadership within the party tends to occur as soon as a candidate enters the race. After all, presidential candidates are looking to win over the party establishment and, more broadly, appeal to the loyal base of the party. Trump, however, was not interested in decorum or what others had done before him. He was determined to be the exception to the rule.

Trump and the Republican Party were strange bedfellows from the start. Perhaps this was due to the fact that Trump was once a registered Democrat— and twice a registered Independent—and he had previously donated to a number of Democratic campaigns, including Hilary Clinton's. From early on in his candidacy, Trump fielded consistent attacks from fellow Republicans, who openly questioned his true Republican and conservative bonafides. Republican Senator Rand Paul, for example, issued a three-page statement in August of 2015, calling Trump a "fake conservative,"[11] a line of attack that would become commonplace throughout his campaign and echoed by several other fellow Republicans, including former governor Jeb Bush. Similarly, Senator Susan Collins suggested in August of 2016 that "Donald Trump does not reflect historical Republican values nor the inclusive approach to governing that is critical to healing the divide in our country."[12] Rand Paul and Susan Collins were not alone. Various other high-level Republicans—including Senators John McCain, Ted Cruz, and Lindsay Graham; Speaker of the House Paul Ryan; Governor John Kasich; and former 2012 Republican presidential candidate Mitt Romney—spent much of the 2016 election cycle lambasting Trump for his questionable Republican or conservative credentials and proclaiming that he was a poor representative for their party.

What these critics and naysayers perhaps did not realize at the time, however, was that they were helping Trump's case, rather than subverting it. He was not looking to fit the mold of a traditional Republican politician. He was trying to break it. This was his appeal to voters. He was a businessman who abhorred politicians. He was an outsider, the antipolitician who was using the Republican Party to get to Washington and take a wrecking ball to the system. Reflecting on why so many Republicans opposed his campaign, Trump made it clear:

> All the people who've rigged the system for their own personal benefit are trying
> to stop our change campaign because they know that their gravy train has
> reached its last stop. It's your turn now. This is your time. The fact that so many

encrusted old political insiders oppose our campaign is the best proof you will ever need that we are fighting for real change—not partisan change.[13]

It made sense, then, to both Trump and his supporters that he would be at odds with his party. After all, it was filled with the same politicians who, according to him, were the cause of so many of the problems in America. It was essential that he differentiate himself from them. In May of 2016, for example, Trump tweeted: "I will win the election against Crooked Hillary despite the people in the Republican Party that are currently and selfishly opposed to me!"[14] For Trump, Republicans attacking him only served to reinforce his belief that establishment politicians were simply trying to sabotage his campaign to protect themselves and to ensure that business as usual continued in Washington. In his campaign announcement, Trump was clear about what set him apart from his Republican challengers:

> Well, you need somebody, because politicians are all talk, no action. Nothing's gonna get done. They will not bring us—believe me—to the promised land. They will not… So, I've watched the politicians. I've dealt with them all my life. If you can't make a good deal with a politician, then there's something wrong with you. You're certainly not good. And that's what we have representing us [Republicans]. They will never make America great again. They don't even have a chance. They're controlled fully—they're controlled fully by the lobbyists, by the donors, and by the special interests, fully.[15]

Trump, therefore, saw no reason to abide by the same decorum that other candidates had traditionally followed. Throughout the Republican primaries, Trump crossed line after line that no Republican candidate before him would ever dare cross. He portrayed his Republican opponents as do-nothing politicians and, time and again, attacked them directly and often personally. In his words: "I am glad that I make the powerful a little uncomfortable now and again—including some powerful people in my own party. Because it means I am fighting for real change."[16] The message was clear: Trump would be the man who finally shook up Washington.

In one confrontation with former Florida governor Jeb Bush, during a February 2016 debate in Greensville, South Carolina, Trump was particularly ruthless in his attacks. Bush had criticized him, saying: "And while Donald Trump was building a reality TV show, my brother was building a security apparatus to keep us safe. And I'm proud of what he did. And he [Trump] has had the gall to go after my brother."[17] Trump quickly interrupted: "The World Trade Center came down during your brother's reign, remember that? That's not keeping us safe." It was a low blow and the crowd noticed, answering immediately with a mixture of boos and cheers. Not only was Trump going after Bush, he was doing the previously unthinkable. He was attacking a former Republican president, a standard-bearer of the Republican Party. And it wasn't the first time. Throughout the campaign, for example, he criticized the Bush administration's decision to invade Iraq, saying, "Obviously the War in Iraq was a big, fat mistake… George Bush made a mistake. We can make mistakes, but that one was a beauty. We should have never been in Iraq. We have destabilized the Middle East." Trump, by contrast, at least in his view, was "the one that made all of the right predictions about Iraq."

George W. Bush was certainly not the only Republican standard-bearer that Trump went after during the election. In 2015, at a Family Leadership Summit, Trump took on former Republican presidential nominee John McCain in the wake of a spat the two had been having in front of the American public. Trump stated: "I supported him for president. I raised a million dollars for him. That's a lot of money. I supported him. He lost. He let us down. But, you know he lost. So, I never liked him as much after that because I don't like losers."[18] The moderator interjected, defending McCain, saying, "He's a war hero." Trump's now famous response was: "He's not a war hero. He's a war hero because he was captured. I like people who weren't captured, Ok? I hate to tell you." A few days later, the Trump campaign followed up with a letter to reporters calling McCain "yet another all talk, no action politician who spends too much time on television and not enough time doing his job."[19]

In March of 2016, Trump turned his sights on yet another high-profile Republican, former Republican presidential candidate Mitt Romney, when the former governor was set to give a speech at the University of Utah to label Trump as "a phony, a fraud."[20] Trump quickly went on the offensive, tweeting: "Failed candidate Mitt Romney, who ran one of the worst races in presidential history, is working with the establishment to bury a big 'R' win!"[21] Eight minutes later, he reiterated: "Establishment wants to kill this movement!"[22] No Republican, not even ex-presidents and recent Republican presidential nominees, was off-limits to Trump's scathing attacks on the political establishment. Trump was not about to bow to the Republican Party. They, in time, would have to bow to him.

This dynamic was never more evident than when Trump had to deal with the fallout within his party over the now famous Access Hollywood tape, during which he was captured on a hot microphone describing acts of sexual assault that he had committed against women and bragging about there being no consequence. Republicans from all levels of government came out to decry what Trump had said and several high-level party members in Congress rescinded their endorsements. The Republican fallout was so palpable that many in the media started calling it a "GOP Civil War."[23] Speaker of the House Paul Ryan, for example, condemned the comments. Although he did not go so far as to rescind his endorsement, he did pledge to stop actively campaigning for Trump and said he would no longer support him publicly. Trump's response was vicious, accusing Ryan of "fighting the Republican nominee."[24] Three days after the release of the tape, Trump tweeted: "Despite winning the second debate in a landslide (every poll), it is hard to do when Paul Ryan and others give zero support!"[25] and "Disloyal R's are far more difficult than Crooked Hillary. They come at you from all sides. They don't know how to win—I will teach them!"[26] Trump's strategy was an odd one. He was taking the establishment elites within his party head-on and, seemingly, without any reservations. According to Trump, the Republicans were out to get him just as much as the Democrats. Again, it fed his larger argument that the American people needed someone not only different from the Democrats in power but from *all* politicians in power, including Republicans.

In May of 2016, Paul Waldman of the *Washington Post* expressed bemusement at Trump's tendency to go after his own party:

> [I]t might be tempting to see his willingness to go after fellow Republicans as laudable candor. He doesn't engage in the rote back-and-forth cross-party sniping we're so used to—he criticizes everybody! But the thing about criticizing people from the other party is that it has a purpose. It's meant to persuade people that your side is right and their side is wrong. But what's the purpose of criticizing your own allies? There is none. It's just about lashing out, personal pique, indulging your hurt feelings.[27]

Trump and his supporters, however, could not have disagreed more. To Trump, it was a strategic choice to be an equal opportunity attacker. His argument to voters was not that he could play by the rules of Washington politics. It was hinged upon the idea that Trump was different from them all, different from all those politicians who had, for so many years, run Washington into the ground. To him, it made sense to bring Republicans into the fray. After all, Republicans were politicians too. And politicians, the lot of them, Democrats and Republicans alike, according to Trump, were the real culprits in American politics. They were who everybody should blame. Politicians had brought the system to a grinding halt and they stood in the way of making it work again. And so, throughout the campaign Trump kept politicians of all stripes in his crosshairs. It was integral to his case that he, and he alone, was the true outsider candidate and, therefore, the only one who could fix Washington. This was fundamental to the exceptional me strategy.

Drain the Swamp: Targeting Politicians and the Washington Establishment

Given the clear disdain and, at times, hostility Trump exhibited toward the political establishment in Washington, we begin our analysis by assessing the ways Trump differed from Kerry, Obama, and Romney in how they discussed "politicians" in Washington and attributed blame to them for the nation's problems. At the outset it is important to recognize that Mitt Romney, Donald Trump, and even Barack Obama all attempted to make the case that they were the Washington outsider candidates—Mitt Romney and Donald Trump because of their business backgrounds and Obama because of his newcomer status as a US senator and his grass-roots organizing background. This meant that each sought, to a certain extent, to differentiate their own campaign identities from those of career politicians in Washington. They were the outsiders who, according to them, could bring novel approaches and solutions to Washington. The rub, however, is in how extensively they did so and how they framed their attacks. This is where Trump, without question, stood apart from the others.

Figure 3.1 shows the percentage and rate by which each candidate sought to blame politicians in Washington for the problems in the country. These included any reference to "politicians" in which no party affiliation was mentioned. In other words, we identified when candidates spoke of "politicians" in general, with no language that specified whether they were Democratic or Republican.[28] Perhaps not surprisingly, John Kerry almost never attacked Washington politicians because, well, he had been one of them since 1985 when he was first elected as a US senator from Massachusetts. The real comparison, therefore, is between Obama, Romney, and Trump, as they all, again, sought to portray themselves as Washington outsiders. What is clear from the data is that Trump focused far more attention on vilifying politicians than either Obama or Romney. In particular, Trump invoked the idea that politicians were culprits almost three times as often as Obama and over eight times as often as Romney. To be clear, it is not that Obama and Romney went easy on politicians in Washington. One of Romney's go-to phrases during his campaign, for example, was: "Career politicians got us into this mess and they simply don't know how to

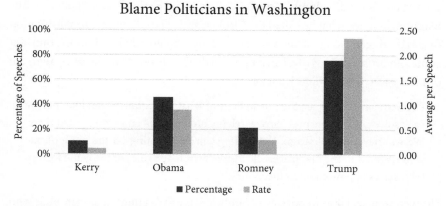

Figure 3.1 Percentage and rate of invocations of "politicians" across all speeches from 2004 to 2016.

get us out."[29] Furthermore, Romney alluded to a line of attack that Trump would take up four years later when he said:

> Politicians are routinely elected on promises to change Washington, but when they come here, they become creatures of Washington. They begin to see government as the answer to every challenge and the solution for every problem. At every turn, they try to substitute the heavy hand of the federal government for free citizens and free enterprise. They think government knows better—and can do better—than a free people exercising their free will.[30]

Similarly, Obama often portrayed politicians as people who were self-serving. For example, he argued:

> I realize that politicians come before you every election saying that they'll change all this. They lay out big plans and hold events with workers just like this one, because it's popular to do and it's easy to make promises in the heat of a campaign. But how many times have you been disappointed when everyone goes back to Washington and nothing changes? Because the lobbyists just write another check. Or because politicians start worrying about *how* they'll win the next election instead of *why* they should.[31]

By and large, however, Obama and Romney kept their critiques relatively tempered, often focusing on simply portraying politicians as inauthentic and prone to offering false promises while serving their own interests or those of lobbyists.

Trump offered similar critiques, but this was just his baseline. As his campaign progressed, he took his criticisms to a whole new level. Trump commonly called politicians "stupid," "dumb," "weak," "all talk, no action," and "failed," while blaming them for what he called the "broken and corrupt" system in Washington that was "rigged" to favor the very politicians who guarded it. Trump's outright contempt for politicians of all stripes was palpable throughout the campaign. On one occasion, for example, he stated:

> Everywhere I look, I see the possibilities of what our country could be. But we can't solve any of these problems by relying on the politicians who created them. We will never be able to fix a rigged system by counting on the same people who rigged it in the first place. The insiders wrote the rules of the game to keep themselves in power and in the money.[32]

He even went as far as to portray the politicians in Washington as criminals who would finally be brought to justice once he was elected. This was evident when he went on to say:

> On Election Day, the politicians stand trial before the people. The voters are the jury. Their ballots are the verdict… Come November, the American people will have a chance to issue a verdict on the politicians that have sacrificed their security, betrayed their prosperity, and sold out their country.

To Trump, politicians were not only criminal, they no longer had any sense of loyalty to the nation. They were part of the "corrupt Washington establishment" that, he argued, feared a Trump presidency that would likely take them all down. According to Trump: "The fact that Washington and the Washington establishment has tried so hard to stop our campaign is only more proof that our campaign represents the kind of change that only arrives once-in-a-lifetime."[33] Trump represented something completely different. Something exceptional.

As these criticisms of politicians and the Washington establishment increasingly became a part of Trump's rhetorical repertoire, he needed a catchy slogan to bring it all together. "Drain the Swamp" was just the ticket. The phrase was nothing new to Washington politics. According to Eric García of Roll Call: "Since the nation's capital was built on a literal swamp, the phrase has become a staple for political outsiders, promising to come to Washington and clean up the mess."[34] It was first popularized by Ronald Reagan in 1983 when he said that he had come to Washington "to drain the swamp." Nancy Pelosi had also used the phrase in 2007 when she spoke of needing to "drain the swamp" after years of GOP control of the House of Representatives.[35] Given the intense visibility and attention that it received during the 2016 presidential election, one might assume that Trump talked about draining the swamp in Washington from the inception of his campaign. But this catchphrase did not actually appear in his remarks on the campaign trail until just twenty-two days before the election.

On October 17, 2016, Trump revealed his new campaign slogan at a campaign rally in Newton, Pennsylvania. After introducing a proposed ethics reform package, Trump slowly and deliberately said: "It's time to drain the swamp in Washington, D.C."[36] The crowd erupted with applause. Trump/Pence signs rose and shook above the crowd as the audience began chanting, "Drain the Swamp! Drain the Swamp!" Trump paused to let the chant grow louder and louder in the auditorium. He then turned, walked slowly toward the American flag at the back of the stage with his arms wide open, and then hugged it. The crowd erupted again. The slogan was a hit and Trump knew it. As the cheers died down, Trump approached the podium and asked the crowd: "Is there any place more fun to be than a Trump rally? Right?" Trump clearly liked his new slogan.

The next day Trump made it official with a tweet and a new hashtag: "I will Make Our Government Honest Again—believe me. But first, I'm going to have to #DrainTheSwamp in DC."[37] The slogan was set. It was a political winner. And Trump's crowds loved it. People started showing up to his campaign rallies with signs, hats, and T-shirts, reading, "Drain the Swamp" and "Hire Trump to Drain the Swamp." It was his crowd's reactions that had sealed the deal. At a rally in Raleigh, North Carolina, the day before the election, Trump reflected on how his slogan came about:

> I want the entire corrupt Washington establishment to hear the words we're all about to say. This is a phrase, I told you. I didn't like it. I thought it was hokey. But it's not hokey. It's called "drain the swamp." We're going to go to Washington. We're going to drain the swamp. Can't believe it. I told the story. I hated that expression. I said no way I'm going to say that, no way. That's so hokey. And I said it. The place went crazy. Then I said it to another place. It went crazier. Then I said it with more confidence because you know confidence is—and it went wild. Now I love the expression. I think it was genius. Drain the swamp. Drain the swamp.[38]

"Drain the Swamp" had become, according to Trump, "the hottest expression." It was a clear and succinct way of portraying the same narrative he had been building since the day he launched his campaign. Politicians in Washington, regardless of political party, were all the same. They were the real culprits in the American system, they were to blame for the woes of the country, and they needed to be removed. "We will drain the swamp in Washington D.C.," Trump said, "and replace it with a government of, by, and for the people."[39]

By promising that he would "drain the swamp" and casting politicians of all stripes in Washington as the enemy, Trump was laying the groundwork for the exceptional me strategy.

Make America Exceptional Again

Throughout the 2016 election cycle, one message was coming through loud and clear from the Trump campaign: Elect me and I will take this downtrodden country out of the hands of corrupt Washington politicians and make it great (exceptional even) again. This was Trump's mantra. Even though it was a campaign slogan essentially borrowed from Ronald Reagan's 1980 campaign slogan, "Let's Make America Great Again," Trump claimed it as his own. In April of 2019, Trump reflected on his choice during the election to borrow, and slightly alter, Reagan's slogan at a Make America Great Again rally in Green Bay, Wisconsin:

> And it has been said—Make America Great Again, the greatest theme. Ronald Reagan used, let's... Make America Great. Close, but not the same. The apostrophe is too complicated. He used it a little bit. We seriously used it. MAGA. And MAGA we got for free, because my whole deal was Make America Great Again. All of a sudden people started going #MAGA.[40]

"Make America Great Again" was a tailor-made promise for the modern jeremiad. According to Trump, the nation was in tatters and politicians of all stripes were to blame, which made Trump uniquely qualified to restore America's greatness. MAGA was clear and succinct, and his crowds adored it. It was a flexible slogan too. Throughout the campaign, Trump invoked some variation of the slogan over 230 times. Trump often replaced the word "great" with a number of alternatives. Take, for example, this message, in which Trump frequently used to close his rallies:

> This is the change I am promising all of you: an honest government, a thriving economy, and a just society for each and every American. I am asking for your vote so I can be your champion in the White House. Together, we will make America wealthy again. We will make America strong again. We will make America proud again. We will make America safe again. And we will make America great again. Thank you, and God bless.[41]

Nonetheless, it is one thing for a candidate to promise that they will make America great again, but it is quite another to promise to make it exceptional again. In other words, any country can be great—as Trump promised to bring about—but only one can be the greatest. Trump promised that too. Consistent with his narrow conception of American exceptionalism, Trump declared that under his administration, he would restore America's superiority in world affairs: "We will build the greatest infrastructure on the planet earth—the road and railways of tomorrow. Our military will have the best technology and the finest equipment—we will bring it back all the way."[42] He also promised to "double our growth and have the strongest economy anywhere in the world."[43] In short, "American will no longer settle for anything less than the best." Clearly, in Trump's view, the United States still had potential and American exceptionalism could be restored. There was just one catch: the politicians who had run Washington for so many years had proven themselves incompetent and incapable. Put simply, "They will never make America great again. They don't even have a chance."[44] And so, according to Trump, there was one person—and one person alone—who could rescue the country from the gutter and restore American exceptionalism. "I know these problems can all be fixed," Trump said, but, "only by me."[45] He went on:

> I will be the greatest jobs president that God ever created, believe me. So we're going to have millions and millions of jobs, jobs like you have never seen in this country before, because our jobs are being stolen from us, our companies are being stolen from us, our manufacturing is down by 40 percent and 50 percent and numbers that nobody even believes. Those days will be over if Donald Trump is elected president of the United States, believe me.

According to Trump, there was something exceptional about him that made him uniquely capable of restoring the country to the greatness that it once had. This was the promise of the exceptional me strategy.

Self-Exceptionalism

Presidential candidates tend to employ a wide variety of tactics to build their credibility in the eyes of voters, but one that virtually every candidate uses is the argument that their experiences and accomplishments make them undeniably qualified to become president. John Kerry, for example, spoke of both his military service and his almost twenty years in the Senate as proof that he was qualified to take over as commander-in-chief at a time when the country was still at war in Iraq and Afghanistan. Barack Obama touted his experience in community organizing and his bipartisan achievements in the Illinois State Legislature and the US Senate as evidence that he was qualified to unify the country and address what he believed to be the most pressing issue in the nation at the time—inequality. Mitt Romney highlighted his experience working as a Republican governor in a Democratic state and his successes as a businessman to illustrate his executive experience and ability to manage large organizations. Similarly, Donald Trump touted his successes in the real estate business to argue that he was qualified to manage the rebuilding of the country's infrastructure.

Scholars often refer to this type of political behavior as *acclaiming*, or the act of praising one's self and one's own accomplishments to positively differentiate oneself from their political opponents.[46] It is an integral part of every campaign and serves to help candidates appear more "presidential" to the American electorate. Our focus in this chapter, however, is on a more extreme form of acclaiming. Specifically, we are interested in a form of acclaiming that we call self-exceptionalism.[47] Self-exceptionalism, we argue, takes acclaiming and ratchets it up a notch. Specifically, it involves candidates not merely just acclaiming their successes but also portraying themselves as exceptional in some important way. This might include candidates identifying unique characteristics or attributes about themselves, portraying themselves as superior to all other candidates, or even, in rare cases, suggesting that a higher power might be in favor of their candidacy.[48] In short, self-exceptionalism entails candidates presenting themselves as exceptionally qualified to lead the country in a successful direction.

Referring to oneself as exceptional, however, has traditionally been seen as a risky move for presidential candidates because, as one might expect, such claims can come off as pompous and unnecessarily self-aggrandizing and they risk alienating voters. Indeed, modesty and humility are two traits that voters tend to value in their presidential candidates. Candidates, therefore, tend to self-acclaim at this level only rarely, if ever. Nonetheless, Trump defied these norms. Indeed, self-exceptionalism was undoubtedly his favorite tactic throughout his campaign. As Figure 3.2 indicates, there really is no comparison between how often Trump invoked self-exceptionalism relative to his predecessors.[49] Notably, Kerry, Obama, and Romney only scarcely employed this tactic, and when they did, the nature of these references was extremely limited. At times, both Romney and Obama referred to themselves as "the only candidate" in the race to take a clear stance on an issue or to offer a specific policy that other candidates had not addressed. Obama twice referred to his campaign as "historic," and Romney

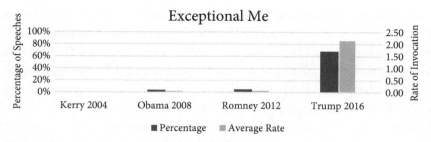

Figure 3.2 Percentage and rate of invocations of self-exceptionalism across all speeches from 2004 to 2016.

once described his efforts in managing the 2002 Olympics in Salt Lake City as "the world's largest athletic event."[50] Thus, self-exceptionalism references were exceedingly rare for these candidates. In contrast, Trump was undeniably "all in" on self-exceptionalism throughout his campaign. Specifically, he described himself, his campaign, or his closest political confidants as exceptional in 68 percent of his speeches, and at an average rate of over two times per speech. Self-exceptionalism, therefore, was a Trump-specific rhetorical tactic. And, even though Trump liked to say, "I don't have to brag. I don't have to, believe it or not,"[51] clearly, he did. It was the centerpiece of his exceptional me strategy. Below we illuminate the distinct ways that Donald Trump invoked self-exceptionalism during his 2016 campaign.

Exceptional Me

It is important to note that, from the outset, Trump had little interest in displaying any modesty or humility throughout his campaign. Simply put, it was just not in him to do so. Instead, he sought to paint a larger-than-life portrait of himself for his audiences. One way he did this was to refer to himself in the third person, as if "Donald Trump" was some extraordinary, even mythical, persona who had no bounds. Trump referred to himself in the third person over seventy times throughout the campaign in a number of different circumstances.[52] When speaking on the war in Syria, for example, he offered: "Mark my words. Nobody would be tougher on ISIS than Donald Trump. Nobody."[53] The most common way that Trump invoked self-exceptionalism, however, was to overtly describe himself—whether in first or third person—as being exceptional as an individual, as a businessman, and as a candidate. For example, Trump commonly said: "I will be America's greatest defender and most loyal champion."[54] With regard to his professional preparation, Trump famously offered: "I went to an Ivy League School. I'm very highly educated. I know words—I have the best words."[55] Trump also often touted his singular expertise on specific issues. On terrorism, Trump stated: "I've studied this issue in great detail. I would say, actually, greater by far than anybody else, believe me, oh, believe me."[56] Similarly, Trump said: "[N]obody in the history of this country has ever known so much about infrastructure as Donald Trump."[57] On the border wall that he vowed to build once he became president, he argued: "I would build a great wall, and nobody builds walls better than me, believe me."[58] According to Trump, everything he did was exceptional. Put simply: "I could do the greatest things."[59] Trump's explicit celebration of himself was perhaps best encapsulated in his speech at the Republican National Convention when he proclaimed: "I have joined the political arena so that the powerful can no longer beat up on people that cannot defend themselves. Nobody knows the system better than me, which is why I alone can fix it."[60] It was a foregone conclusion, then, that Trump—and Trump alone—could save the country from its problems.

Voters did not just have to take Trump's word for it. Indeed, he regularly boasted how others were touting his exceptionalism as well. For instance, Trump regularly talked of his business acumen as being second to none, declaring: "Many people have said that I perform better under pressure than anyone they've ever seen. I've proven that over and over again."[61] Furthermore, Trump highlighted how others were praising his campaign: "Even the pundits, even the ones that truly dislike Donald Trump have said, it's the single greatest phenomenon they have ever seen."[62] On his performance in the second presidential debate against Hillary Clinton in St. Louis, Missouri, Trump offered this: "Pat Buchanan wrote the big article today, you saw it—I'm not bragging, I'm just saying—maybe a little bit, but here—he said it was the single greatest debate performance in the history of presidential politics."[63] Similarly, in reference to the electoral impact of the Republican National Convention, he offered: "Biggest—they say the biggest bounce in memory." Finally, in late 2015, Trump released a letter about his health to the public from his doctor, Harold Bornstein—who later revealed that Trump had dictated the letter—stating that "his physical strength and stamina are extraordinary" and that "If elected, Mr. Trump, I can state unequivocally, will be the healthiest individual ever elected to the presidency."[64] For Trump, this line of argument helped fuel the idea that it was not just him touting his exceptionalism, "many people" had noticed it and they were declaring it too. In essence, Trump was employing the age-old rhetorical fallacy of *argumentum ad populum*: If others are saying it, it must be true.

Exceptional Accomplishments

To further bolster Trump's "exceptional me" argument, he often boasted of his singular accomplishments in business and politics. With regard to his real estate ventures, he frequently referred to them as "the best in the world," "the most sought after," and in the "best locations." Trump even emphasized that he was sacrificing his lavish lifestyle to run for president:

> I didn't have to do this. When I did this, believe me—you see this incredible resort. It's one of the great in the world. When I did this, I could be here enjoying myself. I don't have to be with you guys. I didn't need this. I have places that are the best in the world, OK. I could be doing other things. I'm doing this because we're going to make America great again.[65]

At times, Trump would feign humility while doubling down on the argument that he and his ventures were, in fact, exceptional. Take, for example, when he spoke of his business book:

> You see, I know about deal making, that's what I do. I wrote the Art of the Deal. One of the bestselling all-time, and I mean, seriously, I'm saying "one of," because I'll be criticized if I say "the," so I'm going to be very diplomatic, "one of," I'll be criticized, I think it is number one, but why take a chance. One of the all-time bestselling books about deals and deal making.[66]

Trump also frequently went out of his way to make clear that he was—or would be, if elected president—exceptional compared to other presidents and politicians of the past. In reference to his performance in the Republican primaries, for example, Trump claimed:

> [W]e got almost 14 million votes. That's more than any other person in the history of the Republican Party in the primary system running for president. Think of it. That's more than Ronald Reagan, who we love. That's more than Richard Nixon. It's more than Dwight D. Eisenhower. You know, he won the Second World War, in all fairness. Pretty good. It's more than the Bushes.[67]

On another occasion, he reflected further on the history of this achievement: "That's a long time. You know, starting with Honest Abe Lincoln, right. That's a long time. I got more than Honest Abe."[68] Putting aside the fact that the population of the United States under the presidency of Lincoln was around 31 million and that more than half of that population did not have the legal right to vote—such details can matter little in the overall persuasiveness of campaign messages—Trump was making the case to voters that he stood head and shoulders above even the most revered icons of the Republican Party. More often, though, Trump was more general in these comparisons. He frequently promised that he would do more than any other president in history. When speaking on the Second Amendment, for example, Trump promised: "Donald Trump will protect it more so than any president that has ever served."[69] In this light, Trump was one-of-a-kind and he was going to bring about change that no one before him was capable of accomplishing.

Exceptional Promises

Another facet of Trump's exceptional me strategy was to speak of his campaign promises and future policies as exceptional in some way. One line of argument that Trump offered was that he would work for the American people more than any president before him had done. On the issue of urban crime, Trump stated:

> Take a look at some of these cities where you see things happening that are horrendous. And if you talk about them, they say bad things about you. They call you a racist. They call you all—and by the way, speaking of that, nobody will do more for the African-American citizens of this country than Donald Trump, nobody, nobody. Nobody will do more for the Latino community than Donald Trump, I can tell you.[70]

In a similar light, Trump regularly spoke directly to the African American community, offering: "I will fight for you as no one ever has before."[71] He offered that he would do the same for Christian Americans: "A Trump administration, our Christian heritage will be cherished, protected, defended, like you've never seen before. Believe me. I believe it. And you believe it. And you know it. You know it."[72] Trump also touted his policy proposals as larger in scope and reach than ever before. Trump emphasized, for example, that he had "the most pro-growth economic plan in American history,"[73] and he promised the "largest regulatory reform in American history." In short, his plan was "the most pro-growth, pro-jobs, pro-family plan put forth perhaps in the history of the country."[74] Trump also vowed to appoint the "best people," stating:

> I will appoint the best judges and prosecutors and federal investigators who will make this [crime] their personal mission. There is one thing which can no longer be denied: if you keep voting for the same people, you will keep getting the same results. To those suffering, I say: what do you have to lose by voting for Donald Trump? I will fix it. I will fight for you as no one ever has before.[75]

Perhaps the quintessential example of Trump referring to his policies and abilities to enact them as exceptional was when he said (on two separate occasions): "I will be the greatest jobs president that God ever created, believe me."[76] The language of exceptionalism, therefore, was clearly infused in how Trump talked about his promises and policies.

The Exceptional Campaign

Throughout his campaign, Trump lavished praise on his "historic" campaign, his "unprecedented" political movement, and the "best" people who were involved in it at every turn. This was another important component in his exceptional me strategy. Take, for example, how Trump spoke of the people involved in his campaign:

> I mean, we have great people. We have the most loyal people. We have the smartest people. You know, so many of my people, they're so smart. They like to say, well, Trump, I don't know if he's got this right. Let me tell you, we have the smartest people. We have the people that are the smartest, and the strongest, and the best and the hardest working. We have the smartest people. We'll put I.Q.s among—some of us, we couldn't say all of us, right—against any I.Q.s that we, we have to deal with.[77]

Trump also frequently praised his crowds, but in a way that went far beyond what presidential candidates have traditionally done. Indeed, from the earliest days of his campaign through Election Day, Trump spent an exorbitant amount of time talking about the exceptional size of his crowds. The day Trump announced his candidacy, for example, he looked over his crowd and commented: "There's been no crowd like this."[78] At virtually every campaign event, Trump would often dedicate the first moments of his campaign speeches to talking about the "massive" crowds that were "setting records" wherever he went. Taking it a step further, Trump even made sure to point out that his crowds were larger than everyone else's, from Jay-Z and Beyoncé ("I get bigger crowds than they do."[79]) to Hillary Clinton ("She's never had a crowd like this in her life."[80]). To Trump, his crowds were something to behold. They were truly exceptional.

Trump also frequently proclaimed in his stump speeches: "this is a movement like they've never seen in this country before, and every place is packed, and the greatest people on Earth."[81] And he would typically close his speech with the following:

> Imagine what our country could accomplish if we started working together as one people, under one God, saluting one American flag. You're going to look back at this rally for the rest of your life. This is a movement like the world has

never seen before. You're going to look back at this election, and say this is by far the most important vote you've ever cast for anyone at any time. We will make America wealthy again. We will make America strong again. We will make America safe again. And we will make America great again.[82]

Trump's message, then, was meant to empower his supporters with the feeling that they were participating in something special, something that had never happened before in American politics. Perhaps the most illustrative example came during his final campaign speech the day before the election when he reflected at length on just how exceptional his campaign had been:

> There has never been a movement like this. Even these dishonest people in the media say there has never—Bill O'Reilly. He said it's the single greatest political phenomena that he's witnessed in his life. That's a pretty good statement. But others have said it. Others have said it. Others have said it. And it's not going to happen again. It won't be able to happen again. Four years it'll never happen. So you got to get out there and you got to vote. Got to get out. Somebody said what you've done has never been done before. It doesn't matter if you win or lose. I said believe me, it matters. No, they said that. It'll be down in the history books. I said you know what? You may be right about that. But if we don't win I will consider this the single greatest waste of time, energy. Wow do I—you need energy for this. The single greatest waste of time, energy and money. You know, we have a movement going on like they've never seen before in this country. Drain the swamps, you've gotta a "drain the swamp" sign back there, we're going to drain the swamp, believe me. But this is a movement like they've never seen in this country before, and every place is packed, and the greatest people on Earth, and we're going to turn our country around, we're going to turn it around fast.[83]

Trump was no doubt disciplined and consistent in how he communicated his exceptional me strategy throughout his campaign. Whether it was himself, his campaign team, his supporters, or the Trump movement in general, each was portrayed as exceptional, one-of-a-kind, better than all the rest, and the true and only answer to the nation's fall from grace. Clearly, if anything was exceptional, it was Trump and everything related to him.[84]

Unexceptional Others

Another crucial element within Trump's exceptional me strategy was his use of the language of exceptionalism to describe the other players involved in the presidential election, but always, of course, in a negative light. Trump's use of the language of exceptionalism, therefore, was not restricted to himself, his campaign, or those around him; he also used the language to denigrate his political opponents as well as the media. Barack Obama, for example, was someone whom Trump routinely characterized as unexceptional. Trump attacked Obama on a number of fronts, from Obamacare and his handling of the economic recovery to his record on foreign policy. For example, Trump said this about Obama's legacy as president:

> I think President Obama has been the most ignorant president in our history. His views of the world, as he says, don't jive. And the world is a mess. You look at what's happening with the migration, with Syria, with Libya, with Iraq, with everything he's touched. He has been a disaster as a president. He will go down as one of the worst presidents in the history of our country. It is a mess.[85]

Similarly, on the Iran nuclear deal, Trump argued: "it will go down in history as one of the worst deals ever negotiated."[86] On Israel: "Obama, in my opinion, is the single worst thing politically speaking that's ever happened to Israel. He has been a disaster for Israel."[87] Furthermore, Trump criticized Obama's efforts on economic recovery, frequently saying that it was "the worst so-called recovery since the great depression."[88] Obama, according to Trump, was a complete disaster.

Hillary Clinton, however, as one would expect, tended to be in Trump's crosshairs the most when it came to his use of unexceptionalism. He called her, for example, the "all-time worst" on a number of occasions and across a broad range of issues. He routinely attacked Clinton's track record as secretary of state, for example, stating:

> Her tenure as Secretary of State may be regarded as the most disastrous in U.S. history. Look at the world before and after she became Secretary of State. Pre-Hillary, in early 2009, Iraq was seeing a reduction in violence. Libya was stable. Syria was under control. The group we know today as ISIS was close to being extinguished. Iran was being choked by sanctions. Now, fast-forward to present time. After Hillary, here is what the world looks like: Iraq is in total chaos. Syria is in the midst of a disastrous civil war and a refugee crisis now threatens Europe and the United States. ISIS has been unleashed onto the entire world.[89]

In addition, Trump would often label Clinton's policies as being exceptionally bad. At the same time, he would be remiss if he did not also seize the opportunity to laud his own achievements while attacking his opponent. For example, Trump offered this: "We've received the first-ever endorsement from our ICE and Border Patrol officers. They tell us the border crisis is the worst it's ever been—it's a national emergency. They also warn America that Clinton's plan is the most radical proposal in U.S. history."[90] At another rally, Trump attacked Clinton—and her husband's legacy—when referring to NAFTA: "Hillary Clinton pushes for NAFTA—or the Trans-Pacific Partnership, which will also be a disaster—NAFTA's the worst trade deal ever signed, ever made, by anybody in the world."[91] In Trump's view, Hillary Clinton and her political record were a "historic failure."[92] Put simply: "The election of Hillary Clinton would lead, in my opinion, to the almost total destruction of our country as we know it. She would be the most dishonest and the most corrupt person ever elected to high office. And I don't think it would be close."[93]

Trump's other favorite target was the news media. Because Trump viewed the media as disloyal to both him and the nation, he frequently portrayed them as "the worst" and the "world's most dishonest people."[94] Take, for example, the following statement by Trump, which he often offered in some variation throughout his campaign:

> It's time to reject the media and political elite that has bled our country dry. And these are among the most dishonest people. They don't give you the truth, folks. They don't give you the truth. They rarely give you the truth. You know it. And they know it. That's the scary part. They know it.[95]

Such statements were always a hit with the crowds, fueling inevitable booing directed at the media corps in the back. His main gripe, however, was that they were not showing his crowd sizes in their coverage of his campaign. They never show the crowds, he would say. Trump best summarized his view that the media were exceptionally bad when he said:

> Another important issue for Americans is integrity in journalism. These people are among the most dishonest people I've ever met, spoken to, done business with. These are the most dishonest people. There has never been dishonesty— there has never been dishonesty like we've seen in this election. There's never been anywhere near the media dishonesty like we've seen in this election. Don't worry, they won't spin the cameras and show the kind of massive crowds. They won't do that.[96]

In portraying his political opponents as unexceptional, Trump must have thought that it would make his own exceptionalism shine even brighter by comparison. By declaring his opponents to be the worst the world has ever seen while, at the same time, proclaiming himself to be the best there ever was, Trump's method was obvious: he was seeking to set himself on an exceptional pedestal. To Trump, there was no gray area in the political arena, no place for nuance. Trump saw virtually everything in extremes, from the putrid state of American exceptionalism to Trump himself, his movement, and his opponents. Trump wanted to leave no room for doubt for his supporters and potential voters. He was the only person alive who could save America and make it great again.

A Jeremiad in Tatters: The Exceptional Me Strategy Emerges

Over the past two chapters we have shown how Donald Trump strayed from the structure of the modern jeremiad to create his own exceptional me strategy. Whereas typical opposition candidates stick strictly within the confines of the three rhetorical tactics of the modern jeremiad—embrace American exceptionalism in all its forms, carefully make the case that the country was being misled or damaged by the opposing party in power, and position oneself as the solution to the problem—Trump took a different path. Figure 3.3 vividly illustrates these different political strategies on a number of fronts. First, the data in the figure show how Trump was substantially less likely to invoke American exceptionalism than any of the other opposition presidential candidates—John Kerry, Barack Obama, Mitt Romney. Furthermore, when Trump did on occasion invoke American exceptionalism, he focused almost all of his attention on speaking of American superiority. Otherwise, Trump rarely paid any attention to the various facets of American exceptionalism that each of his predecessors routinely invoked. Specifically, Trump rarely spoke of the unique qualities that make the United States singular within the international community, and very seldom did he mention America's special role as global leader or suggest that America stands as the "city on a hill" for others around the world to follow. Notably, for Trump, winning mattered more than anything else. In the first chapter of his campaign book, *Crippled America: How to Make America Great Again*, titled simply, "Winning Again," he made it clear and simple: "Winning matters. Being the best matters."[97] To Trump, American exceptionalism was a zero-sum game.

In Trump's exceptional me strategy, American exceptionalism was all about winning, which, according to Trump, America was not. Scholars have pointed out that when opposition candidates employ the modern jeremiad, they typically couch their relatively few references to the nation as being unexceptional in a broader story of American exceptionalism.[98] This allows

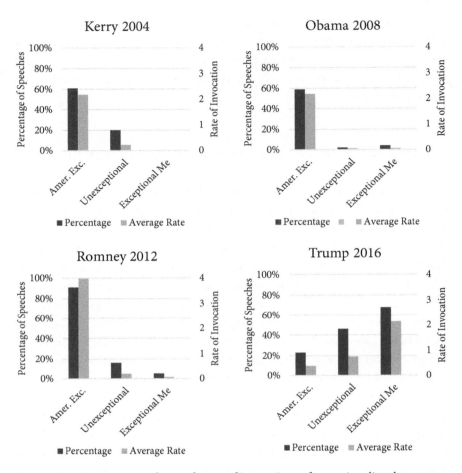

Figure 3.3 Percentage and rate of types of invocations of exceptionalism language across all speeches from 2004 to 2016.

them to point out what is wrong with the nation while not running the risk of seeming unpatriotic or insufficiently supportive of American exceptionalism. This was not at all what Trump did. Figure 3.3 shows that Trump was twice as likely to refer to the United States as unexceptional than he was to refer to it as exceptional. In other words, Trump's principal approach to American exceptionalism was to discredit it. Again, Trump was clear on this point: "The idea of American Greatness, of our country as the leader of the free and unfree world, has vanished."[99] Furthermore, Trump's approach to assigning blame for America's decline was vastly different from the modern jeremiads of his predecessors. Specifically, Trump did not simply blame the Democrats in power for the country's ills, as one would expect. Instead, he spread the blame around, often attacking those within the Republican Party and portraying Washington politicians as the culprits for the America's decline. The modern jeremiad was getting a bit too clunky for Trump.

Our analysis has also shown that, unlike his predecessors, Trump made the argument that the status of American exceptionalism was not necessarily tied to anything inherent within the nation itself. Rather, it was tied to Trump and his own self-exceptionalism. Instead of proving his stripes as a true believer in American exceptionalism and drawing upon this idea to inspire and motivate citizens during his campaign, he focused his attention on building the case that he was the only person qualified to save the nation from disaster. Time and time again, Trump argued that he alone could fix the country. It was clear that the modern jeremiad did not entirely fit his vision for his presidential campaign. The nation was clearly in need of a savior, according to Trump, but in the exceptional me strategy, that savior could not be found in any political party or campaign platform. The savior was not American exceptionalism, replete with its promise that the American people had the inherent, unparalleled ability to overcome any challenge and rise from difficult challenge themselves. No, there was only one savior out there. It was Donald Trump.

Throughout the 2016 Make America Great Again campaign, Trump's exceptional me strategy was undeniably clear to his supporters and potential voters. The country was in tatters and American exceptionalism was in the gutter. In fact, the country had become unexceptional and politicians of all political stripes were to blame. They were all—Democrats and Republicans alike—part of the Washington establishment that had put their own interests before the interests of the nation, thus causing its decline. There was an answer, though. The country could be made great again, but there was only one person in all of politics who could do it. Trump was a once-in-a-lifetime candidate, he argued, who was exceptionally successful at business and life. He had created the greatest political movement in the history of the country, and his opponents who were trying to undermine and ultimately take down his campaign—from Democrats and Republicans to the media—were the worst possible human beings, representing the same establishment that had taken advantage of Americans for years. In other words, Trump was the only option. Only he could fix it. As Trump argued:

> Some people warned me this campaign would be a journey to hell. But they are wrong, it will be a journey to heaven because we will help so many people. In my former life, I was an insider as much as anybody else, and I know what's like to be

an insider. Now I am being punished for leaving their special club and revealing to you their great scam. Because I used to be part of the club, I'm the only one who can fix it. I'm doing this for the people, and this movement is just right and we will take back this country for you and Make America Great Again. The corrupt establishment knows that we are an existential threat to their criminal enterprise. They know, that if we win, their power is gone and returned to you.[100]

This was the exceptional me strategy at work.

Act Two

The Trump Presidency: Exceptional Me 2.0

4

Exceptional We: Building the Case for an Exceptional Nation

And as we begin the new year, our economy is booming, wages are soaring, workers are thriving, and America's future has never, ever looked brighter, ever. We're the envy of every country in the world.

—Donald Trump[1]

Two days before taking the oath of office on January 20, 2017, Donald Trump filed for copyright protection of a new campaign slogan: "Keep America Great!"[2] Trump was already thinking about reelection, and this new slogan was designed to seamlessly take the place of "Make America Great Again" for his 2020 reelection bid. The logic and overall political strategy behind this new slogan were simple. In his 2016 presidential bid, Trump had traveled the nation promising crowd after crowd that he was going to "Make America Great Again." Now that he was president, he would be expected to fulfill that promise. In other words, at some point in his presidency—presumably thanks to his policies and actions as president—the country would have to become "great" again. As Trump emphasized in his inaugural speech: "We're going to start winning again. Winning like never before."[3] The argument that he was restoring American exceptionalism, however, would need to be rolled out over time as his presidency gained traction and he had achieved some political victories. Indeed, Trump could not simply proclaim that American exceptionalism had been restored by virtue of his election; he had to get to work, building a case for how he, as president, had made it exceptional again. He would have to bide his time, gradually transitioning from the narrative he had spun during his campaign of a lost American exceptionalism and a country in tatters to a much more vivid and resonant one in which the United States had reemerged as the greatest and most powerful country in the world. "Keep America Great!" would have to wait to be unveiled. It wasn't time.

A month after his inauguration, Trump delivered his first major address to the nation as president, speaking before a joint session of Congress. Trump began the speech by laying the foundation upon which his new communication strategy would emerge, focusing on trying to spur a new sense of hopefulness about what his presidency would bring: "A new chapter of American greatness is now beginning. A new national pride is sweeping across our nation. And a new surge of optimism is placing impossible dreams firmly within our grasp. What we are witnessing today is the renewal of the American spirit."[4] He then spoke of his campaign, celebrating his supporters who had participated in an "historic movement the likes of which the world has never seen before." Trump then pivoted, digging back in on the same bleak and dismal narrative that he had told time and again on the campaign trail about an America in utter disrepair:

> [W]e must honestly acknowledge the circumstances we inherited. Ninety-four million Americans are out of the labor force. Over 43 million people are now living in poverty, and over 43 million Americans are on food stamps. More than one in five people in their prime working years are not working. We have the worst financial recovery in 65 years. In the last eight years, the past administration has put on more new debt than nearly all of the other Presidents combined.

This sentiment was also evident in other speeches that Trump gave at the time. At a Make America Great Again rally in Melbourne, Florida, on February 18, 2017, for example, Trump stated: "We don't win anymore. We don't win at trade. We don't win in any capacity. We don't win anymore. We're going to start winning again."[5] At another rally in Harrisburg, Pennsylvania, a couple of months later, Trump argued: "For decades our country has lived through the greatest jobs theft in the history of the world. Our factories were shuttered, our steel mills closed down, and our jobs were stolen away and shipped far away to other countries."[6] He then added: "We are not going to let other countries take advantage of us anymore."

Such doom and gloom—mixed with assurances that the tide was about to turn—in the opening days of the Trump presidency was strategic for two important reasons. First, it set the bar as low as possible for the Trump presidency by portraying the nation in the worst terms imaginable, ensuring that even the most modest of improvements made by Trump would be perceived as monumental achievements by comparison. Second, it allowed Trump to essentially use other administrations—Obama's in particular—to deflect blame onto for any problems that might arise while taking full credit for any successes. Perhaps this is why, at his first solo press conference as president, Trump offered this: "To be honest, I inherited a mess. It's a mess. At home and abroad, a mess."[7] Trump then stated: "[W]e'll take care of it folks. We're going to take care of it all. I just want to let you know, I inherited a mess." What was noticeably scarce in all of Trump's early communications, however, were celebrations of American exceptionalism. It wasn't quite time. Trump's argument was hinged upon the idea that he was taking over a country that was, in fact, not exceptional at all, but could be made so again. In essence, Trump was setting the stage for the updated, presidential version of his exceptional me strategy. He was just waiting for the right time to roll it out in all its glory.

Roughly three years later, Trump's tune had changed entirely. On December 10, 2019, for example, Trump held a MAGA rally at the Kellogg Arena in Hershey, Pennsylvania. He walked out to a raucous applause as Lee Greenwood's "God Bless the U.S.A." played him onto stage. The speech ran just over two hours in length and touched on a range of issues, including the fact that House Democrats had just officially released two articles of impeachment—abuse of power and obstruction of Congress—against Trump earlier in the day. Earlier, Trump tweeted this in response:

> To impeach a President who has proven through results, including producing perhaps the strongest economy in our country's history, to have one of the most successful presidencies ever, and most importantly, who has done NOTHING wrong, is sheer Political Madness! #2020Election.[8]

It was no surprise, then, that at the rally, Trump spoke of "impeachment" throughout the speech, but his central message was not to be outshined: American exceptionalism had been restored under his presidency. In the speech, Trump invoked American exceptionalism a full twenty-seven times—by far the most in any speech that he had given to that point—and he spoke at length about how the country had become great again. For instance, Trump highlighted America's military superiority, saying:

> We build the greatest weapons, the greatest planes, the greatest ships, we build it in the United States. There is nobody who comes close. We have the greatest military equipment than anywhere in the world. Rockets, missiles, no place builds it like us we are the best in the world and we sell it to allies. And they all want to buy from the United States. We are so hot.[9]

The idea that America was "hot" was simply a way of saying that American exceptionalism was a recent phenomenon, one that took place, of course, under his administration. On the economy, Trump was even more explicit. He mentioned, for example, that "right now we are by far the largest economy in the world." He then added:

> We have now the hottest economy. You know what I mean: dictators and presidents and kings and queens and prime ministers. They all come into that beautiful oval office, so beautiful, right? So respected. And the first thing they almost always say, "sir, congratulations on your economy, were trying to do the same thing." And I say "you will not be able to do it." They won't be able to. Let them give it a shot, but they all say "congratulations on the great job you've done."

Trump also noted: "We are now number one in the world in energy." Moments later, he added: "The United States is now—and I said it and I'll say it all night long, number one producer of oil and natural gas in the world and there's nobody even close." According to Trump, America was back. It was "now" stronger and more prosperous, he argued, than ever before. And it was all, according to Trump, thanks to him.

In this chapter, we begin to lay out how Trump modified the campaign version of his exceptional me strategy to fit his presidency. We start by tracking the trajectory of Trump's invocations of American exceptionalism throughout his first term in office. Specifically, we systematically analyze and compare Trump to other post–Second World War presidents, focusing on their invocations of American exceptionalism in major speeches to the nation. Notably, we find that unlike most of his predecessors, Trump did not come into office trumpeting American exceptionalism. In fact, Trump very gradually made the case that American exceptionalism was returning as the first term of his presidency progressed. Furthermore, we demonstrate how Trump—again, unlike his predecessors—continued to show a more narrow understanding of American exceptionalism, portraying it as a fairly single-faceted idea that focused principally on the idea of American superiority, or the idea of "winning" within the global arena. By comparison, we demonstrate how previous presidents tended to wax philosophical about this concept, tying it to various aspects of the nation and often referring to the United States as the global leader and a model for the rest of the world to follow. We also reveal how Trump tended to speak of American exceptionalism in more malleable terms, defining it as something that can be won or lost by the person occupying the presidency. Previous presidents, by contrast, have historically regarded it as something that is inherent or fundamental to the nation itself and, thus, not conditional to the whims of any given president.

This set Trump up, we argue, for his next step, which was to claim credit for the return of American exceptionalism. Specifically, given that Trump had made the case that American exceptionalism is something contingent upon the attributes and abilities of the president, it then allowed him to argue that he was responsible for making America great (exceptional) again. As our findings indicate, this was completely at odds with how all of his predecessors since the Second World War had approached American exceptionalism. No president before Trump claimed such blatant credit for American exceptionalism in any consistent or meaningful way. Trump, however, did so at a remarkably high rate relative to his predecessors. In each case, we take a deeper dive into how these dynamics played out in his messaging in tweets and in the various Make America Great Again rallies that he continued to hold throughout his presidency. These communications represent a different side of Trump—one that was just as strategic, but much less restrained and scripted than in his official speeches as president. Overall, our findings offer important insights into the broader communication strategy employed by Trump during his first term in office and how Trump built the case that he had restored American exceptionalism at some point during his presidency. After all, his decision to trademark, "Keep America Great!" just days before his inauguration and make it the centerpiece of his reelection bid, depended on it.

Setting the Tone: The Inaugural Address

No speech is more important for setting the tone of a presidency than a president's inaugural address. It serves as the first opportunity for an incoming president to speak directly to the American people and lay out their vision for the country. As a result, a president tends to approach the inaugural address with a level of forethought and seriousness rarely seen, if ever, during the rest of their presidency. New presidents tend to see inaugurals, then, as monumentally important events. It is the only moment of their presidency when the entire nation is on the edge of their seats waiting to find out what to expect from their new president, to see what kind of leader they intend to be, and to determine if they can feel confident getting behind their new commander-in-chief. And even in the age of fractured media consumption, where citizens can regularly avoid watching political speeches, large swaths of the American public still take the time to tune in to presidential inaugurals live. The inaugurals, therefore, tend to be well-manicured moments of political theater during which the new president attempts to seize on the symbolic importance of the moment to make a good first impression on the American public as their president. They clearly know that such impressions could very well persist throughout the rest of their presidency. It is, therefore, crucial for a president to deliver a memorable speech on this occasion.

It is also in the inaugural where presidents tend to lay out a complex story of American exceptionalism, illustrating to the American public that they understand the uniqueness of the nation, its unprecedented accomplishments, and the special role it should play in the world. The American people have, no doubt, come to expect this type of language from their president, not just in the inaugural address but throughout their presidency. In the eyes of the public, presidents should serve as the foremost champions of American exceptionalism, carrying its flag both at home and abroad. According to presidential communication scholars David Domke and Kevin Coe, this is because: "Presidents are the nation's foremost political storytellers, spinning narratives about America's past, present, and future."[10] Presidents, therefore, regularly use the inaugural address as a platform to spin creative new ways to retell the story of America's special history, its exceptional form of government, and the unique people who drive it forward. Notably, in the modern era, there are two presidents who above all others offered the most explicit and forceful narratives about American exceptionalism in their first speech before the nation—Ronald Reagan and Barrack Obama. Their inaugural addresses, therefore, serve as useful points of comparison when analyzing how Trump used his inaugural address to lay the groundwork for the exceptional me strategy.

When Ronald Reagan took the podium in front of the Capitol Building in 1981 to deliver his inaugural address, the country was still reeling from a decade of political turmoil and economic woes. The memories of Richard Nixon's resignation—coupled with Gerald Ford and Jimmy Carter's rocky presidencies— were still raw in the minds of most Americans. As a result, confidence and trust in the government, especially toward the presidency, appeared to have reached historic lows. Reagan, therefore, attempted to use his inaugural address to ameliorate this malaise and restore Americans' faith in their country. He did so primarily, we argue, by emphasizing the idea of American exceptionalism in both subtle and conspicuous ways. This was evident from the outset:

> To a few of us here today this is a solemn and most momentous occasion, and yet in the history of our nation it is a commonplace occurrence. The orderly transfer of authority as called for in the Constitution routinely takes place, as it has for almost two centuries, and few of us stop to think how unique we really are.

In the eyes of many in the world, this every 4-year ceremony we accept as normal is nothing less than a miracle. Mr. President [Carter], I want our fellow citizens to know how much you did to carry on this tradition. By your gracious cooperation in the transition process, you have shown a watching world that we are a united people pledged to maintaining a political system which guarantees individual liberty to a greater degree than any other.[11]

Reagan then spoke at length about what makes the United States so unique, invoking such phrases as "special among the nations of the earth," "this last and greatest bastion of freedom," and "the world's strongest economy." Perhaps his most poignant reference to American exceptionalism came when he said:

If we look to the answer as to why for so many years we achieved so much, prospered as no other people on Earth, it was because here in this land we unleashed the energy and individual genius of man to a greater extent than has ever been done before. Freedom and the dignity of the individual have been more available and assured here than in any other place on Earth. The price for this freedom at times has been high, but we have never been unwilling to pay that price.

Reagan's message was clear: the United States had been through difficult times before, but it had always overcome those challenges because of the inherently special nature of the country.

When Barack Obama took the oath of office in January of 2009, the country was going through a similar period of friction and strife. The American people had grown weary from two ongoing wars, a health care crisis, and the ominous Great Recession that had hit various parts of the country over the preceding year. Nonetheless, similar to Reagan, Obama did not dwell on these daunting challenges. Instead, he sought to restore confidence among Americans, appealing to and bolstering the idea of American exceptionalism at virtually every turn. As Obama stepped up to the podium to deliver his address, he immediately sought to reassure the American people that there was no cause for alarm, that American ingenuity was second to none. He offered:

We remain the most prosperous, powerful nation on Earth. Our workers are no less productive than when this crisis began. Our minds are no less inventive. Our goods and services no less needed than they were last week or last month or last year. Our capacity remains undiminished. But our time of standing pat, of protecting narrow interests and putting off unpleasant decisions, that time has surely passed. Starting today, we must pick ourselves up, dust ourselves off, and begin again the work of remaking America.[12]

For Obama, there was something special embedded in the character of the country that made it worthy of optimism:

> As for our common defense, we reject as false the choice between our safety and our ideals. Our Founding Fathers, faced with perils that we can scarcely imagine, drafted a charter to assure the rule of law and the rights of man, a charter expanded by the blood of generations. Those ideals still light the world, and we will not give them up for expedience's sake. And so to all the other peoples and governments who are watching today, from the grandest capitals to the small village where my father was born, know that America is a friend of each nation and every man, woman, and child who seeks a future of peace and dignity, and we are ready to lead once more.

American exceptionalism, therefore, was not at risk here. Rather, it was proof positive of America's ability to lift itself out of difficult times. For Obama, though his role was to lead, it was in the hands of the American people to move the country forward in a positive direction.

There were several important parallels between the inaugural addresses given by Reagan and Obama and the one that Trump delivered. Each followed a similar pattern, almost as though the same template had been given to each of them before they (and their team of speechwriters) crafted their respective speeches. Each spoke of the crisis that the country was experiencing at the particular moment. Each alluded to the many Americans who had continued to struggle despite the efforts of Washington. All of them promised that the time had come to change direction in America and that their administrations would solve the problems that had long plagued the country. For Trump, this was perhaps most evident when he said:

> [F]or too many of our citizens, a different reality exists: Mothers and children trapped in poverty in our inner cities; rusted-out factories scattered like tombstones across the landscape of our Nation; an education system, flush with cash, but which leaves our young and beautiful students deprived of all knowledge; and the crime and the gangs and the drugs that have stolen too many lives and robbed our country of so much unrealized potential.[13]

He then paused quickly, for effect, no doubt, before offering in a slow and deliberate tone: "This American carnage stops right here and stops right now." As Reagan and Obama before him, Trump was taking over from a president of the opposing political party and was promising a stark change from the outgoing administration. Trump took this a step further, however, offering a sort of rejection of how presidents from both parties since the end of the Second World War had approached American exceptionalism:

[T]hat is the past. And we are now looking only to the future. We, assembled here today, are issuing a new decree to be heard in every city, in every foreign capital, and in every hall of power. From this day forward, a new vision will govern our land. From this this day forward, it's going to be only America first. America first.

It was a decree. The United States would no longer seek to lead the world. It would turn inward and focus primarily on the problems at home. It may have been a surprise to many, but it was the same tune he had played throughout his campaign. The United States, according to Trump, should focus on competing with and standing above other nations, not leading them. He solidified this new vision with his only reference to American exceptionalism in the entire speech:

> We will seek friendship and good will with the nations of the world, but we do so with the understanding that it is the right of all nations to put their own interests first. We do not seek to impose our way of life on anyone, but rather to let it shine as an example—we will shine—for everyone to follow.

American global leadership, therefore, would not be a priority for the incoming Trump administration. Trump had a different vision for American exceptionalism. It was about winning, but Trump was not quite ready to tout America's superiority in world affairs. Again, it was counterproductive to his messaging strategy. The purpose of Trump's inaugural was not to build the case that the country was already exceptional. Trump used it to signal a change, one where the fading light of American exceptionalism would be halted and, at some point during his presidency, set afire again.

From Unexceptional to Exceptional

Trump's inaugural address was the perfect stage to roll out the first step of the exceptional me strategy. Unlike presidents before him, Trump made no claims of American superiority in the early days of his administration. There were no suggestions that the country's economy was the strongest in a sea of strong international competitors. He made no references to the military as the strongest and most equipped in the world. There were no proclamations that the United States was the greatest country on earth. And he had all but rejected the idea of American leadership in world affairs. To be sure, these were all ideas that virtually every president that came before Trump—certainly since the Second World War—had routinely embraced and promoted early on in their presidencies. Such references would suggest that the country was already exceptional as he took office. Again, this would have served to undermine his broader communication strategy. Trump had, after all, made it clear throughout his campaign that the country was unexceptional and losing in world affairs, but that when he took office, that was all going to change. A turnaround was afoot. Early in his presidency, for example, Trump offered:

> Instead of peace, we've seen wars that never end and conflicts that never seem to go away. We don't fight to win. We fight politically correct wars. We don't win anymore. We don't win at trade. We don't win in any capacity. We don't win anymore. We're going to start winning again. Believe me.[14]

To further illustrate the complexity of these dynamics, we examined how Trump spoke about the United States as being either exceptional or unexceptional in his major speeches to the nation, with a specific eye on trends over time. Figure 4.1 offers an initial look at this aspect of the exceptional me strategy. Specifically, each solid black dot represents the number of times Trump referenced American exceptionalism in a given speech. The hollow dots represent the number of times Trump referenced unexceptionalism in that same speech. The trend lines indicate either an increase or a decrease over time. As the figure indicates, Trump was only slightly more likely to invoke American exceptionalism than unexceptionalism at the beginning of his presidency. As his time in office progressed, however, his invocations of American exceptionalism increased substantially while his references to unexceptionalism declined.

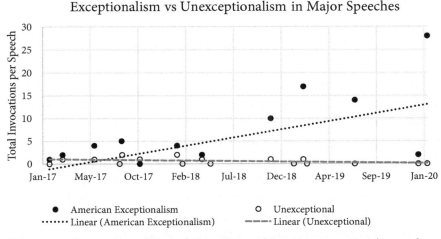

Figure 4.1 Comparison of Trump's invocations of American exceptionalism and unexceptionalism in major speeches from January 2017 to February 2020.

These trends are even more clear when we look at how Trump invoked these ideas in the various Make America Great Again rallies that he held throughout his first term in office. Figures 4.2 and 4.3 track Trump's invocations of American exceptionalism and unexceptionalism in the ninety MAGA rallies he held before his State of the Union address in 2020. There are a number of important findings in these figures. Figure 4.2, for example, shows how Trump's references to the country as being unexceptional steadily decreased throughout his time as president. Specifically, during his first year in office, Trump invoked American unexceptionalism in 90 percent of his MAGA rallies and at an average rate of over three references per speech. By 2020, it had dropped to 20 percent of speeches and at an average rate of around one reference in every two speeches. Such a dramatic shift is revealing. In essence, as Trump's reelection bid heated up, his talk of an unexceptional America had all but disappeared. His comments at a 2019 MAGA rally in New Hampshire epitomized this transition:

> Before the election, our factories were closing. Hey, who knows it better than you? You're like central casting for the closing of factories. Our jobs were vanishing. Our military was totally depleted. When I took over, our military was sad. We weren't flying half of our planes, they were old. They were tired. Our equipment was tired. Our people weren't tired, though. Our people weren't tired. But everything we had, it was depleted. Now we've rebuilt our military like never before.[15]

In other words, Trump had inherited a country that was suffering and in disarray, but now, due to his policies and actions, America was making a

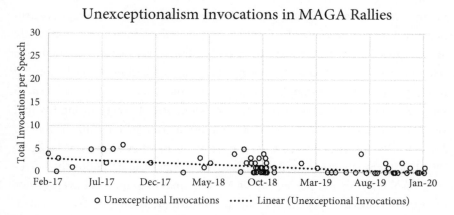

Figure 4.2 Over time trend in Trump's invocations of American unexceptionalism in Make America Great Again rallies from January 2017 to February 2020.

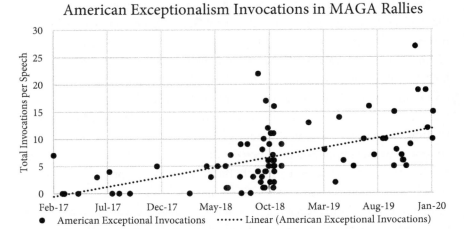

Figure 4.3 Over time trend in Trump's invocations of American exceptionalism in Make America Great Again rallies from January 2017 to February 2020.

remarkable comeback. Once the ball was rolling and enough concrete indicators became available for Trump to point to as "evidence" of this comeback, Trump essentially opened the floodgates, relentlessly bombarding Americans with facts and figures that supported his argument that America was becoming exceptional again.

Trump's references to American unexceptionalism were falling because, according to him, the country was bouncing back from the brink. It was becoming exceptional again. "This big ship is turning a lot faster than anyone thought possible,"[16] Trump offered in late 2018. Figure 4.3 provides a sharp picture of this dynamic. Specifically, as Trump's invocations of unexceptionalism decreased, his invocations of American exceptionalism increased significantly as his presidency progressed. In essence, there was almost a symbiotic relationship between these two concepts in Trump's speeches. At the beginning of his presidency, for example, there were various speeches in which Trump made not one reference to American exceptionalism. In fact, during his first year of office, he invoked American exceptionalism in only 40 percent of MAGA rally speeches and at an average rate of under two times per speech. By 2020, Trump had increased his references to American exceptionalism five-fold, invoking it in 100 percent of his MAGA speeches and at an average rate of over ten times per speech. At a rally in late 2018, for example, Trump stated: "America's extraordinary comeback is the envy of the entire world. The whole world is talking about—we're the hottest nation in the world. We're the hottest."[17] Similarly, at a rally in July 2019, Trump emphasized:

We have been blessed with the greatest republic on the face of the earth. But it was going in the wrong direction, and now we are turning it around. It is going better than ever before, and we're going to keep it that way. We're going to keep it that way. With your help, with your devotion, with your drive, we are going to keep on working. We are going to keep on fighting, and we are going to keep on winning.[18]

Trump's use of American exceptionalism in his speeches was clearly increasing and changing. Now that he was in office, the country was finally regaining its exceptionalism. At a rally in January 2020, Trump remarked: "America is winning again. America is respected again. And America is thriving again like never before. We're doing great. We're the envy of the world."[19] America was back and, according to Trump, better than ever before.

Championing the Exceptional Nation

So, Trump had finally warmed to American exceptionalism, working diligently throughout his first term to spin the narrative that it was returning. As we've seen, presidents regularly rely on the power of American exceptionalism to inspire the American people to dream big and accomplish the unthinkable. After all, if not America, the argument goes, then who? Perhaps this is why Americans tend to possess an outsized sense of their place in the world. Presidents routinely invoke American exceptionalism to generate public support for their presidencies. When Americans feel good about their nation, they tend to feel better about their president. It is, therefore, generally good politics for a president to celebrate the nation in these terms. If a president is seen as a strong champion of American exceptionalism, it can also help their chances for reelection. This seemed to be the sole focus of Trump's approach as he prepared for the 2020 election.

As the next step in our analysis, we assessed the manner and extent to which Trump invoked American exceptionalism relative to every president since the Second World War, focusing on their political speeches during their first terms in office. Specifically, we examined every word of all major presidential speeches to the nation from the day Harry Truman took office on April 16, 1945, through Donald Trump's third official State of the Union address on February 4, 2020. In total, we analyzed 217 speeches. We noted every time a president referred to the United States as being singular or unique in some way, superior to other countries, a model for the world to follow, and as the leader of the international community. Our overall findings are in Figure 4.4.

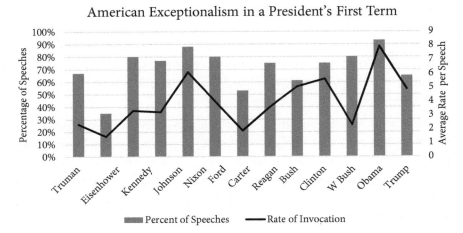

Figure 4.4 Percentage and rate of all types of American exceptionalism language across all major presidential speeches to the nation during a president's first term in office from 1945 to 2020.

The larger picture in Figure 4.4 is a compelling one. It demonstrates that every president, including Trump, invoked American exceptionalism extensively during their first term in office. Some presidents, however, stick out more than others. Obama and Nixon, for example, both saw American exceptionalism as central to their overall rhetorical strategies while in office, invoking the idea in over 85 percent of speeches and at an average rate of at least six invocations per speech respectively. In addition, compared to his contemporaries, Trump registered somewhat low in his invocations of American exceptionalism. This stems in large part, as we have shown, from the fact that Trump entered office portraying America as unexceptional before gradually building the case that American exceptionalism had returned over the course of his presidency. Overall, Trump invoked the idea in 65 percent of his speeches and at an average rate of just under five invocations per speech. Given how infrequently Trump embraced American exceptionalism during his campaign, these numbers are notable. Specifically, during his campaign, Trump only invoked the idea in 23 percent of his speeches. In effect, Trump almost tripled the visibility of American exceptionalism from his campaign messages to those during his presidency. A significant increase in the average rate of his invocations occurred as well. Specifically, Trump went from an average of around one invocation in every three speeches during the campaign to an average of just under five invocations per speech as president. This was over a twelvefold increase. Simply put, American exceptionalism came to be viewed by Trump as a much more powerful rhetorical tool during his presidency than during his 2016 presidential campaign.

To obtain a more robust understanding of these dynamics, we next examined how presidents in their first terms invoked the distinct types of American exceptionalism. In other words, we parsed out the relative amount of attention presidents in their first terms paid to the different types of American exceptionalism—singular, superior, model, and leader. Figure 4.3 shows the percentage breakdown of the various types of American exceptionalism each president favored. What is evident in this figure is that every president had their own particular style when it came to invoking American exceptionalism. Bill Clinton, for example, preferred to focus on America's leadership role in the world. He often stated that "America must continue to lead the world we did so much to make,"[20] and he was responsible for coining the phrase America is "the world's indispensable nation,"[21] and he spoke of it widely. George W. Bush, however, tended to characterize the United States as an exemplar nation that other countries should aspire to. He stated, for example: "This ideal of America is the hope of all mankind. That hope drew millions to this harbor. That hope still lights our way. And the light shines in the darkness. And the darkness will not overcome it."[22] At the same time, Bush routinely spoke of American leadership in the world, which was reflected in this statement: "I believe that America is called to lead the cause of freedom in a new century."[23]

Dwight Eisenhower and Ronald Reagan, however, were perhaps the most versatile in their invocations of American exceptionalism, emphasizing all four types at a relatively equal rate. Ronald Reagan, in particular, stands out as one of the foremost champions of American exceptionalism. As the following quote illustrates, what was remarkable about Reagan was his ability to weave together multiple facets of American exceptionalism into a single statement: "I've always believed that this land was set aside in an uncommon way, that a divine plan placed this great continent between the oceans to be found by a people from every corner of the Earth who had a special love of faith, freedom, and peace."[24] Elsewhere, Reagan succinctly noted: "We are first. We are the best. And we are so because we're free."[25] As these data indicate, presidents before Trump were more than willing to wax philosophical about the idea of American exceptionalism, citing various aspects that made the country special, the world's iconic leader, and in all cases foremost among nations.

Trump's strategic approach to American exceptionalism was clearly quite different from his predecessors. It was narrowly focused on American

American Exceptionalism Types in Major Speeches

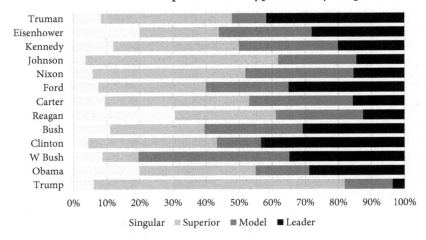

Figure 4.5 Percentage of the different types of American exceptionalism invocations that presidents invoked across all major speeches to the nation during their first term in office from 1945 to 2020.

superiority, or the idea of winning within the global community. This was, by far, Trump's favorite tactic, and, again, it set him apart from other presidents. As Figure 4.5 illustrates, Trump focused a full 76 percent of his invocations in major speeches on the idea of American superiority, while paying little to no attention to the ideas of American singularity—the characteristics and attributes that make America unique or special—or its role as the leader in the international community. In particular, the overwhelming majority of Trump's invocations of American exceptionalism were focused on two aspects: the economy and the military. Trump routinely portrayed the US economy as the "hottest," "largest," or "most prosperous" in the world. This was reflected in the following statement: "I will say this: The United States has a lot to offer, with the greatest and most powerful economy in the history of the world."[26] Often, he linked such statements to actions his administration had taken to cut taxes and regulations, which, according to him, were fueling unprecedented growth in the economy. When Trump spoke about the military, the message was usually clear and concise: the United States had "the greatest military in the world."[27] If we take into account his messaging in tweets and MAGA rallies, Trump's clear preference for American superiority is even more evident. Figure 4.6 shows that when Trump was unscripted, essentially bound only by his own

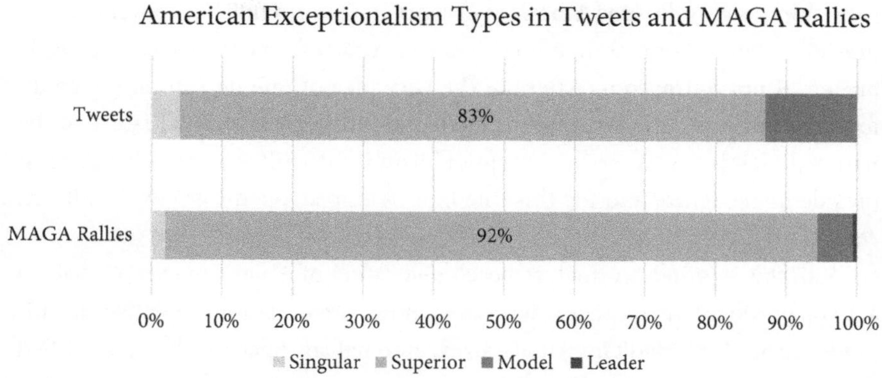

American Exceptionalism Types in Tweets and MAGA Rallies

Figure 4.6 Percentage of the different types of American exceptionalism invocations that Trump invoked in tweets and Make America Great Again rallies between January 2017 and February 2020.

conception of the world, American exceptionalism clearly meant American superiority. In other words, Trump's conception of American exceptionalism had remained narrow, focusing on the parts of the idea that were seemingly more malleable—that is, more dependent upon the actions and policies of the president. This, of course, was by design because it enabled Trump to then claim credit for restoring American exceptionalism.

Exceptional Because of Me

Throughout the 2016 campaign, Trump devoted much of his energy toward explaining how and why America was no longer exceptional. On the rare occurrence that he did invoke American exceptionalism, he, of course, did not take credit for it. After all, how could he? He was not the man in charge. But as soon as Trump took office, armed with a 2020 campaign slogan of "Keep America Great!," Trump understood full well that he would have to build a convincing case that America had become exceptional again during his presidency if he intended to win reelection. And how would Americans know who to thank if he did not tell them? The next step in his exceptional me strategy, therefore, was to inform the American people that the return of American exceptionalism was brought about entirely by his presidency and its policies. Here, Trump differed greatly from his predecessors. Taking credit for something as grandiose as American exceptionalism is a fine line to walk for any president. Such claims from a president can come off to citizens as excessively brazen, if not outrageous. After all, the very idea of one person taking credit for something as complex, multifaceted, and interwoven into the fabric of the national identity as American exceptionalism is difficult to comprehend. Most presidents recognize and toe this fine line. Trump stepped right over it. It was central to his strategy.

With this in mind, we analyzed each invocation of American exceptionalism across presidential speeches to assess how often Trump, relative to his predecessors, took credit for American exceptionalism. Specifically, we identified times where it was clear that a president was crediting their own policies or their administration for the return of American exceptionalism in some form. Figure 4.4 indicates the percentage of American exceptionalism references in which each president took credit. As the findings in Figure 4.4 reveal, this was something that was exceedingly rare before Trump took office. When it did occur, there was often a level humility or modesty involved. Presidents, for example, have occasionally taken credit for restoring American leadership in world affairs. Barack Obama, for example, stated:

> That's the leadership we are providing: engagement that advances the common security and prosperity of all people. We're working through the G-20 to sustain a lasting global recovery. We're working with Muslim communities around the world to promote science and education and innovation. We have gone from a bystander to a leader in the fight against climate change.[28]

Similarly, Harry Truman spoke of how his administration deserved credit for stimulating the world economy: "To restore world trade we have recently taken the lead in bringing about the greatest reduction of world tariffs that the world has ever seen."[29] Lyndon Johnson, on three occasions, took credit for restoring American superiority. For instance, he took credit for the "unprecedented progress of our free enterprise economy"[30] that occurred during his tenure as both vice president and president. Similarly, in his 1965 State of the Union address, he offered:

> Our Nation was created to help strike away the chains of ignorance and misery and tyranny wherever they keep man less than God means him to be. We are moving toward that destiny, never more rapidly than we have moved in the last 4 years. In this period we have built a military power strong enough to meet any threat and destroy any adversary. And that superiority will continue to grow so long as this office is mine and you sit on Capitol Hill.[31]

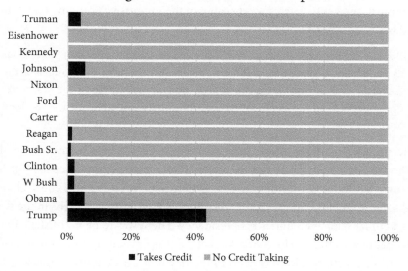

Figure 4.7 Percentage of American exceptionalism invocations that presidents explicitly took credit for across all major presidential speeches to the nation during their first term from 1945 to 2020.

Again, Johnson was referring to policies enacted under both the Kennedy and Johnson administrations, but the message was clear: they deserved credit for restoring American exceptionalism. In each of these rare examples, though, credit taking tended to be couched in the broader domestic or foreign policy needs and goals of the country.

Trump, again, was vastly different. First of all, as reflected in Figure 4.7, he took credit for American exceptionalism 43 percent of all of his invocations, which was more than eight times more often than any of his predecessors. Trump was not only unrestrained in his efforts to take credit for American exceptionalism, he was shameless. He would simply be remiss if he passed up an opportunity to slip in claims that he had brought about the return of American exceptionalism. When speaking to the American people about the immigrant "caravans" from Central America that were approaching the border, for example, Trump argued:

> And we've already dispatched, for the border, the United States military. And they will do the job. They are setting up right now, and they're preparing. We hope nothing happens. But if it does, we are totally prepared. Greatest military anywhere in the world, and it's going to be, and is now, in great shape. No longer depleted like it was when I took over as the President of the United States.[32]

In that same speech, he went on to say that the reason so many immigrants were coming to the United States was because of the impressive economy that Trump had built. He argued:

> But this is a perilous situation, and it threatens to become even more hazardous as our economy gets better and better. A lot of the cause of this problem is the fact that we right now have the hottest economy anywhere in the world. It's doing better than any economy in the world. Jobs, unemployment—you look at any number.

The phrase "right now" was one of Trump's go-to ways of indicating that although the country was not exceptional before he became president, it had become so under his administration. Other times, he was much more blatant. Take, for example, Trump's regular references to the "historic" highs in the stock market that happened under his presidency. There was to be no mistake that it was because of him: "The Stock Market went up massively from the day after I won the Election, all the way up to the day that I took office, because of the enthusiasm for the fact that I was going to be President. That big Stock Market increase must be credited to me. If Hillary won—a Big Crash!"[33] In short, Trump took credit at every turn.

The transition between Trump's 2018 and 2019 State of the Union addresses serves as a perfect example of how Trump rolled out the credit-taking tactic of the exceptional me strategy in a gradual, albeit deliberate, manner. At his 2018 address, Trump had only been in office for one year. Six days before his speech, Trump attended the World Economic Forum in Davos, Switzerland, tweeting before his departure: "Will soon be heading to Davos, Switzerland, to tell the world how great America is and is doing. Our economy is now booming and with all I am doing, will only get better… Our country is finally WINNING again!"[34] America, according to Trump, had turned a corner. At the same time, Trump was embroiled in controversy. A report from the *New York Times* had accused Trump of seeking to dismiss Special Council, Robert Mueller.[35] He had also just overseen his first government shutdown ten days earlier, and he was openly feuding with celebrities, tweeting two days before his State of the Union: "Somebody please inform Jay-Z that because of my policies, Black Unemployment has just been reported to be at the LOWEST RATE EVER RECORDED!"[36] The State of the Union, therefore, was Trump's opportunity to speak directly to the American people about the progress he had made in restoring American exceptionalism. The White House had billed the speech beforehand as conciliatory and unifying, notwithstanding Trump's boastful tone in the tweets he had released days before the speech. The idea that an American resurgence was already happening was evident in the speech from the outset:

> Less than one year has passed since I first stood at this podium, in this majestic Chamber, to speak on behalf of the American people and to address their concerns, their hopes, and their dreams. That night, our new administration had already taken very swift action. A new tide of optimism was already sweeping across our land. Each day since, we have gone forward with a clear vision and a righteous mission: to make America great again for all Americans.[37]

In other words, things were changing and the country was finally moving in a positive direction. Trump's claims about the nation were grandiose, for sure, but his claims of an emerging American exceptionalism were still tame. He noted, for example: "Over the last year, the world has seen what we always knew: that no people on Earth are so fearless or daring or determined as Americans." It was Trump's use of the words "over the last year" in reference to his time in office that make this one of his more subtle claims of credit for restoring American exceptionalism. This measured tone, however, would not last.

One year later, as scandal and turmoil appeared poised to engulf the Trump presidency, Trump remained laser-focused on his objective of persuading Americans that the nation had returned to greatness. He started the year off with a morning tweet on New Year's Day in what seemed like an attempt to set the tone for his third year in office:

> HAPPY NEW YEAR TO EVERYONE, INCLUDING THE HATERS AND THE FAKE NEWS MEDIA! 2019 WILL BE A FANTASTIC YEAR FOR THOSE NOT SUFFERING FROM TRUMP DERANGEMENT SYNDROME. JUST CALM DOWN AND ENJOY THE RIDE, GREAT THINGS ARE HAPPENING FOR OUR COUNTRY![38]

It was day eleven of a partial government shutdown that already had Trump at odds with the incoming Democratic majority in the House of Representatives. In addition, the Mueller investigation was still ongoing, and Trump had been forced to replace several people in his White House cabinet. Specifically, in 2018, Trump had dismissed Secretary of State Rex Tillerson and Attorney General Jeff Sessions. Meanwhile, Chief of Staff John Kelly and Secretary of Defense James Mattis had recently resigned. These changes signaled a fundamental shift in the Trump administration. The Associated Press referred to it as the end of the "contain and control" phase of the Trump administration in which the "Axis of Adults" would no longer be around Trump to constrain his worst impulses,[39] and "Yes Men" would be employed to take their place.[40] Trump could finally be himself without restraints.

His second State of the Union address was the ideal time to unleash the new Trump. The speech, however, started with a conciliatory tone and a call for bipartisan unity, which likely surprised those expecting Trump in the raw. Early in the speech, for example, Trump stated: "There is a new opportunity in American politics, if only we have the courage, together, to seize it. Victory is not winning for our party, victory is winning for our country."[41] He then spoke of the seventy-fifth anniversary of D-Day where "15,000 young American men jumped from the sky, and 60,000 more stormed in from the sea, to save our civilization from tyranny." This was followed by a statement that could have been from any president: "In the 20th century, America saved freedom, transformed science, redefined the middle class, and when you get down to it, there's nothing anywhere in the world that can compete with America." Trump's normal, boastful tone seemed to be taking a back seat to a narrative about collaboration, unity, and the American spirit. It did not last long. Trump then pivoted to speaking about his first two years in office:

> Wages are rising at the fastest pace in decades and growing for blue-collar workers, who I promised to fight for. They're growing faster than anyone else thought possible. Nearly 5 million Americans have been lifted off food stamps. The U.S. economy is growing almost twice as fast today as when I took office. And we are considered, far and away, the hottest economy anywhere in the world. Not even close.

Trump was unequivocal, at every turn, about who deserved the credit:

> My administration has cut more regulations in a short period of time than any other administration during its entire tenure. Companies are coming back to our country in large numbers thanks to our historic reductions in taxes and regulations. And we have unleashed a revolution in American energy. The United States is now the number-one producer of oil and natural gas anywhere in the world. And now, for the first time in 65 years, we are a net exporter of energy. After 24 months of rapid progress, our economy is the envy of the world, our military is the most powerful on Earth, by far, and America is again winning each and every day.

Trump then paused and continued, "Members of Congress: The state of our union is strong." The audience—Republicans, mainly—erupted with applause and Mike Pence immediately rose from his seat behind Trump to applaud. Chants of "U.S.A! U.S.A! U.S.A.!" filled the chamber. Trump's message was clearly resonating with the Republican members in Congress. Only a year earlier, Trump had spoken of a rising tide of optimism and change within the country, but he had largely held back from making any full-throated claims that America had become exceptional again. This time there were no restraints. American exceptionalism was back and, according to Trump, he was to thank.

Again, these dynamics were even more evident in Trump's MAGA rallies. In a similar fashion to his major speeches to the nation, Trump took credit for 42 percent of all invocations of American exceptionalism in his MAGA rallies. Furthermore, Figure 4.8 demonstrates that his credit taking for American exceptionalism increased steadily as Trump's presidency progressed. In fact, after November of 2018, Trump took credit for American exceptionalism at least once in every MAGA rally he held. With his eyes set on reelection, Trump's main focus was on building the argument that he was responsible for a historic surge in the country's economy. In early 2019, for example, Trump offered this: "In the last two years we have embarked on an unprecedented economic revival. Unprecedented. America is now the hottest economy anywhere on the planet earth. There is nobody close."[42] Trump also liked to claim that without him, American exceptionalism would not have returned. In late 2018, for example, Trump stated: "China was catching us rapidly before I became president. And right now we are going so fast, we are the fastest developing country in the world. Can you believe that? Boom. Fastest in the world."[43] And again, you did not just

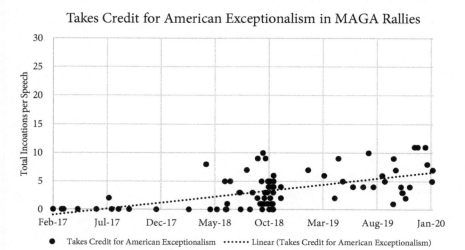

Takes Credit for American Exceptionalism in MAGA Rallies

● Takes Credit for American Exceptionalism ⋯⋯⋯ Linear (Takes Credit for American Exceptionalism)

Figure 4.8 Over time trend in Trump's credit taking for American exceptionalism in Make America Great Again rallies from 2017 to 2020.

have to take Trump's words for it. Many people, according to Trump, were also giving him credit. One of Trump's favorite stump stories, for example, was to say that foreign leaders from all corners of the world regularly congratulated him on his success with the country. For instance, Trump offered this after a meeting with NATO officials:

> I said you got to pay your bills, folks, got to pay up, got to pay up. But they liked it, they liked it. But everyone that reached me says hello, Mr. President, congratulations on what you've done for the economy. It's the talk of the world, talk of the world. Now that we have the best economy in the history of our country.[44]

Trump also regularly offered a variation of the following claims:

> The United States has the hottest economy on earth. You know these prime ministers and presidents and kings and queens and, sometimes dictators. We take them as they come. We take them as they come. They always start off, sir, congratulations on the great job you've done with the economy. The hottest numbers, the hottest economy in the world. We have the number one economy anymore in the world, anywhere in the world. Had our opponents got elected, you would right now be the number two economy to China and we are now so far ahead.[45]

If one were listening closely to what Trump was saying, the message was clear: Trump had restored American exceptionalism, other countries were taking notice, and there was no one, other than Trump himself, who could have done it.

The "Exceptional" Presidency

Orrin [Hatch] is—I love listening to him speak...he actually once said I'm the greatest president in the history of our country and I said, "Does that include Lincoln and Washington?" He said, "Yes." I said, "I love this guy."

—Donald Trump[1]

Trump's exceptional me strategy reached its peak form in his State of the Union Address on February 4, 2020. The atmosphere in the House of Representatives chamber was mired by talk of Trump's ongoing impeachment hearing in the Senate, even though it was a foregone conclusion that he would be acquitted by Senate Republicans one day later. Before the speech, Republicans had warned Trump not to engage in settling scores with Democrats as retribution for the impeachment inquiry and, instead, encouraged him to focus his message on the future of the nation and making the case for his reelection bid. Aside from snubbing Nancy Pelosi's attempt to shake his hand as he approached the lectern, Trump stayed on message throughout the speech. The theme "The Great American Comeback" was evident from the outset, as Trump made clear at every turn that the country was no longer the mess he had supposedly inherited. It was officially great again and he was the reason for its comeback. Trump, for example, offered this early on:

> I am thrilled to report to you tonight that our economy is the best it has ever been. Our military is completely rebuilt, with its power being unmatched anywhere in the world — and it is not even close. Our borders are secure. Our families are flourishing. Our values are renewed. Our pride is restored... The vision I will lay out this evening demonstrates how we are building the world's most prosperous and inclusive society — one where every citizen can join in America's unparalleled success, and where every community can take part in America's extraordinary rise.[2]

All facts and evidence aside, Trump was proclaiming that he had, in effect, restored American exceptionalism, and after just three years in office. In the midst of these claims, Trump offered a claim of grandeur related more to his presidency than to the nation itself: "And for all these reasons, I say to the people of our great country, and to the members of Congress before me: The State of our Union is stronger than ever before." Simply put, it was not just that American exceptionalism had been restored under his watch. The unmistakable takeaway here was that this was *the best version of America in its history* and Trump, of course, was taking credit.

Trump was laying claim to the notion that he was, in fact, the best president in American history. After all, according to Trump, this was the best that America had ever been, and it was due to the policies and actions of his administration. The fact that Trump believed that he was better than all other presidents was not at all concealed in his rhetoric. He was unapologetic about it. He stated, for example:

> Incredibly, the average unemployment rate under my administration is lower than any administration in the history of our country. If we had not reversed the failed economic policies of the previous administration, the world would not now be witness to America's great economic success.

He then rattled off a laundry list of other ways that the country was better off now than ever before. He spoke of "slashing a record number of job-killing regulations" and "enacting historic and record-setting tax cuts," and he emphasized that "jobs, like so many elements of our country, are at a record high." In essence, all of his accomplishments were "historic" and "unprecedented," or "the greatest in the history of the nation." To cap it off, Trump concluded: "[L]adies and gentlemen, our ancestors built the most exceptional republic ever to exist in all of human history. And we are making it greater than ever before." Thus, the nation had become exceptional again (and more exceptional than ever before), all because of Trump's "exceptional" presidency.

The next day, Trump's State of the Union Address was the talk of Washington. Many focused on the overtly braggadocios tone of the speech. Michael Shear of the *New York Times*, for example, wrote: "President Trump claimed credit for a 'great American comeback'... boasting of a robust economy, contrasting his successes with the records of his predecessors and projecting optimism."[3] Others took a cue from Trump and described the speech as a singular phenomenon. CNN put it plainly: "We've never seen a State of the Union like this."[4] John Harris of POLITICO seemed to embrace Trump's exceptionalistic language, going as far as to say: "This was the most defiant, most boastful, most ostentatiously theatrical, most overtly campaign-oriented, most *am-I-hearing-this-right?* outlandish—the most flamboyantly bizarre—State of the Union Address of All Time."[5]

Indeed, the speech was so over-the-top, across the board, that journalists responded immediately by aggressively fact-checking Trump's claims, a norm that had been established during the Trump presidency because of Trump's penchant for exaggerating his accomplishments and emitting outright lies. Surely, such a move would serve to keep Trump in check and, more broadly, place his suspect claims in proper context. Trump, however, was keen to two truths that seemed to have eluded many journalists, pundits, and the like. First, Trump understood that in the modern media environment, what is actually true matters much less than what people believe to be true, especially at the ballot box. Second, he knew that if he repeated the same claims over and over again with confidence (*argumentum ad nauseam*), even if they were false, large swaths of the American public would believe them to be true.[6] In fact, Trump had tipped his hand about this strategy in his book *The Art of the Deal*, when he offered:

> I play to people's fantasies. People may not always think big themselves, but they can still get very excited by those who do. That's why a little hyperbole never hurts. People want to believe that something is the biggest and the greatest and the most spectacular. I call it truthful hyperbole. It's an innocent form of exaggeration—and a very effective form of promotion.[7]

In the immortal words of *Seinfeld* character, George Costanza: "It's not a lie if you believe it."[8] CNN's conservative host S. E. Cupp seemed to capture this idea perfectly in her tweet during the address: "This #SOTU speech is winning. I mean, let's be clear—it's full of lies and half-truths. But for millions of Americans the stuff he's saying tonight sounds really, really good. Like, four more years good. Democrats ignore this at their peril."[9] This was perhaps not lost on Speaker of the House, Nancy Pelosi, as she was ripping up Trump's speech at the end of the address. Trump was spinning a narrative—one that he had meticulously crafted his entire life—that focused less on what was actually true and more on what he wanted the American people to believe was true. He wanted them to believe that he had accomplished bigger and better things than any of his predecessors, that the country under his direction was doing better than ever before, and that he was, in his own words, "the greatest president in the history of our country."[10] And for many Americans, that was all they needed to know.

The Exceptional Me Strategy Takes Form

This chapter documents the next steps in the evolution of Trump's exceptional me strategy during his presidency, focusing on how it was employed to promote his agenda as president and lay the groundwork for his potential reelection in 2020. We begin by comparing Trump to his predecessors to see whether and to what extent other presidents invoked self-exceptionalism while in office relative to him. Our findings show that, yet again, Trump was unique in his use of this communication strategy. Previous presidents, for example, often displayed humility in their communications about the enormity of the job as president. As President Truman once stated:

> I accept with humility the honor which the American people have conferred upon me. I accept it with a resolve to do all that I can for the welfare of this nation and for the peace of the world. In performing the duties of my office, I need the help and the prayers of every one of you. I ask for your encouragement and for your support. The tasks we face are difficult. We can accomplish them only if we work together.[11]

President Johnson noted: "I am here today to say I need your help. I cannot bear this burden alone. I need the help of all Americans, and all America."[12] Trump, in contrast, portrayed himself as more exceptional than the office itself. We show, for example, that although Trump's invocations of American exceptionalism steadily increased during his time in office, these references still paled in comparison to his efforts to portray himself and his presidency as exceptional. Indeed, as we point out in the introduction, in Trump world, no one was more exceptional than Trump, even the United States of America. Trump, for example, routinely referred to himself as "your favorite president," proclaimed that his election was "the greatest moment in American history," and, time and again, characterized his policies and actions as "unprecedented" and "historic." In other words, Trump's presidency was *the* exceptional presidency.

Next, we show that when Trump invoked America, the point of comparison was rarely about the country relative to the world. Instead, it was almost always about Trump relative to the presidents who came before him. For instance, rather than saying, "We have the greatest economy in the world," Trump often stated, "We have the best economy in the history of our country."[13] As the story goes, Trump was responsible and deserved credit for not only making America great (or exceptional) again but also for *making it greater (or more exceptional) than ever before*. Finally, we show how Trump sought to build the case that without him in office, the nation would almost certainly fail. The argument here was that just as Trump was able to quickly—indeed, miraculously—restore American exceptionalism during his first term in office, the nation would easily descend into chaos and destruction immediately if he were to lose reelection. As our evidence shows—from the economy, the military, and health care to numerous other issue areas—Trump made clear throughout his first term in office that the stability and livelihood of the nation was entirely dependent upon him retaining the presidency. Just as presidents before him had proclaimed that America was the one indispensable nation to lead the world, Trump argued, in effect, that he was the one indispensable person to lead the country.

Exceptional Presidencies

It is, of course, customary for presidents in their first term in office to build a case for reelection by emphasizing and celebrating their accomplishments. After all, the American people have come to expect this and it would be foolish to do otherwise. To be clear, however, it is one thing to tout one's own accomplishments as president but quite another to portray oneself as the greatest president of all time. In Chapter 3, we explored the concept of *self-exceptionalism* in the context of Trump's 2016 presidential campaign—how he spoke of himself, his campaign, and the movement that he had inspired—relative to presidential candidates that came before him. Here, we extend this analysis to examine how this communication strategy was adapted to fit the Trump presidency. Specifically, we assess the manner and extent to which Trump, relative to his predecessors, engaged in what we refer to as *presidential exceptionalism* during his first term.

Presidential exceptionalism as a communication strategy, we argue, tends to manifest in three important ways. First, it involves presidents referring to themselves as exceptional individuals. This might be, for example, "I am the most qualified person to deal with this issue." Second, it includes presidents characterizing their administration as exceptional relative to other presidencies. A president might say, for example, "My administration has accomplished more than any other previous administration." Third, it entails presidents portraying the nation as better off than ever before due to their policies and actions. An example would be, "the country is now stronger and more prosperous than ever before." Each of these versions of presidential exceptionalism serves to achieve a larger objective, which is to differentiate oneself from others and to, more importantly, suggest that nobody else—past or present—could do the job of president as well as them. As our data will show, this is a rhetorical tactic that presidents have rarely used—that is, until Trump took over the presidency.

The office of the presidency typically instills within those who inherit the position a profound sense of self-awareness and humility, given the enormity of the challenges and responsibilities that come with it. Perhaps this is why former presidents have been so reluctant to speak out or criticize sitting presidents. As former President George W. Bush, once stated: "I don't think it's good for the country to have a former president undermine a current president. I think it's bad for the presidency for that matter."[14] The decorum of the presidency, therefore, has traditionally dictated that each president be overtly respectful of their predecessors and not try to "one-up" them at every turn. Trump, however, was not interested in adhering to tradition or presidential decorum. It would defeat the mainline argument of his messaging. In fact, he seemed intent on blowing the lid off these constraints as he embarked on his exceptional me strategy.

To gain a complete picture of just how different Trump was compared to his predecessors in his invocation of presidential exceptionalism, we examined how often presidents employed this concept in their major speeches to the nation and how this compared to their references to American exceptionalism. The findings in Figure 5.1 clearly show that typical presidential behavior has been to only rarely invoke the idea that one's own presidency is exceptional. For most presidents, we only see a few references to presidential exceptionalism during their first term in office. Trump, however, invoked presidential exceptionalism a total of 125 times in his major addresses to the nation. Lyndon Johnson, the next closest, made only sixteen references of this kind. Furthermore, typical presidential behavior entails an explicit embrace of American exceptionalism that far exceeds references to presidential exceptionalism. Their presidency is more about the country than it is about themselves and their accomplishments. Trump, without question, violated both of these rules. He not only invoked presidential exceptionalism at a rate that was essentially off the charts when compared to his predecessors but he was the only one to offer himself and his administration more praise than he did to the nation. Notably, he was over one-and-a-half times more likely to invoke presidential exceptionalism than American exceptionalism. As it had been during his 2016 campaign, this was Trump's favorite rhetorical tactic as president.

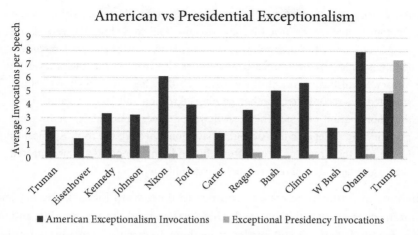

Figure 5.1 Average rate of invocations of American and presidential exceptionalism across all speeches from 1945 to 2020.

A closer look reveals not only significant differences in how frequent Trump invoked this idea relative to his predecessors but also considerable differences in the content and tone of these references. For other presidents, references to their exceptional presidency, by and large, were used as a way of celebrating the nation as a whole, while also directing the American people's attention to the work that still needed to be done. In his first State of the Union Address in 1964, for example, Lyndon Johnson stated:

> In 1963, for the first time in history, we crossed the 70 million job mark, but we will soon need more than 75 million jobs... Wages and profits and family income are also at their highest levels in history, but I would remind you that 4 million workers and 13 percent of our industrial capacity are still idle today. We need a tax cut now to keep this country moving.[15]

The tone of Johnson's remarks was celebratory, to be sure, but it also illustrated the challenge that hitting such a historical mark could be for the country. Rather than basking in the glow of his own accomplishments and suggesting that no further work was needed because he had already completed it, Johnson opted to focus on the welfare of the nation moving forward and the work that still needed to be done. Similarly, Richard Nixon noted: "Our Administration, as you know, has provided the biggest tax cut in history, but taxes are still too high."[16] And Bill Clinton emphasized that, despite passing "the toughest crime bill in history," we "still leave too many of our people behind."[17] Contrast these statements with the following from Trump during his first State of the Union Address:

After years and years of wage stagnation, we are finally seeing rising wages. Unemployment claims have hit a 45-year low. And something I'm very proud of: African American unemployment stands at the lowest rate ever recorded. And Hispanic American unemployment has also reached the lowest levels in history. Small-business confidence is at an all-time high. The stock market has smashed one record after another, gaining $8 trillion and more in value in just this short period of time. The great news for Americans: 401(k), retirement, pension, and college savings accounts have gone through the roof. And just as I promised the American people from this podium 11 months ago, we enacted the biggest tax cuts and reforms in American history.[18]

The tone of Trump's remarks, in contrast to those from Johnson, Nixon, and Clinton, was unmistakably boastful. There was no modesty, no humility, and no recognition of what was still needed to be done. In essence, virtually everything that he had touched, according to Trump, had turned to gold. Indeed, in a matter of just eight short sentences, Trump identified six records that *he* had supposedly set as president (e.g., unemployment levels for African Americans and Hispanic Americans, small business confidence, the stock market, tax cuts, and reforms), not to mention countless other accomplishments that did not quite meet the threshold of "historic" or "best ever" (e.g., unemployment claims, 401(k), retirement, pension, and college savings accounts). And this all occurred, according to Trump, due to the policies he put in place during just one year in office.

Trump's efforts to sell himself as *the* exceptional president, however, began well before his first State of the Union Address. On February 28, 2017, for example, just one month after taking office, Trump proclaimed: "The stock market has gained almost $3 trillion in value since the election on November 8—a record."[19] A few months later, Trump suggested that his administration had achieved "a record reduction in illegal immigration on our southern border" and brought "jobs, plants, and factories back into the United States at numbers which no one until this point thought even possible."[20] By August 2017, just seven months into his presidency, Trump had reached his stride. In a speech that was billed as a response to the violence that had erupted in the wake of the "Unite the Right Rally" in Charlottesville, Virginia, two days earlier, Trump stated:

Our economy is now strong. The stock market continues to hit record highs, unemployment is at a 16-year low, and businesses are more optimistic than ever before. Companies are moving back to the United States and bringing many thousands of jobs with them. We have already created over 1 million jobs since I took office.[21]

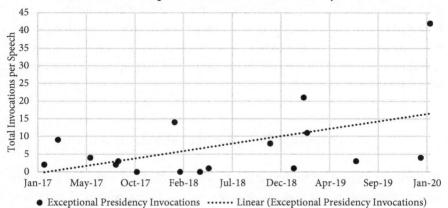

Figure 5.2 Over time trend in Trump's invocations of presidential exceptionalism in major speeches to the nation from 2017 to 2020.

As we will see, such claims—many of them dubious, others requiring much needed context—would become the norm in Trump's public communications throughout his first term in office.

Over the course of his first three years in office, as reflected in Figure 5.2, Trump's invocations of presidential exceptionalism continued to increase significantly in his major speeches to the nation. In his 2019 State of the Union Address, for example, Trump invoked this idea a full twenty-one times. Indeed, it was full display in the following statement:

> Over the last two years, my administration has moved with urgency and historic speed to confront problems neglected by leaders of both parties over many decades. In just over 2 years since the election, we have launched an unprecedented economic boom, a boom that has rarely been seen before. There's been nothing like it.[22]

By the time of the 2020 State of the Union Address, however, Trump was completely unrestrained, invoking presidential exceptionalism a total of forty-two times—double that of the year before. He had essentially collected a "greatest hits" of statistics and so-called accomplishments designed to support the notion that both he and his presidency were indeed exceptional. Armed with these claims, he was prepared to unapologetically shower them over the American people in his march toward reelection, which is exactly what he did in his 2020 State of the Union Address. To put this in proper perspective, no other president since the Second World War had ever invoked this idea more than five times in a speech, including in their State of the Union Addresses, the prime venue for presidents to make the case for how well they are doing as president and how well the country is doing under their leadership. Make no mistake, this was strategic. Trump was laying the foundation for his 2020 reelection campaign and serving notice to all those who dare to challenge him.

The Perpetual Campaigner: MAGA Rallies

Trump's major speeches to the nation, however, provide us with only a cursory view of just how robust and multifaceted his use of this rhetorical tactic was during his first term in office. After all, these speeches tend to be highly scripted and restrained in their language, something that Trump had always resisted in his communications. While our analysis of major presidential speeches offers valuable insights into just how different Trump was compared to his predecessors in his invocations of presidential exceptionalism, it is in his Make America Great Again rallies that we see the rest of the story. It is in these rallies where the unrestrained version of Trump and his unapologetic presentation of the exceptional me strategy were on full display. It was here that Trump became famous for his rambling soliloquies, impromptu jokes, and searing attacks on the media, Democrats, the political establishment, and anybody else who he thought had done him wrong. Most importantly, given the relatively unscripted nature of these events, it is at MAGA rallies where we get a closer look at Trump's own thoughts and beliefs.

Unlike presidents before him, Trump became a perpetual campaigner, speaking at rallies on average more than once a month during his first three years in office and, all the while, maintaining an unwavering focus on making the argument for his reelection. As the difficulties of the presidency mounted and attacks from his opponents increased, Trump used his rallies to air his grievances and to connect again and again with his ardent supporters. Standing in front of his adoring fans seemed to reinvigorate Trump, reminding him that regardless of the trials and tribulations in Washington, his base was undeterred in their support for him. They loved the unscripted Trump. His "modern day presidential" persona was on full display and it made his crowds go wild. MAGA rallies allowed Trump to let loose and speak, at length, about his favorite subjects: himself and his exceptional presidency. In Figure 5.3, we see just how common it was for Trump to invoke presidential exceptionalism at these events and, more

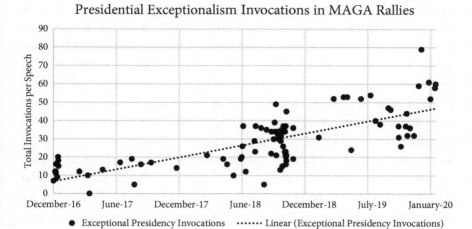

Figure 5.3 Over time trend in Trump's invocations of presidential exceptionalism in major speeches to the nation from 2016 to 2020.

importantly, how these invocations increased dramatically over time. Indeed, in the last five rallies leading up to his 2020 State of the Union Address, Trump averaged an incredible sixty-two references to presidential exceptionalism per speech. Again, when given the choice, Trump wanted to talk about himself and his exceptional presidency.

Figure 5.4 gives us an even clearer picture of the extent to which Trump sought to promote the idea that he was the exceptional president. The findings here are unambiguous: across major speeches, MAGA rallies, and

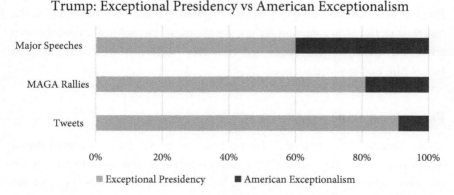

Figure 5.4 Proportion of Trump's invocations of Presidential Exceptionalism versus American Exceptionalism by type of communication from 2017 to 2020.

tweets, Trump was much more likely to lavish exceptional praise on himself and his presidency than on the nation itself. Notably, it was in the moments that Trump was channeling his unscripted and unrestrained self (rallies and tweets) that he became much more interested and intent on communicating presidential exceptionalism over American exceptionalism. In effect, as these results indicate, the more that Trump was left to his own devices—both literally and figuratively—the more likely it was that he would glorify himself and his presidency over the nation. To see what this looked like in real terms, below we document the innumerable different ways that Trump spoke of himself and his presidency as exceptional in his rallies. It is important to note at the outset that the examples we provide below are but a small sample of the barrage of exceptional presidency references (over 3,000 in total)[23] that Trump communicated in these venues.

Exceptional Me

While in office, as the preceding sections have well-documented, Trump, without question, consistently and unapologetically presented himself and his presidency as exceptional. This manifested, we argue, in four important ways. First, Trump often emphasized his exceptional skills and attributes to give the impression that he was the very best person who had ever occupied the White House. Second, Trump routinely suggested that his election and the "movement" that swept him into office were beyond anything America had ever seen. Third, throughout his time in office, Trump sought to give the clear impression that his accomplishments as president surpassed anything that any president before him had ever achieved. Fourth, Trump portrayed himself, time and again, as the target or victim of persecution, be it from the press, the political establishment, government bureaucrats, judges, or Democrats, the likes of which no president before him had ever experienced.

Exceptional Trump

As we illustrated in Chapter 3, Trump had a penchant for showering himself with exceptional praise throughout his campaign. It was no different in his constant campaigning while in office. Indeed, Trump seemed to turn up the volume, using the power of the bully pulpit to amplify his claims. During his time in office, Trump repeatedly boasted about his unique set of personal qualities and characteristics—from his intelligence, education, and wealth to his knowledge of business, trade, and how to negotiate—to build the case that he was an exceptional man—indeed, *the* exceptional man. Trump was known for his braggadocios personality, but he took this to another level when he was standing in front of his supporters. In such moments, he was unrestrained in speaking about himself, offering things like, "I am the most brilliant guy in the world,"[24] and, "I'm smarter than anybody."[25] Put simply: "You know I think I'm a totally brilliant human being. I think I'm the smartest person, so I came up with a plan... I came up with this incredible plan. Only I could think of this."[26] In essence, Trump thought he was smarter than everybody. And he wanted everyone to know it.

To cap it off, Trump developed a fondness for calling himself "your favorite president."[27] On the surface, this was a seemingly harmless and somewhat playful expression. But placed in proper context, his frequent use of this phrase was part of a much larger pattern in which Trump sought to find creative and, no doubt, strategic ways to talk about himself as exceptional. Perhaps the most notable example of Trump using this expression occurred in the lead-up to his "Salute to America" event on July 4th, 2019, when he tweeted:

> HOLD THE DATE. We will be having one of the biggest gatherings in the history of Washington, D.C., on July 4th. It will be called "A Salute to America" and will be held at the Lincoln Memorial. Major fireworks display, entertainment and an address by your favorite President, me![28]

Although billed as a day of celebration for the country, previous presidents had traditionally avoided holding any kind of public event on Independence Day, especially one of this size and magnitude. This was because previous presidents simply did not want to politicize a day that Americans of all stripes celebrated together. But this was yet another piece of presidential decorum that Trump ignored. He wanted a day of pomp and circumstance, during which he could stand on stage and be viewed as the essence of American patriotism. While it was called, "Salute to America," it came off more like a salute to Trump.

Trump's self-praise often came at odd moments and in relation to things that, seemingly, had no reason to be talked about in exceptional terms. For instance, in an interview with Sean Hannity as the COVID-19 pandemic was in its infancy, Trump offered: "Somebody said, you're the cleanest person in the country."[29] It apparently was not sufficient to simply say that he was a clean person. He needed to be the cleanest and to show that someone else had noticed it. He also often claimed that he was the "least racist person in the world."[30] Again, simply saying that he was "not racist" would have had the same effect. Somehow to Trump, saying that he was "the least racist person" made the claim more true or irrefutable. It seemed that, in Trump world, everything had to be presented in the most extreme version possible. If it had anything to do with Trump, it had to be exceptional.

The Exceptional 2016 Campaign (Again)

MAGA rallies were also a place where Trump loved to bask in the glory of his "historic" win in the 2016 election. In these venues, he would go on and on, waxing nostalgic about his victory and recounting every detail of his "unprecedented" campaign to his adoring audiences.[31] And it was all exceptional in every way. In one rally, for example, Trump noted:

> You know, I've always said 2016 was the most important election, maybe in the history of our country. A lot of people thought that. So I don't know. I can't say this is more important. What we did was a miracle. Not to us, it wasn't. But a lot of people said it was the greatest election we've ever had. There's never been anything like it. Never been such excitement.[32]

Inevitably, Trump always got around to talking about his 2016 victory, at times revisiting the story two or three separate times in the same speech. Time and again, Trump proclaimed that it was "the greatest election in our country's history,"[33] "the most exciting evening of our lives,"[34] and even "the most exciting night in the history of politics."[35] Even into the fourth year of his presidency, Trump was still at it. He still wanted to recount his 2016 victory for his supporters, but now he had a strategic segue. He would talk about the splendor of the 2016 election to get his supporters excited about his reelection. At a rally in early 2020, for example, Trump offered:

> We are asking all Americans to join our incredible movement. That's what it is. It's one of the greatest moments. It's probably the greatest movement in history. The 2016 election was probably, I mean you could say, the greatest election in the history of our country. And now we have to do it again to keep it going. It's like a giant tree, you plant it, but it takes time to grab on. We need this next election so badly. The good news is, it's much easier, because here I've done it all. I've achieved more than I promised.[36]

According to Trump, he was leading "the greatest revolution ever to take place in our country"[37] and "possibly the greatest political movement anywhere,"[38] but he needed to keep it going.

The Exceptional Presidency

Trump was also constantly preoccupied with how he compared as president to all of his predecessors. And he wanted to control the narrative from the outset. It was clear that Trump was fixated on convincing the American people, and his supporters in particular, that his presidency was by far the greatest in American history. One of Trump's common refrains, for example, was convincing people that he had accomplished more in his time in office than every president before him. This appeared early and often throughout his presidency.[39] Just two months after taking office, for example, he told his supporters: "We have done far more—I think maybe more than anybody's done in this office in 50 days, that I could tell you."[40] Four months later, he noted: "I think that with few exceptions, no president has done anywhere near what we've done in his first six months. Not even close."[41] From the very beginning, even before the dust had settled from the 2016 presidential election, Trump was selling his presidency as the greatest ever. At seven months: "I don't believe that any president has accomplished as much as this president in the first six or seven months."[42] This obsessive pattern would continue unabated thoughout his presidency. At three years, in the lead-up to his 2020 State of the Union Address, Trump proudly proclaimed: "Nobody, in the first three years of a presidency, has done what we've done, nobody."[43] Throughout our analysis we noted that Trump made this claim—each, it should be noted, on numerous occasions—at fifty days, six months, seven months, one year, five-hundred days, two years, two-and-a-half years, three years, and finally: "We have done more than any first term administration in the history of our country."[44] Apparently, every day was a day that the Trump presidency surpassed every other presidency in history.[45]

The Exceptional Republican

Trump seemed particularly fixated throughout his presidency on comparing himself and his administration favorably to the two most iconic figures in the history of the Republican Party: Abraham Lincoln and Ronald Reagan. It seemed from the outset that Trump was threatened by the prospect that Lincoln and Reagan may be more popular than him within the Republican ranks and he wanted to put a stop to it. The most prominent way that he did this was to refer to public opinion polls and what others were saying about his presidency. This was certainly one of his favorite topics to discuss. At one rally, for example, he stated: "They just came out with a poll, did you hear? The most popular person in the history of the Republican Party is Trump. Can you believe this? So I said, 'Does that include honest Abe Lincoln?'"[46] At another rally, Trump said:

> I have a 95% approval rating. Can you believe that?... Do you know who second is? Ronald Reagan at 87%... Then, one of these characters back there, they put me in a contest with the late great Abraham Lincoln, right? Who do you like better, Trump or Abraham Lincoln? All I know is, we won against Abraham, Honest Abe. We won, 53 to 47. Can you believe that, Abraham Lincoln? I went back to the First Lady, I said, "First Lady, I just beat Abraham Lincoln in a poll."[47]

Lastly, citing "the great Lou Dobbs" from Fox News, Trump offered this:

> I was watching the other night the great Lou Dobbs, and he said, "When Trump took over, President Trump," he used to say, "Trump is a great president." Then he said, "Trump is the greatest president since Ronald Reagan." Then he said, "No, no, Trump is an even better president than Ronald Reagan." And now he's got me down as the greatest president in the history of our country, including George Washington and Abraham Lincoln.[48]

Clearly, Trump was vying for the top spot as the most popular figure in the history of the Republican Party.

Trump's crosshairs, however, were most commonly fixed on Reagan, the sweetheart of the modern Republican Party. Trump desperately wanted to be seen as better than Reagan. Throughout his rallies, Trump mentioned Reagan time and again, finding creative ways to suggest that he had accomplished more than Reagan. He was certainly clever, if not skillful, about it, though, carefully claiming superiority without unnecessarily stepping on the toes of those who still put Reagan on a pedestal. At one rally, for example, Trump offered: "[A] thing comes out, a big poll, and a couple of polls, a number of polls that, 'He's the most powerful, most popular, Republican in the history of the party'... more popular than a man I like, Ronald Reagan."[49] At another rally, Trump wanted to highlight his tax cuts, which he characterized as the "largest tax cuts and reform in American history." But he couldn't just leave it there. Trump also went out of his way to mention: "the tax bill was so massive, bigger than Reagan, bigger than—biggest one ever done."[50] He also emphasized: "We've already implemented 64 percent of our top agenda items. And that's a much faster pace than even Ronald Reagan."[51] Such comparisons, we argue, were not merely random or insignificant.[52] They were strategic and part of a larger plan. Trump wanted to make clear that he had surpassed even Lincoln and Reagan as the most beloved and celebrated figure that Republicans—and, indeed, Americans—had ever seen. Perhaps this is why Trump at one point "jokingly" floated the idea—bear in mind, this was in 2017, less than one year into his presidency—that he should eventually be on Mount Rushmore:

> I'd ask whether or not you think I will some day be on Mt. Rushmore, but, but here's the problem. If I did it joking, totally joking, having fun, the fake news media will say, "he believes he should be on Mt. Rushmore." So I won't say it, okay? I won't say it. But every president—they'll say it anyway tomorrow. "Trump thinks he should be on Mt. Rushmore." Isn't that terrible? What a group. What a dishonest group of people.[53]

Given Trump's obsession with being perceived as *the* exceptional president, as well as his repeated efforts to compare himself favorably to Lincoln and Reagan, it is fair to say this was likely no joke.

The Exceptional Victim

According to Trump, he was not only exceptional in his achievements as president, he was also exceptional in how poorly his political opponents and the media had treated him. This likely stemmed from the fact that his presidency was mired in controversy since well before it even began. There were the accusations that the Trump campaign had colluded with Russia, which prompted the Mueller investigation. There were his many controversial executive orders, which often triggered claims of executive overreach. And there was the Ukraine scandal, which ultimately led to his impeachment. Notably, throughout his first term, there was a sense of inevitability that he would eventually be impeached by the Democrats, who, in his view, were desperate to overturn the 2016 presidential election. Trump repeatedly denounced the many forces that he perceived to be seeking to undermine him and his presidency. In both tweets and rallies, Trump liked to refer to the Mueller investigation as "the worst and most corrupt political Witch Hunt in the history of the United States."[54]

Trump's response to impeachment was no different. Trump suggested, for instance, that it was both "the greatest hoax ever perpetrated on our country"[55] and "the most unfair Witch Hunt in the history of Congress."[56] Trump, therefore, was the most unfairly treated president in American history. Put simply: "There has been no President in the history of our Country who has been treated so badly as I have. The Democrats are frozen with hatred and fear. They get nothing done. This should never be allowed to happen to another President. Witch Hunt!"[57] In essence, Trump was not only a victim, he was the victim*est* of them all. Nonetheless, this was not done to merely elicit sympathy or support. It was strategic, designed to cultivate the impression that Trump was exceptional in how he handled this persecution.[58] Specifically, Trump sought to portray himself as stronger and more resilient than any president before him in how he dealt with this treatment: "A regular president would have been under a table, thumb in the mouth, saying, take me home mommy, this is too tough for me."[59] Trump, though, was a different kind of president. He was exceptional.

Trump's America: "Better Than Ever Before"

Trump's 2016 presidential campaign slogan, Make America Great Again, no doubt put pressure on him to deliver—or, at least, proclaim that he had delivered— impressive accomplishments once he entered office. A primary component, we argue, in this broader communication strategy was his emphasis on the idea that America, under the Trump presidency, had not just become great again but that it was doing *better than ever before*. A few weeks after his election, for example, Trump stated: "We're gonna have a country that was never so great. You watch—in so many different ways."[60] Days later, at another rally, he vowed to "show the world that America is going to be strong again, stronger than ever before."[61] To be sure, in the days, months, and years that followed, so much of Trump's presidency was devoted to persuading Americans that these statements had, in fact, become reality. Whether it was the economy, the military, or even the environment, Trump was determined to make clear to the American public that he had made America better than ever before. The shift toward "proving" that he had delivered on these promises occurred within weeks after he entered office. And, predictably, by his fourth year, Trump was proudly proclaiming: "America is thriving like never before"[62] and "we're having probably the best years we've ever had in the history of our country."[63]

An Economy Like Never Before

From the outset, Trump was determined to convince the American public that he was responsible for creating an unprecedented economic boom in America during his presidency. Trump regularly offered numerous facts and figures about how well the economy was doing under his presidency, taking credit at every turn, even when it came to economic trends that began well before his presidency. As we have already noted, a common focus for Trump was celebrating and taking credit for a rise in the US stock market. This was perhaps most evident when

Trump stated: "We have set 141 records on the stock market, highest levels ever in recorded history. 141 records. That means, in less than three years, for 141 days, we set a record. Think of it, we've set 141 records. Who the hell can do that?"[64] Trump also regularly took credit for "record" employment numbers, suggesting that his administration had achieved "the highest jobs, the best jobs, the best employment number ever, the best unemployment numbers ever."[65] Perhaps it was no surprise, then, that Trump tweeted in late 2019: "The workers will vote for me in 2020 (lowest unemployment, most jobs ever)."[66] After all, it was clear that Trump believed that a strong economy—or at least the perception of one—was crucial to his reelection chances in 2020.

Trump also seemed almost obsessed with discussing how these economic numbers applied to certain demographics within the United States.[67] Perhaps this was because he struggled to gain traction with minority voters and because he had only won a majority of two major demographics in the 2016 election: whites and males. During the 2016 campaign, for example, Trump had argued that African Americans should take a chance on his candidacy. After all, according to Trump, what did they have to lose? He frequently revisited this idea in his rallies as president: "I said to them, 'What the hell do you have to lose? Vote for me. What do you have to lose?'… And now, I just said African-American unemployment is at the lowest level in history."[68] Trump was both making a play for African American voters and, as some have suggested, trying to deflate accusations that he was racist by showing how much he was doing for them.[69] Perhaps the most iconic, and truly odd, reference to this came when he said this:

> African-American unemployment has reached its lowest rate ever recorded in the history of our country. And African-American poverty has reached its lowest rate ever recorded. And Kanye West, who gets it. And big Jim Brown… but they get it! How do you win when you hear those numbers? Because the democrats for 100 years have been promising African-Americans, Hispano-Americans, Asians. They've been promising everything, nothing happens. Here we are, less than two years, the best employment numbers, the best numbers they've ever had in virtually every category. Every category. Hispanic-American and Asian-American unemployment rates have also reached all-time lows. How do you beat us in 2020?[70]

According to Trump, he was not just doing historic things for African Americans; minorities of all kinds were benefiting in unprecedented ways thanks to him. In addition, Trump regularly spoke of how his economic policies and achievements had led to "historic" results for women. He often spoke of how there were "more women in the workforce than ever before."[71] At times, however, he had to do a bit of an awkward dance when unemployment numbers for women had yet to hit historic proportions. A perfect illustration of this occurred during a rally in May 2018 in which Trump stated:

> We love women. Women. The lowest unemployment rate in 18 years. I'm sorry we didn't make it in history but we're catching—it will soon happen. I'm disappointed with that. Can you imagine? My most disappointing stat is women. It's the lowest unemployment rate in 18 years because all of the others are history. But I have the feeling the women will soon be history too, because that's what's happening.[72]

Trump's obsession here with whether or not these numbers were "historic" is notable because it reflects how deeply important it was for him for everything to be perceived as exceptional.

There were, of course, many other economic indicators that Trump routinely cited as evidence that the nation's economy was doing better than ever before. At a rally in November 2018, for example, Trump stated: "Wages, wages, beautiful wages for the first time in years, wages are rising. Confidence is soaring. You saw the confidence level. Business confidence, consumer confidence, every form of confidence is at an all-time high."[73] In a tweet in October 2019, he proclaimed: "Just out: MEDIAN HOUSEHOLD INCOME IS AT THE HIGHEST POINT EVER, EVER, EVER! How about saying it this way, IN THE HISTORY OF OUR COUNTRY!"[74] On other occasions, Trump noted that manufacturing enthusiasm in the United States was "at an all-time high"[75] and that, during his presidency, "earnings for the bottom 10 percent are rising faster than earnings for the top 10 percent for the first time ever."[76] Taken together, Trump's prolific and overwhelming use of these facts and figures, many of which were embellished or unverifiable, enabled him to arrive at one simple, overarching conclusion: "We now have the greatest economy in history!"[77]

The Military Is Back and Better Than Ever!

Trump devoted considerable time and energy during the early part of his presidency decrying the decrepit state of the US military and promising to rebuild it into something "bigger, better, stronger than ever before."[78] Despite the fact that, by virtually any measure, the United States possessed by far the most powerful military in the world when Trump stepped into office, he was determined to construct an alternate reality, one in which the US military had lost its edge and was in serious decay. As he stated in late 2017 at a speech before the US Coast Guard: "We're at $700 billion for the military. And, you know, they were cutting back for years. They just kept cutting, cutting, cutting the military. And you got lean, to put it nicely. It was depleted, was the word. And now it's changing."[79] This narrative essentially allowed Trump to position himself to be the savior of the US military—the only one who could not only restore its dominance, but make it better than ever before. This rhetorical strategy—or sleight of hand—was on full display, for example, during a rally in 2018 when Trump stated: "[Y]ou know what was happening to our military. It was depleted. It was tired. It was exhausted. The planes were old. Everything was tired. We are rebuilding America's military might like it's never been rebuilt before."[80] This notion that he was in the process of building the military like never before was a familiar and pervasive theme in Trump's communications throughout 2018.

By the middle of 2019, an important, albeit somewhat subtle, rhetorical shift occurred in Trump's statements about the US military. At a rally in May, for example, Trump made sure to note the state of the military before he took office: "[W]hen we took over two-and-a-half years ago, the military was depleted. The equipment was old, the planes were old." He was setting the stage. Later in the speech he was finally ready to proclaim: "The military is more powerful right now than ever before."[81] Trump had, in effect, transitioned from promising to rebuild the military "like never before" to claiming that he had, indeed, delivered on that promise "like never before." A few months later, Trump emphasized:

> Our military was totally depleted. When I took over, our military was sad. We weren't flying half of our planes, they were old. They were tired. Our equipment was tired. Our people weren't tired, though. Our people weren't tired. But everything we had, it was depleted. Now we've rebuilt our military like never before.[82]

Trump then seemed to take this to another level when his reelection campaign was in full swing. In January 2020, for example, he offered this:

> After years and years of devastating defense cuts, we have fully rebuilt the United States military. Some of it's still coming in. We have everything. We've got new planes, we've got new rockets, new missiles, we've got new everything, and it's either here or coming in, $2.5 trillion in new investments. So, our military is now stronger and more powerful than ever before. And if you remember, three years ago when I took over, we were depleted. Our military was totally depleted.[83]

Less than a week later, Trump reinforced these ideas, stating: "So after years of devastating defense cuts, we have fully rebuilt the United States Military to a point that it has never been before and it's now more advanced, more lethal, and more powerful than ever."[84] In just under three years, Trump, in his telling of the story, had miraculously transformed the military from a beleaguered, rapidly decaying mess to the best it had ever been.

The Kitchen Sink

Trump heaped exceptional praise upon himself for his work on the economy and military more than anything else during his first term in office because he knew that it would play well in the 2020 elections, but he also spread the love around, so to speak. Here is but a small sampling of the multitude of "exceptional" ways that the country, according to Trump, was doing better than ever before under his administration:

- "And today, our nation is stronger today than ever before."[85]
- "America's future has never, ever looked brighter, ever."[86]
- "America is respected again, respected like never before."[87]
- "America now is winning again like they haven't won before."[88]
- "The American dream is back, it is bigger and better and stronger than ever before."[89]
- "[T]he American nation remains the greatest symbol of liberty, of freedom and justice on the face of god's earth. And now we have spirit like we've never had before."[90]
- "We're restoring America's industrial might like never before."[91]
- "America's steel and aluminum mills are roaring back to life like nobody has ever seen."[92]
- "The USMCA is another colossal victory for American agriculture like you have never had before."[93]
- "We are delivering a policy of American energy independence like you've never seen before."[94]
- "We are coming out with so many health care plans. It is so much better than anything you've ever seen before."[95]
- "We're approving more generic drugs than ever before in the history of our country."[96]
- "We have taken historic steps to secure our border, impose needed immigration control like you've never seen before"[97]
- "We are removing illegal border crossers from Central America at a pace never done before."[98]

- "We have never had a better relationship with China than we do right now."[99]
- "The wall is being built like you've never seen before."[100]
- "[T]he poor are doing the best they've ever done."[101]
- "Our veterans, for the first time, are taken care of at a level that has never happened in our country before."[102]
- "[R]ight now we have the cleanest air and the cleanest water that we've ever had."[103]

In virtually every area, America, according to Trump, was doing better than ever before, and he was shouting it to the American people *ad nauseam*. Although many of these statements were exaggerations—others, patently false, as many journalists regularly pointed out—Trump was trying to control the narrative as well as the national mood by painting a picture of an America that was soaring to heights never seen before. And, it was no coincidence that all of it, every historic accomplishment imaginable, just so happened to have transpired under Trump's exceptional presidency. After taking stock, there seems to be only one question left unanswered: was there anything about Trump or his presidency that, in his view, was *not* exceptional?

Without Me, It All Fails

Perhaps the most extreme and, one could argue, sinister facet of Trump's exceptional me strategy was his argument that if he were not president, the country would fall inevitably into ruins. Similar to what an authoritarian leader might do, Trump was making the case that the welfare of the nation depended entirely upon him and him alone. This strategy, we argue, primarily manifested in two important ways. First, it involved Trump portraying his 2016 election as a miracle for the nation. Specifically, Trump argued that had he not been elected, America would have never recovered and it would have continued to dive in a perpetual downward spiral. Throughout his presidency, for example, Trump liked to heap blame on Hillary Clinton, claiming that the country would have fallen into ruins had she become president. At one rally, for example, Trump offered:

> If crooked Hillary would've won, your economy would have crashed. You were going down. The regulations were taking it down. The taxes were taking it down.

Instead of being up 92% or whatever you're up, a lot, you would have been down, you would have been at less than half. It was crashing. For all those people that would say, "Oh, it's the Obama... " Let me tell you something. You were dying.[104]

At another rally, Trump stated: "And you know today with the new stock market at an all-time high, it's... I will tell you something... if we didn't win this election, that stock market would be in one-half. It was heading in the wrong direction. It was going to fail."[105] In addition, Trump argued: "Your economy is the greatest on earth. And let me tell you it, if my crooked opponent would have won the election right now China would be by far the number one nation from an economic standpoint in the world."[106] Notably, these statements occurred more than three years after his election, each serving as a reminder that Trump had, in his view, saved the nation.

This idea that Trump had "saved the nation" was something that Trump loved to talk about. At multiple rallies, for example, Trump told the story of meeting a man backstage before the rally who thanked him for "saving the country." This man was always "big," "tough," or "strong," and, according to Trump, "crying" when he said it. This story first appeared at an October 2018 rally in Tennessee, in which Trump said:

> We were losing our country. I've had so many people come up to me, great people, some of them strong and tough—and, you know, these aren't emotional people—they have tears in their eyes, say, "Mr. President"—I saw one tonight, came up to me, a man, strong, tough cookie, I wouldn't want to fight him, OK? And he said, "Mr. President"—he's crying—he said, "thank you for saving our country." So many people say that.[107]

A few weeks later, at a rally in Montana, Trump claimed to have met a similar guy backstage:

> You know, I just walked in, and a big, strong guy grabbed me. And he was almost crying. It happens every time. And many times. And he said, "sir, Mr. President, thank you so much for saving our country." And, you know... I hear it all the time, those exact words. "Thank you for saving our country."[108]

Months later at an event in Texas, Trump again repeated this story, but with a twist:

> This guy is like a monster. No, no, it's true... This guy is like a monster. He is like this monster, big, strong guy. He says to me, "Thank you very much." I don't know what to say, but that's ok. And he's crying. And he said—I'm walking up, and it happens all the time. "Thank you very much, Mr. President." I said, "For

what?" He said, "You have saved our country. Our country was going in the wrong direction. You have saved our country." I have had so many people say that.[109]

Trump would go on to repeat versions of this story in multiple other venues as well. Whether or not all of these interactions actually occurred seems inconsequential.[110] Trump wanted to build a specific narrative and, as the saying goes, "you should never let the truth get in the way of a good story." Trump, apparently, had saved the country from certain failure and as a result, big, burly, tough men—even monsters—everywhere were not able to contain their emotions.

The second way Trump made the case that the country would fail without him was to speak in great detail of the disastrous consequences the nation would face if he did not win reelection. He prophesized that if he lost the presidency, the country would fall into economic collapse, illegal immigrants would start streaming across the border, health care premiums would skyrocket, drugs and crime would infest American communities, and the world would turn their backs on the United States. In a speech at a rally in late 2019, for example, Trump sought to link his 2016 election with the 2020 race and, in doing so, combine both elements of his "without me, it all fails" message:

> [Y]ou know, the markets have gone through the roof since November 9th. That's the day after I won the election. So, I won the election. The markets went up thousands of points. Things started happening… And let me tell you, if for some reason I wouldn't have won the election, these markets would have crashed. And that'll happen even more so in 2020. See the bottom line is I know you like me and this room is a love fest. I know that. But you have no choice but to vote for me because your 401(k)s down the tubes. Everything's going to be down the tubes. So, whether you love me or hate me, you gotta vote for me.[111]

Elsewhere, Trump took these ideas to a much more urgent and almost apocalyptic level. At one rally, for example, he stated: "[W]e must devote everything we have toward victory in 2020. We have to win. You know, we have to win. Because all of these things that we've done can be undone. And you can have a country that goes to hell very very fast, very very fast."[112] At another, he argued: "At stake in our present battle is the survival, frankly, of our nation. Look, I can make this speech really short. All I have to do is say, 'Hello Iowa, you have no choice. You have to vote for me. Otherwise everything that you've built in your entire life will be gone.'"[113] At yet another rally, Trump took this argument even a step further:

You know, I don't think we've ever done better as a country, certainly the economy and lots of other things. Look at all of those beautiful red hats. Those beautiful red hats. Look at them. Boy, oh boy. And I like the white ones too. Make America great again. Lifts those whites up there. But it can disappear quickly. You know, what we did was unprecedented in the history of our country, really in the history of the world, what we did with this election. And the strides that we're making have never, ever been made like this before. But it can also disappear if you put fools and if you put the wrong people in. It can disappear.[114]

Perhaps the best example of his effort to convince Americans that without him, the nation would fail, Trump offered this at a July 2019 rally in North Carolina:

Everything that we've built, low taxes, strong military, taking care of our vets, all of the things we've done can be decimated very quickly if the wrong person gets in, especially now. You know, I've always said 2016 was the most important election, maybe in the history of our country… What we did was a miracle. Not to us, it wasn't. But a lot of people said it was the greatest election we've ever had. There's never been anything like it. Never been such excitement. Never been such excitement. But you know what? If we don't win in 2020, everything that we've done—seriously, though, everything that we've done, your 401s, they're going to crash, the whole thing it's going to come down like a stack of cards.[115]

In effect, this was "I alone can fix it" on steroids. Without Trump as president, the well-being and livelihood of all Americans would be in peril. As Trump had made clear, America had no choice but to reelect him. If not, they would stand to lose everything. The nation was Trump and Trump was the nation. If one fell, so too would the other.

"Me the People"

We are going to declare our independence from failures of the past and create a New American Future. Once again, we will have a government of, by, and for the people.

—Donald Trump[1]

On January 20, 2017, the eyes of the world turned to Washington, D.C., to witness the swearing in of Donald J. Trump as the forty-fifth president of the United States of America. As Trump stepped up to the podium, it was unclear what the tone of his message would be. Would he pivot from the harsh rhetoric of his campaign to a more conciliatory tone in an attempt to unify the nation around his presidency, or would he sow the same seeds of division that had taken center stage only months prior? Would he mirror the tone of humility taken by so many presidents before him, or would he focus on simply exalting himself as exceptional? Trump started with a call to all Americans:

We, the citizens of America, are now joined in a great national effort to rebuild our country and restore its promise for all of our people. Together, we will determine the course of America and the world for many, many years to come. We will face challenges, we will confront hardships, but we will get the job done.[2]

He went on to thank President Barack Obama and First Lady Michelle Obama for their help with the transition of power. This, however, would be the end of his conciliatory remarks. Trump then pivoted to drive a clear wedge between himself and the presidents who came before him. He sought to make clear that his would be an "exceptional" presidency in one clear way:

Today's ceremony, however, has very special meaning. Because today we are not merely transferring power from one administration to another or from one party to another, but we are transferring power from Washington, DC, and giving it back to you, the people.

Trump was, in effect, saying that the power was being returned to the American people by giving him the reins. He was arguing that his will as president would represent the will of the entire American public, all while disregarding the fact that he was about to preside over a deeply divided nation. According to Trump, he was not one of the politicians who inhabited Washington, he was the voice of the American people moving to Washington to confront them:

> For too long, a small group in our Nation's Capital has reaped the rewards of government while the people have borne the cost. Washington flourished, but the people did not share in its wealth. Politicians prospered, but the jobs left, and the factories closed. The establishment protected itself, but not the citizens of our country. Their victories have not been your victories, their triumphs have not been your triumphs, and while they celebrated in our nation's capital, there was little to celebrate for struggling families all across our land. That all changes, starting right here and right now, because this moment is your moment: It belongs to you. It belongs to everyone gathered here today and everyone watching all across America. This is your day. This is your celebration. And this, the United States of America, is your country. What truly matters is not which party controls our government, but whether our government is controlled by the people.

According to Trump, he was not just a representative of the American people, he *was* the American people incarnate. His voice was their voice. His will was their will. The American people were now in control, through his hands. As Trump succinctly stated: "January 20, 2017 will be remembered as the day the people became the rulers of this nation again." This was perhaps the ultimate form of self-exceptionalism because it allowed Trump to position himself as being the one and only person who could speak for the entirety of the American people. Again, it mattered little that the majority of Americans neither voted for him nor saw him as representing their values or voices. This was evident in the next line of the speech, which was telling of a different aspect of his strategy: "The forgotten men and women of our country will be forgotten no longer. Everyone is listening to *you* now." It was clear, Trump was talking more to his supporters than to the broader American public. This would become more evident as Trump's presidency evolved.

Traditionally, when presidents step into the office of the presidency, they tend to make an immediate and overt gesture to those who did not vote for them, claiming that they will do their best to represent "all of the people," while recognizing that many Americans are weary of a president they did not vote for.[3] Such a step is an explicit recognition that they are now the president of *all* Americans and will have to work hard to win over support from those who oppose them. Presidents before Trump typically used their inaugural address to ease the concerns of those voters. Even Barack Obama, who came in with populist appeals during his campaign, immediately transitioned to a more inclusive and broadly representative tone once he entered the presidency. It is important to note here that in our analysis of major presidential speeches since the Second World War, Trump was the only president to stray from this norm in any meaningful way.

To illustrate these differences, a fitting contrast can be drawn between Trump and Ronald Reagan, a president to whom, as we've shown, Trump was fixated on comparing himself. Reagan, in his inaugural address, employed many of the same ideas that Trump echoed some thirty-six years later. His language, however, focused not on portraying one group of Americans as more important than others but on facilitating national unity and offering to represent all Americans. Reagan, for example, offered this:

> From time to time we've been tempted to believe that society has become too complex to be managed by self-rule, that government by an elite group is superior to government for, by, and of the people. Well, if no one among us is capable of governing himself, then who among us has the capacity to govern someone else? All of us together, in and out of government, must bear the burden. The solutions we seek must be equitable, with no one group singled out to pay a higher price.[4]

In contrast to Trump's overt populist appeals to his supporters, Reagan was saying that the office of the presidency was much bigger than any single person and that it was imperative that inclusivity and broad representation serve as the basis for governing. He argued:

> This administration's objective will be a healthy, vigorous, growing economy that provides equal opportunities for all Americans, with no barriers born of bigotry or discrimination. Putting America back to work means putting all Americans back to work. Ending inflation means freeing all Americans from the terror of runaway living costs. All must share in the productive work of this "new beginning," and all must share in the bounty of a revived economy.

Reagan, therefore, was seeking to be the president of all of the people. Trump was not. Reagan spoke to all "the citizens of this blessed land," saying: "Your dreams, your hopes, your goals are going to be the dreams, the hopes, and the goals of this administration, so help me God." To be sure, the language in both speeches by Reagan and Trump employed many of the same themes related to the American people and the office of the presidency, but the messages could not have been more different. Reagan made obvious gestures to calm partisan divisions and convince Americans who had not voted for him that he would do his best to represent them too. Trump, by contrast, was more focused on throwing more red meat to his base and letting them know that he was there to represent them. They were the true American people.

In this chapter, we examine the extent to which populism was embedded in Trump's exceptional me strategy, focusing on how Trump portrayed himself as "Me the People" throughout his presidency. This, we argue, was designed to further build out his "exceptional" image as president. Specifically, we explore three distinct ways that Trump's exceptional me strategy was inspired by and inherently linked with populism. First, we document how Trump actively sought to portray himself, his values, his policies, and his priorities as being the only true representation of the nation as a whole. As scholar Jan-Werner Müller—an expert on populism in modern politics—has argued, populist leaders such as Trump often "claim that they, and they alone, represent the people."[5] Second, we illustrate how Trump routinely sought to redefine "the people" as including only those who support him and his policies. In essence, to Trump, the "real" American people were those who showed loyalty to him. Finally, we show how Trump consistently sought to define anyone who opposed him as transgressors who were working to undercut the will of the American people. Again, as Müller points out, populist leaders, like Trump, "refuse to recognize any opposition as legitimate." Indeed, they tend to regard their opposition, he argues, "as 'enemies of the people' and seek to exclude them altogether." Given that Trump, and Trump alone, represented the true will of the people, those who opposed him, so the argument goes, also must oppose the will of the American people. This was particularly evident, we argue, in how Trump routinely sought to delegitimize his Democratic opposition in Congress—often referring to them as the "do-nothing Democrats" from the "radical left"—and how he portrayed the news media as the "the enemy of the people."

"Me" The People

Equating himself with the American people was not a new strategy that Trump simply adopted once he became president. The seedlings of this populist approach had been planted early on in his 2016 campaign, when Trump relentlessly targeted the Washington elite as a primary source of America's problems. This idea, however, really took form only once Trump was declared the Republican nominee. It was at that moment that Trump fully proclaimed that he, and he alone, represented the will of the American people. Specifically, Trump fully unveiled this new populist tactic in his acceptance speech at the Republican National Convention on July 21, 2016, when he offered: "My opponent asks her supporters to recite a three-word loyalty pledge. It reads: 'I'm With Her.' I choose to recite a different pledge. My pledge reads: 'I'm with you——the American people.' I am your voice."[6]

After the convention, Trump sought out new ways to claim that he was the one true champion for the people. At times, he would blend it together with some of his other greatest hits: "We will drain the swamp in Washington DC and replace it with a new government of, by, and for the people."[7] That Trump now thought of himself as the embodiment of the American people grew from then on out. A month after the convention, Trump echoed the language of his speech with a new hashtag, tweeting: "We are going to make this government of the people once again! #MakeAmericaGreatAgain #ImWithYou."[8] In addition, Trump increasingly described his agenda as that of the American people, saying: "America will get the respect it deserves. And if we don't, I will walk away from the deal like you've never seen anyone walk before. And, believe me, within a short while, they will come back, but only on my terms, therefore the terms of the American people."[9] In his mind, power would be taken from the hands of Washington politicians, and the American people would now somehow govern through him. Trump had essentially equated his own potential ascension to power as being a rise in popular rule. This equivalency was rampant in how Trump described what his presidency would represent. He went on:

> Decades of political failure and corruption will come swiftly to an end, and a new American future will begin. The citizens of this country will be in charge once more. The special interests have had their day. That chapter in our history is closing. The history book is closing on the failed politicians of yesterday. A new chapter is beginning, and this chapter will be authored by you, the American people. This will be your time. You will be running the show. Not the donors, not the insiders, not the media executives. Once more, we will have a government of, by and for the people. All we have to do is cut our ties to the bitter failures of the past, and anything becomes possible. Change is coming. All the people who've rigged the system for their own personal benefit are trying to stop our change campaign because they know that their gravy train has reached its last stop. It's your turn now. This is your time.

For Trump and his supporters, the 2016 election represented "our one magnificent chance to reclaim our country for We The People."[10] A Trump victory, therefore, would be "a victory for you, the American people."[11] In short: "This election will decide whether we are ruled by a corrupt political class. You're seeing what's happening. Everybody's watching. Or whether we are ruled by the people. We're going to be ruled by the people, folks."[12]

Once he became president, however, Trump took this element of his exceptional me strategy to a whole new level. He routinely portrayed himself as the embodiment of the will of the American people, shunning the notion that governance entails a complex dialogue among duly elected representatives whose views vary according to the diversity of interests present throughout the country. For Trump, his controversial 2016 win meant that the people had spoken and they were one-hundred percent behind him. This was reflected in the following tweet: "When the American People speak, ALL OF US should listen. Just over one year ago, you spoke loud and clear. On November 8, 2016, you voted to MAKE AMERICA GREAT AGAIN!"[13] The only problem, though, according to Trump, was that this truth would be clearer to all Americans were it not for his detractors in the media seeking to damage his image and derail his presidency. In September 2017, for example, Trump tweeted the following adjoined tweets:

> Facebook was always anti-Trump.The Networks were always anti-Trump hence,Fake News, @nytimes(apologized) & @WaPo were anti-Trump. Collusion?[14]... *But the people were Pro-Trump!* Virtually no President has accomplished what we have accomplished in the first 9 months-and economy roaring![15]

According to Trump, then, the people were behind him. It was just the "elites" in the media who clouded that reality. "You know who else loves me?" Trump asked at one of his rallies, "My country. They have never done better, that's who loves me."[16] Similarly, in a tweet, Trump stated: "I LOVE the people, & they certainly seem to like the job I'm doing."[17] And the reason the American public supported him so broadly, he argued, was because he was giving the power of the American government back to them. For example, in almost every MAGA rally Trump held during his presidency and, at times, in tweets, he would offer a variation of the following: "Loyal citizens like you helped build this country, and together we are taking back our country, returning power back to the American people, where it belongs."[18] On one occasion, Trump even went so far as to offer this: "We're gonna have it so that Americans can once again speak the magnificent words of Alexander Hamilton, 'here the people govern.'"[19]

What Trump regularly neglected to offer was any explanation for how the American people were, in fact, regaining this power. It seemed enough for Trump and his supporters that *he* was in power. He knew what they wanted and he was enacting their will through his presidency. There was little need for negotiations with those in Congress who represented different values and political priorities. Trump saw himself as representing them all. Perhaps the most glaring example of this came in his 2019 State of the Union address when Trump made clear that his representation of the American people was complete:

> We meet tonight at a moment of unlimited potential. As we begin a new Congress, I stand here ready to work with you to achieve historic breakthroughs for all Americans. Millions of our fellow citizens are watching us now, gathered in this great chamber, hoping that we will govern not as two parties, but as one Nation. The agenda I will lay out this evening is not a Republican agenda or a Democrat agenda. It's the agenda of the American people.[20]

A few days later, Trump doubled down on this claim in a tweet: "We are fighting for all Americans, from all backgrounds, of every age, race, religion, birthplace, color & creed. Our agenda is NOT a partisan agenda—it is the mainstream, common sense agenda of the American People."[21] It was odd, however, that Trump presumed to have the right to speak on behalf of the entire American people, especially considering the fact that in the 2016 election he had lost the popular vote by close to three million votes and that his popularity with the American public never crested fifty percent in presidential approval polls. Trump, however, saw "the people" through a different lens, one that included only those who supported him.

President of (Some of) "The People"

During his 2016 campaign Trump was clear about what he thought his relationship was with the American people, tweeting early on: "I am for the people and the people are for me. #Trump2016."[22] Throughout the campaign and his presidency, Trump seemed to move fluidly between claims that he was the champion of the American people and other claims that seemed to suggest that he was really only speaking about his own supporters. In his view, they were the true American people, because, well, they supported him. As Jans-Werner Muller has argued: "This is the core claim of populism: only some of the people are really the people."[23] Trump exemplified this when he spoke of his supporters.

One of his favorite claims was that he was the voice of the voiceless in America, the voice of those who had been left behind or felt dismissed during the Obama presidency or even before that. This rhetorical tactic was a mainstay during his 2016 campaign, as he routinely argued that he was sacrificing his lavish lifestyle to be their voice, their messenger. In one campaign speech, Trump offered: "[I] t's not about me. It's never been about me. It's about all the people in this country who don't have a voice. I am running to be their voice. I am running to be the voice for every forgotten part of this country that has been waiting and hoping for a better future."[24] It was an appeal that harkened back to Nixon's claim that there was a "silent majority" within the American public who disagreed with the way the country had been led but needed someone to be their voice. Trump was up for the task. "The silent majority is back," he suggested on a campaign stop in Phoenix, Arizona, "and we're going to take our country back."[25] What Trump seemed to be alluding to was that those in this voiceless majority, his "deplorables," were the true proprietors of the country, that it had been taken from them, and that he would represent them by handing the reins of power back to them.

This sentiment, we argue, was on full display when Trump spoke at a MAGA rally in December 2016, as part of a nine-city "Thank You Tour" after his election:

> We do not know what the page will read tomorrow. But for the first time in a long, long time, what we do know is that the pages will be authored by each and every one of you and you. You, the American people, will finally be in charge again. Your voice, your desires, your hopes and your aspirations will never again fall on deaf ears. The forgotten men and women of our country will not be forgotten anymore, remember that.[26]

In this case and throughout his speeches as president, Trump often referred to "the American people" only to quickly clarify that he was really talking to his supporters. To Trump, it was clear: "We are taking on the failed political establishment and restoring government of, by, and for the people. It's the people. You are the people. You won the election."[27] Winning the election, therefore, meant that he and his supporters were the only ones who counted and so they were in charge. They were the American people. Perhaps the quintessential example of this came in a MAGA rally, when he said:

> The forgotten men and women of the United States are forgotten no more. You are the great people, you are the great people. You work hard, pay your taxes, you do all these things and you were forgotten. They forgot about you. And you're the smartest people. You are the smartest people. You know when they talk about,

they talk about the elite. You ever see the elite? They are not elite. You're the elite. You are the elite. You are smarter than they are. You make bigger incomes. You have got everything going. You know, so, let them keep calling themselves... You ever hear, hey... You go to the best schools. You do a tremendous job. You own companies. You work for tremendous salaries. You do all the things that you do. You are talented. With your hands, with your mind. And then you hear, "the elite has just said." The elite? They are more elite than me? I have better everything than they have including this [points to head]. And I became president and they didn't. Meaning you became president.[28]

Trump seemed to see his supporters as being the only true American people. They were in charge now and, in his words, they were "[t]he people that truly matter."[29] According to Trump: "there are far more great people ('Deplorables') in this country, than bad."[30] His loyal "deplorables," therefore, were the one true people of the nation—the rest were "bad."

Overall, it was loyalty to Trump that earned people their place as the true American people. "Loyal citizens like you," he told his supporters, "helped build this country, and together we are taking back our country, returning power back to the American patriots, which is you."[31] And according to Trump, he was paying them back in spades. "Our movement is America's movement"— he offered in a MAGA rally—"You are loyal and faithful to your country. You love your country. And now, finally, you have a government and you have a president that is loyal and faithful to you."[32] Trump often spoke of himself and his supporters as being one in the same. At times, he would even include his supporters in his exceptional presidency claims:

> I don't believe any administration—and you're with us, we're partners in this whole deal, you know, when we came out, we're partners, this is not me. This is a whole group of people. I don't believe and I don't even think it's close that any president has done what we've done in 500 days.[33]

Trump's relationship with his followers was tantamount to a love affair. Trump loved his rowdy crowds and they loved him right back. They were the Americans he cared about and he had no shame in admitting it. Together they were the true representatives of the country. And Trump never seemed to concern himself with the fact that this exclusionary rhetoric, in which he and his supporters were portrayed as the true Americans, might alienate large swaths of the American electorate. In response, Chris Cillizza of CNN, noting Trump's seeming laser-focus on speaking only to his supporters while disregarding and even insulting those who opposed him, offered this: "Quick reminder: Donald Trump is president of all of America. Not just people who voted for him."[34] Trump, however, seemed content to be the president of his supporters, the true Americans. Everyone else was in the opposition and that seemed completely fine by them.

Enemies of "The People"

The Do-Nothing Democrats

In Trump's conception of America, there were two teams. One consisted of "the American people" (although only comprised of those citizens who supported him), Trump as their collective voice, and those Republicans who were loyal to, and supportive of, his presidency. The other team consisted of Democratic politicians, the news media, Never-Trump Republicans, and anyone else who was critical of his presidency. They were all the "opposition party" to the American people. According to Trump, this latter team was working tirelessly to subvert the will of the American people to undo American democracy with their resistance to him. In other words, to oppose Trump was to oppose the American people. To criticize Trump was to criticize America itself. While this conception of America seemed to deny the existence of over half of the American public who did not approve of Trump—many of whom would have liked to have seen him removed from office either by impeachment or through electoral means—it seemed easier for Trump to ignore or dismiss them. He noted: "Oh, these resisters resist. Hillary resisted. And you know what happened? She lost the election in a landslide. But you know what they're really resisting? They're resisting the will of the American people. That's what they're resisting."[35] Opposition to Trump, therefore, was anti-American. Trump was fixated on "the resistance" that had formed throughout the country in response to his presidency, but instead of seeking out ways to reach them and win them over, Trump instead often drove the wedge even deeper. To put it mildly, Trump was not one to accept criticism or opposition. It was much easier for him to say they had malicious motives and portray them as being against the will of the American people. Trump argued, for example:

> The so-called "resistance" doesn't accept the will of the American people. They don't believe you have the right to run your own country, control your own lives or defend the nation's borders, traditions, and heritage. But the American people will never ever be silenced. You will never be silenced. We'll never be intimidated.[36]

What was absent here was any recognition that the "resistance" was made up of millions of American citizens who also deserved representation from their president. Again, Trump's conception of America equated Democrats and any resistance to his presidency with challenges to the country, its people, and American democracy itself.

Trump's efforts to portray Democrats as subverting the will of the American people was evident throughout all of his communications. It began during the 2016 presidential election when Trump declared himself to be the voice of the people while suggesting that his competitor, Hillary Clinton, was a threat to the country. The idea here was simple: if Trump represented the will of the American people, then it must logically follow that his opponent was against them. This was evident, for example, in the following statement: "Hillary Clinton is not running against me, she's running against change and she's running against all of the American people and all of the American voters."[37] Furthermore, actions that might have benefited Clinton, such as the FBI's decision to end their investigation into her emails, were "a conspiracy against you, the American people."[38] Democrats, therefore, were not merely a part of the swamp; they were using the swamp to hurt the American people.

As president, Trump sought to further bolster this broader argument, emphasizing that Democrats were not only the opposition party to his presidency and Republicans, in general, but that they were in opposition to the will of the American people as well. At times, Trump simply tried to drive a wedge between Democrats and "the people," like when he tweeted: "The Radical Left Dems are working hard, but THE PEOPLE are much smarter."[39] Thus, Democrats, according to Trump, were not part of "the people." At other times, Trump was even more vicious, portraying Democrats as hostile adversaries of the American people, seeking to subvert their will and destroy their democracy. On this, Trump was relentless:

> The Democrats, they call themselves the resistance. That's what they're good at, resisting and obstructing. They are obstructionists. Every day, they are resisting the will of the American people and trying to undermine the verdict of our democracy, delivered so strongly in 2016, like never before delivered. The most remarkable thing about the modern Democrat Party is how truly undemocratic they really have become, right? The so-called resistance is mad because their ideas have been rejected by the American people.[40]

Notably, such opposition, according to Trump, was an assault on democracy itself. Throughout the history of the country, each president has had to field challenges to their presidencies, their policies, and their leadership from members of the opposing party. This is and remains a fundamental part of the democratic process. But Trump, and only Trump, viewed this quintessential democratic practice as undemocratic:

> As our brilliant White House counsel wrote to the Democrats yesterday, he said, "Their highly partisan and unconstitutional effort threatens grave and lasting damage to our democratic institutions, to our system of free elections, and to the American people." That's what it is. To the American people. It's so terrible. Democrats are on a crusade to destroy our democracy.[41]

To Trump, the Democrats, the party of opposition, should simply grin and bear his presidency without challenging his power because, as he saw it, Trump now *was* the country, he *was* the people, and he *was* the democracy. Put simply, Trump viewed his critics as "horrible people," trying to undermine the country by attacking him. It is important to note here that presidents traditionally refrain from these types of no-holds-barred attacks on the opposing party. Attacking legitimately elected opponents so viscously runs the risk of alienating the voters that they represent. To Trump, however, because his opponents were not part of the "real" American people, their constituencies must not meet the criteria either. Trump was fundamentally not interested in working with anyone who dared challenge his presidency.

The Real Opposition Party: The News Media

There was no group of people who embodied this supposed threat to the country more, according to Trump, than the mainstream news media. Attacking the news media became an early feature in his campaign, and, later, it served as a reliable scapegoat for seemingly anything that went wrong for him during his presidency. Indeed, it was the news media, Trump argued, that led him to extensively rely upon Twitter to get his message out. Early in the campaign, Trump tweeted: "The press is so totally biased that we have no choice but to take our tough but fair and smart message directly to the people!"[42] The fact that the news media did not report on Trump in a purely positive manner made them "FAKE" and angered him to no end, prompting a steady and aggressive campaign to portray them as antidemocratic and a threat to the nation. Early in his presidency, Trump railed against the fact that news outlets used unnamed sources to report on the internal dynamics of his White House, stating: "With all of its phony unnamed sources & highly slanted & even fraudulent reporting,

#Fake News is DISTORTING DEMOCRACY in our country!"[43] Similarly, in early 2018, Trump used two adjoining tweets to attack one of his least favorite news sources, the *New York Times*:

The Failing New York Times has a new publisher, A.G. Sulzberger. Congratulations! Here is a last chance for the Times to fulfill the vision of its Founder, Adolph Ochs, "to give the news impartially, without fear or FAVOR, regardless of party, sect, or interests involved." Get…[44] impartial journalists of a much higher standard, lose all of your phony and non-existent "sources," and treat the President of the United States FAIRLY, so that the next time I (and the people) win, you won't have to write an apology to your readers for a job poorly done![45]

Trump's disdain for the news media, however, took many forms. One of Trump's favorite attacks was to characterize them as the opposition: "THE FAKE NEWS MEDIA IS THE OPPOSITION PARTY. It is very bad for our Great Country… BUT WE ARE WINNING!"[46] Considering that Trump believed that he was using Twitter to speak directly to the American people, it was unclear whether Trump meant that the media was in the same camp as the Democrats or if he meant they were the opposition party to the American people. Trump, of course, would be sure to clear up any doubt.

Just one month into his presidency, as more and more reports critical of Trump began to circulate within the larger news media environment, he coined a new nickname for the media: "The FAKE NEWS media (failing @nytimes, @CNN, @NBCNews and many more) is not my enemy, it is the enemy of the American people. SICK!"[47] And, according to Trump, he was not the only one who believed that the media were the adversaries of the American people. At every MAGA rally, for example, his crowds were more than willing to back up his claims that the media were unfair not only to him but to them as well. At a MAGA rally in Fort Myers, Florida, in late 2018, for example, Trump offered this:

We have forcefully condemned hatred, bigotry, racism, and prejudice in all of its ugly forms, but the media doesn't want you to hear your story. It's not my story. It's your story. [Crowd booing] And that's why thirty-three percent of the people in this country believe the fake news is, in fact—and I hate to say this—in fact, the enemy of the people. The left-wing media doesn't want to solve problems. They want to stoke resentment. It has to stop.[48]

What was clear was that, to Trump, news outlets that were at all critical of his presidency were not simply the necessary thorn that every president must deal with within a functioning democracy; their critiques of him made them a threat to American democracy and thus, "the enemy of the people." Trump used this phrase repeatedly in his MAGA rallies and tweets when speaking about the news media. According to Trump: "The Fake News Media has NEVER been more Dishonest or Corrupt than it is right now. There has never been a time like this in American History. Very exciting but also, very sad! Fake News is the absolute Enemy of the People and of our Country itself!"[49] In other words, the media had never been so critical of another president. Again, in Trump's mind, he was exceptional, even when it came to the media's role as watchdog of his presidency.

Early on in the Trump presidency, he attempted to curb criticism of his use of this nickname by making halfhearted attempts to clarify that he did not mean *all* news media outlets when he called them "the enemy of the people." For instance, in 2018, he tweeted: "CNN and others in the Fake News Business keep purposely and inaccurately reporting that I said the 'Media is the Enemy of the People.' Wrong! I said that the 'Fake News (Media) is the Enemy of the People,' a very big difference. When you give out false information——not good."[50] Similarly, he attempted to add others' voices to the fray by tweeting: "They asked my daughter Ivanka whether or not the media is the enemy of the people. She correctly said no. It is the FAKE NEWS, which is a large percentage of the media, that is the enemy of the people!"[51] In essence, to Trump, he was not sowing public distrust of the entire news media—what some refer to as the fourth estate of American democracy—he was merely weeding out the bad news organizations, whose agenda was to undermine him, his movement, and, therefore, the will of the American people. What was evident in our analysis of his speeches and tweets over time, however, was that Trump attacked any and all media outlets, including every major news network and newspaper of record in the United States and even beyond. The only news sources he did not label as "Fake News" were Fox News and other pro-Trump news sources. Similar to how he had redefined the "American people" as consisting of only those who supported him, Trump only regarded those news outlets who reported on his presidency favorably as not fake. Clearly, Trump was mistaking the role that news media should play in American democracy. To him, the news media were not supposed to serve the American public as a whole by acting as a watchdog on his government. Instead, they should function as a propaganda machine for his presidency. And, if they did not comply, he would relentlessly portray them as undermining democracy and subverting the will of the people.

The Greatest Witch Hunts

For Trump, the democratic system within the United States was rigged. Specifically, the checks and balances designed to keep every president from acquiring and exercising too much power—including the media and any political opposition party—were simply trying to subvert the results of his election and bar him from doing the bidding of the American people. Nowhere was Trump's disdain for those who challenged him and his power more evident than in his reactions to the various investigations surrounding his presidency. Trump was incensed from the outset that anyone would dare investigate his exceptional presidency, let alone place his public image at risk. When the Mueller investigation began just under four months into his presidency, Trump erupted and went on the attack. First, he made it about him. For example, the day after Robert Mueller was appointed as special council, Trump had already come up with a slogan for the investigation: "This is the single greatest witch hunt of a politician in American history!"[52] Again, Trump saw no gray. It was another chance to portray him and his presidency as exceptional and he was, no doubt, seizing it. Over time, however, Trump began to frame it in broader terms. Again, given the fact that Trump viewed himself as the embodiment of the American people and, indeed, the country itself, the investigation must be an attack on these entities as well. At one MAGA rally, for example, Trump told his supporters:

> The Democrats don't care about Russia. They only care about their own political power. They went after my family, my business, my finances, my employees, almost everyone I have ever known or worked with, but they are really going after you. That's what it's all about. It's not about us. It's about you. They tried to erase your votes, and erase your legacy of the greatest campaign and the greatest election probably in the history of our country. They wanted to deny you the future that you demanded, and the future that America deserves, and that now, America is getting. Our radical democrat opponents are driven by hatred, prejudice, and rage. They want to destroy you and they want to destroy our country as we know it.[53]

Trump's language here was clear and unmistakable. To him, investigating his campaign and presidency was tantamount to betraying the country.

Throughout the Mueller investigation, Trump was ever on the offensive. To Trump, it was a farce. In his words: "No politician in history, and I say this with great surety, has been treated worse or more unfairly."[54] Trump seemed genuinely surprised that there would be any opposition to him, let alone any investigations into his presidency. According to Trump, it was not only getting in the way of the work he was doing for the American people but it was also—by design—hurting his public image. For instance, during the investigation, Trump tweeted: "While my (our) poll numbers are good, with the Economy being the best ever, if it weren't for the Rigged Russian Witch Hunt, they would be 25 points higher!"[55] Once the investigation ended, Trump let loose. He felt vindicated and saw this as an opportunity to further portray the Democrats as adversaries of the American people. Just a few weeks after the report was released, Trump tweeted:

> Despite the tremendous success that I have had as President, including perhaps the greatest ECONOMY and most successful first two years of any President in history, they have stollen two years of my (our) Presidency (Collusion Delusion) that we will never be able to get back… [56] The Witch Hunt is over but we will never forget. MAKE AMERICA GREAT AGAIN![57]

Again, Trump seemed to be equating himself and his presidency with the American people, suggesting that the Mueller investigation was a direct attack on them. At another MAGA rally, Trump further articulated this line of argument when he offered:

> But the radical, liberal Democrats put all their hopes behind their collusion delusion, which has now been totally exposed to the world as a complete and total fraud. The greatest political hoax in American history. It really has been. This witch hunt was never really just about me. It was always about stopping you, the millions and millions of freedom loving citizens who rose up on that incredible November day. Remember that day? November 8?[58]

But the Democrats were not the only ones to blame. Trump saw the media's constant coverage of the Mueller investigation as part of the problem as well. Their coverage further fueled the flames of controversy surrounding the Trump presidency and, according to Trump, worked to undermine the will of the American people:

> The Mainstream Media is under fire and being scorned all over the World as being corrupt and FAKE. For two years they pushed the Russian Collusion Delusion when they always knew there was No Collusion. They truly are the Enemy of the People and the Real Opposition Party![59]

From the outset, these attacks were unsubstantiated, considering that Democrats and the mainstream media had nothing to do with launching the Mueller investigation. But this mattered little to Trump and his supporters. If nothing else, it was an opportunity for him to turn his people against them and bolster his claims that he was the true representative of the American people and the country itself. In his words: "This was nothing but an effort to sabotage the will of the American people."[60]

With a playbook already in hand, Trump knew exactly how to respond when House Democrats decided to move forward with an impeachment inquiry following accusations that Trump had pressured newly elected Ukrainian president Volodymyr Zelensky to investigate his political rival and former vice president Joe Biden. This time, however, Trump was even more relentless with his attacks. A week after the impeachment inquiry was announced, Trump repeated the same attacks he had waged throughout the Mueller investigation, tweeting:

> As I learn more and more each day, I am coming to the conclusion that what is taking place is not an impeachment, it is a COUP, intended to take away the Power of the ....[61] People, their VOTE, their Freedoms, their Second Amendment, Religion, Military, Border Wall, and their God-given rights as a Citizen of The United States of America![62]

Ten days later, in Minneapolis, Minnesota, Trump held his first MAGA rally since the impeachment inquiry was announced. He began with boasts about the "exceptional" state of the economy: "America has the number one economy anywhere in the world, and it's not even close."[63] He then quickly transitioned to the subject that was on the minds of everyone there: impeachment. He stated:

> These corrupt politicians and the radical leftists got rich bleeding America dry. And they knew that my election would finally end their pillaging and looting of our country. And that's what they were doing. And that's what they continue to try and do. That is why, from day one, the wretched Washington swamp has been trying to nullify the results of a truly great and democratic election, the election of 2016. They're trying. They're not getting very far. They want to erase your vote like it never existed. They want to erase your voice. And they want to erase your future. But they will fail, because in America, the people rule again.

According to Trump, they were not impeaching him because he had unlawfully used his position of power for political gain and obstructed the investigation in the process. Instead, their underlying motivation was to undermine his presidency and the movement that gave rise to it.

On December 17, 2019, the day before the US House of Representatives was set to vote on the two counts of impeachment against him, Trump sent a scathing five-page letter to Nancy Pelosi about the impeachment. He started with a nod toward the exceptional nature of this inquiry against him: "This impeachment represents an unprecedented and unconstitutional abuse of power by Democrat Lawmakers, unequaled in nearly two and a half centuries of American legislative history."[64] He then went on to say that Democrats were "breaking their allegiance to the Constitution" and "declaring open war on American Democracy." According to Trump, the impeachment was rooted in Democrats' unwillingness to accept their loss in 2016:

> Everyone, you included, knows what is really happening. Your chosen candidate lost the election in 2016, in an Electoral College landslide (306–227), and you and your party have never recovered from this defeat. You have developed a full-fledged case of what many in the media call Trump Derangement Syndrome and sadly, you will never get over it! You are unwilling and unable to accept the verdict issued at the ballot box during the great Election of 2016. So you have spent three straight years attempting to overturn the will of the American people and nullify their votes. You view democracy as your enemy!

Again, attacking Trump meant attacking the country, its people, and American democracy itself.

On the day of his impeachment, December 18, 2019, Trump took his show on the road again to host a rally in Battle Creek, Michigan. Trump was actually on stage as the House of Representatives voted to impeach him on two counts: abuse of power and obstruction of Congress. Impeachment was, of course, front and center at the event. He opened with this: "It doesn't really feel like we're being impeached. The country is doing better than ever before. We did nothing wrong. We did nothing wrong."[65] The emphasis on "we" here was notable. It was not just that Trump had been impeached. Apparently, his supporters had been impeached as well. Trump then stated: "With today's illegal unconstitutional and partisan impeachment, the do-nothing Democrats—and they are do-nothing, all they want to do is focus on this, what they could be doing—are declaring their deep hatred and disdain for the American voter." Again, the message was clear: the impeachment was nothing more than a deliberate attempt to undo the 2016 presidential election and, more broadly, circumvent the will of the American people.

Throughout the impeachment trial in the Senate, Trump stayed on the offensive, calling the trial a "hoax" and a "phony Witch Hunt." During the trial, Trump's impeachment lawyer, Alan Dershowitz, even made the case that Trump should be exempt from impeachment because his reelection was "in the public interest" and, therefore, he was allowed to do whatever was needed to be reelected.[66] Trump's claims that he was the embodiment of the American people and that his interests were the equivalent of their interests had come full circle. Similarly, in a letter from President Trump to his supporters sent out by his campaign just before his 2020 State of the Union address, and a day before his eventual acquittal in the Senate, Trump stated:

> Tonight, I'm going to share with you what's really going on in Washington— something the Fake News media will never tell you. The truth is, while my administration is creating jobs and killing terrorists, the Radical Left is obsessed with demented hoaxes, crazy Witch Hunts, and deranged partisan crusades. They're trying to stop OUR NATION from winning in November. We can't let that happen.[67]

Put simply, Trump's presidency, according to him, was what was best for the nation and Democrats and the media would never relent in trying to undercut the will of the American people by opposing his presidency. His acquittal, he declared, was "our Country's VICTORY on the Impeachment Hoax!"[68] In Trump's view, it had all been a "bullshit"[69] effort to undermine the American people and he was going to make sure everybody knew it. In his words: "They want to erase your vote like it never existed. They want to erase your voice. And they want to erase your future. But they will fail, because in America, the people rule again."[70] At every turn, Trump was making strategic claims that because his presidency was so exceptional, he alone represented the power of the collective American people. And he was ready to fight tooth and nail to defend their will. "Me The People" had become the crown jewel of his exceptional me strategy.

The Exceptional Me Strategy:
Amplified and Contested

*Donald Trump is doing exactly what he said he would do as a candidate,
now as the most effective president, the most successful president, in modern
American history.*[1]

—Lou Dobbs, Fox News

Donald Trump has been the most corrupt, unpatriotic president we've ever had.[2]
—Democratic Senator Kamala Harris

On the first night of the 2016 Democratic National Convention in Philadelphia, Pennsylvania, then First Lady Michelle Obama took the stage to deliver a speech in support of her party's presumptive nominee, Hillary Clinton. The air in the arena that night was thick with tension. Throughout the day, a number of Bernie Sanders supporters had been airing their grievances with loud chants of "Bernie! Bernie!" during some of the speeches and booing when Hillary Clinton's name was mentioned on stage.[3] When Obama took the stage, however, the chants and heckles were nowhere to be found. All eyes were on her. The theme of her speech centered on her two daughters, Malia and Sasha, and the America that she thought they deserved. At first, she reflected on what it was like when her husband became president: "I realized that our time in the White House would form the foundation for who they would become, and how well we managed this experience could truly make or break them."[4] She then went on to situate their experiences within the larger political climate of the country at the time:

> That is what Barack and I think about every day as we try to guide and protect our girls through the challenges of this unusual life in the spotlight—how we urge them to ignore those who question their father's citizenship or faith. How we insist that the hateful language they hear from public figures on TV does not

represent the true spirit of this country. How we explain that when someone is cruel, or acts like a bully, you don't stoop to their level. No, our motto is, "when they go low, we go high."

Obama was taking on the public persona that Trump had built for himself throughout his public life, and especially during his campaign. Although Obama never mentioned Trump by name once in her speech, she found creative ways to dress him down as a person and to argue that he did not have the strength of character to be the president of the United States:

> And when I think about the kind of President that I want for my girls and all our children, that's what I want. I want someone with the proven strength to persevere. Someone who knows this job and takes it seriously. Someone who understands that the issues a president faces are not black and white and cannot be boiled down to 140 characters. Because when you have the nuclear codes at your fingertips and the military in your command, you can't make snap decisions. You can't have a thin skin or a tendency to lash out. You need to be steady, and measured, and well-informed.

Later in the speech, Obama delivered perhaps the most poignant line of the entire convention with a jab that cut straight to the heart of Trump's exceptional me strategy: "So don't let anyone ever tell you that this country isn't great, that somehow we need to make it great again. Because this, right now, is the greatest country on earth." The arena erupted.

Obama quite clearly had become wise to an integral part of Trump's exceptional me strategy and she was calling him out on it before the American public. For Obama, Trump's use of American exceptionalism was so obviously self-serving. He was calling into question an idea that was foundational to how Americans viewed themselves and their nation, and he was using it to stoke fear, hostility, and division throughout the American electorate. It was ironic, then, that Obama, not Trump, was the one who was championing American exceptionalism, the one idea that the GOP—not the DNC—had chosen to define their party and serve as the basis for their 2016 campaign strategy. She was picking up the flag of American exceptionalism that Trump had deliberately left in the dust throughout his campaign, and she was waving it proudly before the American people. The next day, the Atlantic called Obama's speech, "A speech for the ages," saying, "It was as pure a piece of political oratory as this campaign has offered, and instantly entered into the pantheon of great convention speeches."[5] The *Washington Post* called Obama, "The Democrats' best weapon against Donald Trump" and argued that "she offered a more effective rebuttal of the Republican nominee and the mantra that animates his campaign than any other Democrat has been able to thus far in 2016."[6] While Obama's speech may have provided a guide for how to counter Trump's exceptional me strategy, the Clinton campaign was never able to capitalize on it.

Six months later, as President Obama prepared to facilitate the peaceful transition of power over to his successor, he delivered a farewell speech to the American people in Chicago, Illinois. Obama spoke at length of the work he had done as president and the work that remained unfinished. He also discussed how the country's history of both successes and failures had shaped what the nation had become. He then offered this: "So that's what we mean when we say America is exceptional. Not that our nation has been flawless from the start, but that we have shown the capacity to change, and make life better for those who follow."[7] There was one issue, over all others, that Obama wanted to focus on: "the state of our democracy." In his words:

> Our Constitution is a remarkable, beautiful gift. But it's really just a piece of parchment. It has no power on its own. We, the people, give it power. We, the people, give it meaning with our participation, and with the choices that we make, and the alliances that we forge. Whether or not we stand up for our freedoms. Whether or not we respect and enforce the rule of law. That's up to us. America is no fragile thing. But the gains of our long journey to freedom are not assured.

It was a call to action. He was asking citizens everywhere to become actively involved in preserving "our bold experiment in self-government" because "our democracy is threatened whenever we take it for granted." It was also a not-so-thinly-veiled attempt to alleviate the anxiety and fears that so many throughout the country were feeling on the eve of the Trump presidency. Obama then offered an alternative to Trump's dark vision for America:

> America, we weaken [our] ties when we allow our political dialogue to become so corrosive that people of good character are even willing to enter into public service; so coarse with rancor that Americans with whom we disagree are seen not just as misguided, but as malevolent. We weaken those ties when we define some of us as more American than others, when we write off the whole system as inevitably corrupt, and when we sit back and blame the leaders that we elect without examining our own role in electing them.

Finally, Obama sought to draw a sharp contrast to a fundamental notion that had propped up Trump's exceptional me strategy since the very beginning: "I am asking you to believe. Not in my ability to bring about change, but in yours."

Nine days later, and just one day before he would pass the reins of the presidency to Donald Trump, Obama sent a "Thank You" letter to the American people. The letter echoed much of what he had expressed in his farewell speech, but with one important difference. The last lines of the letter were laser-focused on undercutting Trump's exceptional me strategy:

> I've seen you, the American people, in all your decency, determination, good humor, and kindness. And in your daily acts of citizenship, I've seen our future unfolding. All of us, regardless of party, should throw ourselves into that work— the joyous work of citizenship. Not just when there's an election, not just when our own narrow interest is at stake, but over the full span of a lifetime. I'll be right there with you every step of the way. And when the arc of progress seems slow, remember: America is not the project of any one person. The single most powerful word in our democracy is the word "We." "*We* the People." "*We* shall overcome." "Yes, *we* can."[8]

Obama, like every president before him, was recognizing that the presidency and the country as a whole were realities much larger then himself—that the principles that serve as the very foundation of American democracy were more powerful and resilient than the political interests or achievements of any single person. Obama's speech, unbeknownst to many at the time, would mark the end of the presidency as we knew it. A new era would be ushered in by a president who openly held disdain, if not outright contempt, for the traditional norms of the presidency, and who was determined to remake the country in his own image. Trump's ascendance into the highest office in the land immediately shook the foundations of American society, and it was clear that the aftershocks would reverberate for the foreseeable future. The exceptional me strategy was about to take on new life.

The Exceptional Me Strategy Amplified

On the evening of January 21, 2017, the day after Trump's inauguration, White House Press Secretary Sean Spicer approached the White House Press Corps for the first time. On that day, millions of protesters descended upon Washington and cities throughout the world for the first Women's March in a show of defiance to Trump on the first day of his presidency. News reports had also been circulating all day about how Trump's inauguration crowd had paled in comparison to Obama's crowd eight years earlier.[9] In response, Spicer called a special briefing on that Saturday to address the issues that the Trump White House thought were the most important to the nation at that moment. Spicer began by saying: "Before I get to the news of the day, I think I'd like to discuss a little bit of the coverage of the last 24 hours."[10] He then went on:

> Yesterday, at a time when our nation and the world was watching the peaceful transition of power and, as the President said, the transition and *the balance of power from Washington to the citizens of the United States,* some members of the media were engaged in deliberately false reporting. For all the talk about the proper use of Twitter, two instances yesterday stand out.

Spicer then denounced a false *Time Magazine* tweet claiming that a bust of Martin Luther King Jr. had been removed from the Oval Office.[11] He also berated the press for what he saw as false reporting on the size of Trump's inauguration crowd. He offered a number of facts and figures about the logistics of the crowd to bolster his claim. Then, in an increasingly heated tone, Spicer offered this: "This was the largest audience to ever witness an inauguration—period— both in person and around the globe!" Day One and Trump's new spokesman was already pedaling his exceptional me strategy to the American public. As president, Trump now had a built-in team of administration officials and cabinet members to echo his messaging. And when Trump wanted to invoke one of his go-to rhetorical tactics, suggesting that "other people were saying" that he was exceptional, his team was always at the ready.

No one in the Trump administration, however, was a bigger cheerleader and megaphone for the exceptional me strategy than Vice President Mike Pence. As Trump would say, "It was not even close." Pence regularly lavished praise onto Trump for his "unprecedented leadership" and his "historic accomplishments" as he traveled the country and beyond, representing the administration. In a speech to the Heritage Foundation in late 2019, for example, Pence touched on various aspects of Trump's strategic messaging. He started by suggesting that "we've rebuilt our military" and that "the truth is, as President Trump has observed, 'Our active-duty personnel are now the best-equipped, best-trained, and most technologically advanced fighting force in the history of the world.'"[12] Pence, however, was just getting started. He then offered this:

> From the early days of this administration, President Trump has rolled back red tape at a historic level. In fact, this President has signed more laws cutting federal red tape already than any President in American history, saving more than $33 billion in regulatory costs. We've also unleashed American energy… And today, the United States, as I mentioned, is the largest producer of oil and

natural gas in the world. And, of course, it wasn't just rolling back regulations and unleashing American energy. This President kept his promise in the early days of this administration when he signed into law the largest tax cuts and tax reform in American history. In fact, businesses saw a corporate tax rate reduction from one of the highest in the industrialized world to 21 percent. It was the largest percentage point reduction in the top marginal corporate rate in the history of this country.

Thus, it was not just Trump. Apparently, Pence too thought everything Trump did was exceptional. And this message was not just for American audiences. In a 2018 speech delivered to the Knesset, Israel's national legislative body, for example, Pence stated:

> I bring greetings from a leader who has done more to bring our two great countries closer together than any president in the past 70 years—the 45th President of the United States of America, President Donald Trump. Thanks to the President's leadership, the alliance between our two countries has never been stronger, and the friendship between our peoples has never been deeper.[13]

Again, Trump's built-in team of surrogates was not only familiar with the exceptional me strategy, they were prepared and, no doubt, determined to carry it out wherever they went, whether it was at home or abroad. After all, their fates were inescapably tied to his.

Early Resistance

Just because Trump's team was on board with Trump's exceptional me strategy, however, did not mean that Congressional Republicans were behind it as well—at least not in the beginning. There would be some early resistance from those who perceived themselves as guardians of Reagan's Republican Party. Most notably, on February 5, 2017, just two weeks into his presidency, Trump took his first substantive step as president toward breaking down the party's conception of American exceptionalism in an interview with Bill O'Reilly on Fox News.[14] It was Super Bowl Sunday and Fox News was set to capitalize on the game's wide viewing audience by airing portions of the interview during the network's pregame broadcast. The interview gravitated quickly to an issue that was at the top of everyone's minds in relation to the new Trump presidency: his relationship with Russian president Vladimir Putin. O'Reilly started with a simple question: "Do you respect Putin?" Trump quickly snapped back with: "I do respect him." O'Reilly, however, was clearly taken aback by this answer, and quickly asked: "Do you? Why?" Trump then went on to explain that it was in the country's interests for him to get along with Russia and Putin, citing their cooperation in combatting ISIS and Islamic terrorism around the world. O'Reilly, however, still wasn't satisfied. "He's a killer though. Putin's a killer," he interjected. Trump nodded his head for a second and then responded: "Lot of killers. We've got a lot of killers. What you think our country's so innocent?" O'Reilly had no response. He seemed to disagree, but could not quite put it into words. Trump then repeated, "You think our country's so innocent?" Again, O'Reilly was surprised by Trump's comments and his response seemed to be an effort to provide Trump with an opportunity to rephrase or at least contextualize what he had said: "I don't know of any government leaders that are killers in America." Trump didn't miss a beat: "Well, take a look at what we've done too. We've made a lot of mistakes." Instead of taking O'Reilly's lifeline, Trump doubled down. He was directly undercutting his party's stance on American exceptionalism, a concept they had spent years claiming as their own. It did not go unnoticed.

Old guard, pre-Trump Republicans emerged immediately to voice their dissent and to reclaim the banner of American exceptionalism that Trump had so brazenly just torn down. Former Republican Governor of Ohio, John Kasich, for instance, tweeted: "America has been a beacon of light and freedom. There is no equivalence with the brutal regime of Vladimir Putin."[15] Similarly, on ABC's *This Week*, Senator Ben Sasse, emphasized: "There is no moral equivalency between the United States of America, the greatest freedom-loving nation in the history of the world and the murderous thugs that are in Putin's defense of his cronyism."[16] On CNN's *State of the Union* with Jake Tapper, Senate Majority Leader, Mitch McConnell, went as far as to call Putin a "thug." He then offered this:

> I don't think there's any equivalency between the way that the Russians conduct themselves and the way the United States does… I do think America's exceptional. America is different. We don't operate in any way the way the Russians do. I think there's a clear distinction here that all Americans understand.

Tapper then pressed him: "[Y]ou say that *all* Americans understand. Are you confident the President understands it, because he just said something that could have been broadcast on RT [Russia Times]?" McConnell's response was evasive, but he eventually settled on: "I obviously don't see this issue the same way he does." It was clear that there was an obvious disconnect between Trump and his party and the old Republican guard was out trying to do clean up, control the narrative, and minimize the damage. Trump, however, never distanced himself from these comments.

Trump's remarks were so profoundly different from how any Republican, especially a Republican president, had ever spoken about Russia that the shock was being felt at the party's philosophical core. Max Boot of *USA Today* perhaps put it best:

> Once upon a time, "moral relativism"—the tendency to draw comparisons between the conduct of the United States and its enemies—was the bane of American conservatives... So it is more than a little ironic that the chief font of ***moral equivalence*** today is a Republican president who has the support of many conservatives.[17]

Two days later, in a speech on the Senate floor, Republican Senator John McCain was not only incensed by Trump's comments, he was noticeably angry about what they meant for his party. "Putin is a killer!," he exclaimed in a loud voice.[18] Then, while thumping his finger on the lectern and his voice increasing in volume, he offered this:

> There is no moral equivalence between that butcher and thug and KGB colonel and the United States of America—the country that Ronald Reagan used to call a shining city on a hill. And to allege some kind of moral equivalence between the two is either terribly misinformed or incredibly biased. Neither, neither can be accurate in any way.

McCain's reference to Ronald Reagan here was significant. McCain and other prominent Republicans were taking a stand, defending what had been so fundamental to the Republican Party for decades. Indeed, it was Reagan's conception of American exceptionalism—that America was a "shining city upon a hill" that should lead the world through its morally superior example—that had guided how Republicans had viewed America's role in the world ever since his presidency. Nonetheless, Trump seemed determined to take a wrecking ball to it. In the words of James Hohmann of the *Washington Post*, "Trump does not subscribe to the notion that our history, our lower-case-r republican values and our unique constitutional system are distinguishing features that make America exceptional." These choice-few Republican responses, however, were not echoed by most within the Republican ranks. It seemed that this would be the last stand of the old guard Republicans who were determined to preserve their status as the party of Reagan and maintain his conception of American exceptionalism. The rest of the party, though, had other ideas. They were turning to Trump. And they were not alone.

Catching on and Turning Up the Volume/Trump's Megaphones

On November 5, 2018, the night before the midterm elections, Trump took the stage again at a rally in Cape Girardeau, Missouri. In the month before the midterms, Trump had become a super campaigner, holding a full twenty-three rallies in a host of states leading up to Election Day. To be clear, Trump was not simply making appearances at rallies in support of Republican candidates. These were full-fledged MAGA rallies, featuring long speeches by Trump himself, and only guest appearances by local candidates who were provided ten minutes or less to come up and address Trump's crowds. This particular rally in Cape Girardeau, however, was a bit different from the rest. For the first time ever, Trump was introduced by conservative radio host Rush Limbaugh, who was one of Trump's warm-up speakers. Limbaugh, who was from Cape Girardeau, began by praising the Trump rally phenomenon, calling the atmosphere "electric," only to be immediately interrupted by chants of "U-S-A! U-S-A!" Limbaugh continued:

> These rallies, I have to tell you, they are the envy of official Washington. You realize, there isn't a single elected official in either party who could do what this is tonight other than Donald Trump. There's no one… He has a connection. There is no other politician with a connection to voters like this. Nobody has it.[19]

The audience erupted. Limbaugh seemed to almost intuitively know the language that Trump and his supporters responded to the most. Talk about how exceptional Trump is and they—Trump and his supporters—will most certainly love you. Limbaugh, however, was not the only special guest from conservative media to make an appearance that night. Fox News' Sean Hannity and Jeanine Pirro would take the stage as well.

The day before the speech, Sean Hannity was clear about the purpose of his attendance at the Cape Girardeau rally, tweeting:

> In spite of reports, I will be doing a live show from Cape Girardeau and interviewing President Trump before the rally. To be clear, I will not be on stage campaigning with the President. I am covering final rally for my show. Something I have done in every election in the past.[20]

Although it was quite apparent from his show on Fox that he was an unapologetic and vocal Trump supporter, Hannity was trying to argue that he understood and was observing his ethical imperative as a journalist to not get directly involved in a political campaign. It did not last long. Half way into his speech, Trump brought Hannity on stage. In a move that further distanced himself from the ethical standards that are supposed to guide journalists, Hannity began his comments with: "By the way, all those people in the back are fake news."[21] He continued: "Mr. President, I did an opening monologue today, and I had no idea you were going to invite me up here. And the one thing that has made and defined your presidency more than anything else: Promises made, promises kept." It was a Trump campaign slogan. Although Hannity had often portrayed Trump and his presidency as exceptional during his shows, he had never gone as far as he did at the MAGA rally that night. To join him on stage and proudly embrace this campaign tagline said it all. Enter Jeanine Pirro. When Trump brought the Fox News pundit to the stage, she wasted no time: "Do you like the fact that we are now in the longest, strongest economic growth streak in American history? Do you like the fact that this man is the tip of the spear who goes out there every day and fights for us?" The crowd went wild. Trump probably couldn't have said it better himself. So, it was official. The already fuzzy separation between conservative media pundits and the Trump presidency was completely gone. They were now in full support of his exceptional me strategy.

These remarks from Limbaugh, Hannity, and Pirro were certainly more the rule than the exception in how conservative media pundits responded to Trump's exceptional me strategy throughout his presidency. Here is but a small sampling of the various claims that those within the conservative media made about Trump and his presidency:

- Lou Dobbs (Fox News): "Prosperity is returning. Donald Trump is doing exactly what he said he would do as a candidate, now as the most effective president, the most successful president, in modern American history."[22]
- Griff Jenkins (Fox News): "The Trump Administration, Trump policies, have put our economy on a trajectory it has never been on before."[23]
- Jesse Watters (Fox News): "This is the best year any president has ever had."[24]
- Matt Drudge (Drudge Report): "Jobs up big, plus 312,000. Record number working. Manufacturing best in 20 years (Previous administration said this could not happen). Hispanic unemployment lowest ever."[25]
- Steve Hilton (Fox News): "The last three years of Trump policy have finally brought real hope and real change. Unemployment this year hit a 50 year low. With President Trump we've seen the lowest EVER African American and Hispanic unemployment."[26]
- Bill Bennett (Pundit and former Secretary of Education): "No President in modern times has kept more promises than Donald Trump!"[27]
- Newt Gingrich (Pundit and former Speaker of the House): "President

Trump represents a force of change in Washington—the likes of which we've rarely seen in American history."[28]

- Stuart Varney (Fox News): "This is as good a time as I can remember to be an American Worker. We have the strongest economy in the world."[29]
- Chris Christie (Pundit and former Governor): "@POTUS has done more to combat the addiction crisis than any other President."[30]
- Christopher Harris (Fox News): "I would argue that it's probably three of the greatest years since maybe Jesus walked the Earth with his ministry."[31]

Perhaps it was no coincidence, then, that Trump tweeted at one point: "Has anyone noticed that the top shows on @foxnews and cable ratings are those that are Fair (or great) to your favorite President, me!"[32] As these examples illustrate, conservative pundits within the broader news media environment eagerly embraced and echoed Trump's claims that he and his presidency were exceptional. Indeed, these news sources were integral to amplifying his exceptional me strategy.

For Republican officials, a similar dynamic played out over the course of the Trump presidency. In particular, with the death of John McCain and the decision by several Trump critics in Congress, including Senators Jeff Flake and Bob Corker, not to run for reelection in 2018, the voices of dissent against Trump within the Republican Party had all but disappeared by the time the dust had settled from the midterm elections. Others, including Senator Lindsey Graham, had gone from harsh critics to staunch Trump supporters. As one headline in the British newspaper, *The Guardian*, read about Graham: "In no single member of Congress has the transformation from Trump skeptic to true believer been so remarkable."[33] Graham had famously stated back in 2015 that Trump was a "race-baiting, xenophobic, religious bigot"[34] and in 2016, prior to the election, he suggested that Republicans should have "kicked him out of the party."[35] Fast-forward a few years and Graham was singing Trump's praises. At one MAGA rally event in 2020, for example, Graham opened for Trump, stating: "Thank you for rebuilding the military and killing the terrorists. Thank you for the strongest economy of my lifetime."[36] Elsewhere, on terrorism, Graham offered that Trump has "had a determination to destroy the Caliphate unlike anybody I've ever met."[37] And in response to Trump's 2020 State of the Union Address, Graham stated: "[A] compelling narrative that every American from every walk of life is doing better economically. Our military is strong since Reagan."[38] Then, perhaps sensing that he had not gone far enough, he corrected himself: "I've never seen it this strong." Graham, like so many other Republican members of Congress, became, as he once acknowledged during an interview, "all in" on Trump and his "exceptional" presidency.[39] Indeed, the Trump train was full speed ahead and the conventional wisdom within the party was: "get on board" or "get run over." While it was unclear whether Republicans in Congress were fully on board with Trump's conception of American exceptionalism in private, in public, they most certainly were—hook, line, and sinker.

To provide a clearer sense of how broad and extensive Republicans' alignment with Trump's exceptional me strategy was during his presidency, here are a few—out of numerous—examples of their statements:

- House Minority Leader Kevin McCarthy: "Thanks to Trump, America is winning like never before… he will continue to pave the path to the best years our country has ever experienced."[40]
- Senator David Perdue: "This is the greatest economic turnaround in our history. We have the highest median income in U.S. history, the lowest African-American unemployment in our history, the lowest unemployment in 50 years. This economy is rocking because of the policies that President Trump has implemented over the first two years."[41]
- Senator Ted Cruz: "We have the lowest unemployment nationally in 49 years. We have the lowest African-American unemployment that has ever been recorded. We have the lowest Hispanic unemployment that has ever been recorded. We have the lowest Asian-American unemployment that has ever been recorded."[42]
- Senator John Barrasso: "[W]e've added 7 million new jobs, consumer confidence & the stock market are at all-time highs, & wages have gone up. The president has been doing an excellent job for America & will continue to do so."[43]
- Congressman Greg Walden: "As I have said before, no president has leaned farther forward to lower the cost of prescription drugs than @ realDonaldTrump!"[44]
- Governor Ron DeSantis: "I want to thank him [Trump] for what he's done for our military, which is stronger than ever."[45]
- Congressman Pete Stauber: "Mr. President… [n]ow, jobs are up, unemployment numbers are at a historic low, small businesses and manufacturers are surging—and optimism is at an all-time high."[46]
- Congressman Lou Barletta: "You know, the economy is soaring under President Trump's economy. It is soaring. The market—the market is up over 20 percent. Unemployment's at 4 percent. Black unemployment's at

an all-time low. Hispanic unemployment's at an all-time low. Women's unemployment's at an all-time low. Small-business confidence is an all-time high. Consumer confidence is at an all-time."[47]

- Congressman Greg Pence: "I rise today to stand in firm support of President Trump's leadership... Not only is America safer, it is more prosperous than ever before and now energy independent."[48]
- Congressman Mike Kelly: "I want to tell you something: Promises made, promises kept. The strongest personality, the strongest president we have seen in our lifetime! Listen, I got to tell you, the last 21 months of my life, I have seen something happen in America that I had never seen before. I have seen the resurrection of the greatest nation the world has ever known. It knows no boundaries. It doesn't differentiate because of the color of your skin, the shape of your eye, what your gender is, where you worship. Every single American and at every single way every single day is stronger because of this man. You're the best. You are the best!"[49]
- Senator Cindy Hyde-Smith: "[I]t is such an honor to work with this man. Is he not the best president we have ever had?"[50]

The exceptional me strategy, in effect, had become the strategy of the Republican Party. Conservative media pundits and Republicans alike had fully embraced the exceptional me strategy, and they were more than willing to serve as megaphones for Trump's self-congratulatory claims. Though it may not have begun this way, Trump now had loyalists seemingly everywhere who were on the ready to use their powerful voices to amplify his efforts to convince Americans that he and his administration were truly exceptional.

The Exceptional Me Strategy Comes Full Circle

The transformation of the Republican Party from the party of Reagan to the party of Trump became increasingly evident as time progressed, resulting in a full embrace of the exceptional me strategy by the time the 2020 presidential election was heating up. There was one moment along the way that stood out above all others as clear evidence of this metamorphosis. It was the culmination, one could argue, of Trump's efforts throughout his presidency to bend the party to his will. And it happened in the most discreet of spaces: Trump's 2020 State of the Union Address. We will get to that. That night, Trump approached the lectern with an air of confidence and Republican members were clearly poised to shower him with their support. After House Speaker

Nancy Pelosi introduced him, "Members of Congress: The President of the United States," Democrats and Republicans alike applauded out of respect. Republican members, however, started cheering loudly and whistling as Trump stood at the lectern taking it all in. After a few seconds, Republican members started clapping in unison and a chant began to emerge from their side of the chamber: "Four more years! Four more years! Four more years!" And if that was not enough, those same members broke out in chants of "U-S-A! U-S-A!" at various points in time during the address. It was starting to feel more like a MAGA rally than a formal State of the Union address. As we have discussed in the previous chapter, Trump's 2020 address was chock full of the "greatest hits" of the exceptional me strategy. He spoke of his own "historic" achievements at length and let the American public know just how exceptional he was as president. And Trump loudly trumpeted the country's restored American exceptionalism, claiming American superiority at every turn and finishing the speech with a meandering narrative about the history of American excellence and ingenuity.

The telling moment, however, came in an inconspicuous interaction that occurred after Trump had already finished his speech and stepped down from the lectern. It happened when most Americans had already tuned out and as pundits and journalists were already chattering about the significance of the night and the implications of Speaker Pelosi's ripping of Trump's speech right behind his back. Once he had taken in the applause at the end of his speech, Trump began to make his way to the chamber's exit through a crowd of adoring Republican fans jockeying to congratulate their president. With his now famed sharpie in hand, Trump walked slowly, shaking hands and signing everything from copies of the speech to people's hats and ties. As he progressed, he was met with almost servile praise by a number of his fellow Republicans. Comments like "Best speech, great speech. Brilliant Mr. President. Absolutely brilliant," "Great speech, unbelievable. Awesome speech," and "Crushed it Mr. President" came at him from all directions. One congressman, perhaps to the chagrin of Trump, even offered: "Reaganesque." Either way, the Republican Party was clearly behind their president. Amidst all of this praise, Congressman Andy Barr of Kentucky emerged from the crowd to get Trump's ear but for moment. He extended his hand to Trump and then offered simply: "Great defense of American exceptionalism. Thank you."[51] It went unnoticed by most, but its significance cannot be overstated. The exceptional me strategy was firing on all cylinders and the Republican Party, with the full support of conservative media, was behind it all the way. It was now the party of Trump. They had swallowed

Trump's conception of American exceptionalism whole, remade their party in its image, and, in doing so, left a massive opening for Democrats to seize upon.

The Exceptional Me Strategy Contested

From the outset of Trump's presidency, Democrats worked tirelessly to construct a counter narrative to Trump's exceptional me strategy and to build the case that he was a danger to American democracy. Senate Majority Leader, Chuck Schumer, for example, proclaimed: "The greatest thing America has is its honor and its values... no person has done more to destroy the honor and values of America than Donald Trump."[52] Speaker of the House, Nancy Pelosi, declared: "We have the most dangerous person in the history of our country sitting in the White House."[53] Perhaps the most vocal critic of Trump, however, was Democratic Congresswoman, Maxine Waters, who challenged his exceptional me strategy at every turn. In one tweet, for example, she argued: "No one can believe this unworthy president. He is the most prolific, consistent, good for nothing liar this country has ever experienced."[54] In a similar vein, she tweeted: "This is the most unpatriotic president that has ever occupied the Oval Office. He doesn't care abt anybody but himself. He's earning money on his golf clubs, hotels, & Trump Org deals while skimming Americans' money, & overusing SecretService to protect him on his many golf trips."[55] For Waters, and so many other Democrats, Trump was indeed exceptional, just not in the way Trump thought. Taking stock of the numerous Democratic attacks on Trump's exceptional me strategy throughout his presidency, there are two moments, we argue, that stand out and offer valuable insight into how the Democrats formulated a coherent and cohesive response to it: Trump's impeachment and the 2020 Democratic presidential campaign.

The Impeachment of Donald J. Trump

Although Democrats attempted to undermine Trump's exceptional me strategy on countless fronts throughout his presidency, it was not until they finally decided to move forward with an official impeachment inquiry in late 2019 that their messaging seemed to consolidate around a singular focus on American exceptionalism. Indeed, when it came to light that Trump had used the powers of the presidency to advance his own political interests, Democrats saw a perfect opportunity to carefully and deliberately craft a narrative that both reestablished the basic tenants of American exceptionalism and portrayed Trump as its singular existential threat.[56] Notably, these themes were on full display when Speaker Pelosi announced her support for the articles of impeachment on December 18, 2019, on the Floor of the House of Representatives. Her opening remarks began with a nod to the words of Founding Father, Benjamin Franklin: "'The Republic for which it stands' is what we are here to talk about today: 'a Republic, if we can keep it.'"[57] Pelosi then offered this:

> When our Founders declared independence and established a new nation, they crafted a system of government unlike one ever seen before: a Republic, starting with sacred words 'We The People.' For centuries, Americans have fought—and died—to defend democracy For The People. But, very sadly, now, our Founders' vision of our Republic is under threat from actions from the White House.

Pelosi was, in effect, challenging Trump's "Me the People" tactic, arguing that not only was he *not* representing the will of the American people, he was, in fact, actively subverting it. She went on: "When the President's wrongdoing was revealed, he launched an unprecedented, indiscriminate, and categorical campaign of defiance and obstruction. Never before in the history of our nation have we seen a president declare and act as if he's above the law." Trump, therefore, was indeed exceptional, but only in that he believed himself to be exempt from the rules that had traditionally governed the presidency. Pelosi then shifted back, claiming that the American people were still in need of guidance and leadership, but this time to safeguard them from Trump's actions. Pelosi then ended her announcement by saying simply: "Today, we are here to defend democracy *for the people.*"

As the impeachment proceedings played out, several Congressional Democrats took up the banner of American exceptionalism to counter Trump's exceptional me strategy. On the day of the House vote to impeach Trump, for example, Congresswoman Ayanna Pressley sought to portray the entire process as evidence of American exceptionalism:

> What we are doing here today is not only patriotic, it is uniquely American. America is a story of ordinary people confronting abuses of power with a steadfast pursuit of justice. Throughout our history, the oppressed have been relegated to the margins by the powerful, and each time, we have fought back, deliberate in our approach, clear-eyed.[58]

Perhaps the most notable Democratic champion of American exceptionalism throughout the impeachment process, however, was Congressman Adam Schiff, who became the public face of the Democratic impeachment team both in the House and Senate. Schiff delivered several notable statements throughout the proceedings, but one that certainly stood out was his concluding remarks during the House impeachment hearings, when he stated:

> We are the indispensable nation. We still are. People look to us from all over the world. Journalists from their jail cells in Turkey. Victims of mass extrajudicial killings in the Philippines. People who gathered in Tahrir Square wanting a representative government. People in China who are Uighurs. People in Ukraine who want a better future. They look to us. They're not going to look to the Russians, they're not going to look to the Chinese, they can't look to Europe with all of its problems. They still look to us and, increasingly, they don't recognize what they see… What they see, they don't recognize. And that is a terrible tragedy for us, but it is a greater tragedy for the world.[59]

Schiff's message was clear: Trump was a threat to American exceptionalism. During the Senate trial, he took this argument to a new level:

> If we don't stand up to this peril today, we will write the history of our decline with our own hand… We also undermine our global standing as a country, long viewed as a model for democratic ideals worth emulating. We have for generations been the "shining city upon a hill" that president Reagan described. America is not just a country, but also an idea. But what worth is that idea if when tried, we do not affirm the values that underpin it? What will those nascent democracies around the world conclude? That democracy is not only difficult, but maybe that it's too difficult. Maybe that it's impossible. And who will come to fill the void that we leave when the light from that shining city upon a hill is extinguished? The autocrats with whom we compete, who value not freedom and fair elections, but the unending rule of a repressive executive.[60]

Schiff's invocation of Ronald Reagan here was significant. In effect, he was reminding Congressional Republicans what their party had stood for before Trump. This, of course, would fall on mostly deaf ears. At the same time, he was conveying to the American public that American exceptionalism was an idea that was larger than any single president and that Trump posed a unique and malicious threat to it. Americans of all stripes witnessed this narrative in real time. Once Trump was acquitted, however, it would fall to the Democratic presidential candidates to carry the narrative to an even wider audience.

The 2020 Democratic Campaigns

Once the 2020 presidential campaign season was in full swing, the Democratic candidates began to fine-tune their attacks on President Trump and his exceptional me strategy. Senator Bernie Sanders—who launched his campaign under the banner, "Not me. Us.," an obvious affront to Trump's exceptional me strategy—was perhaps the most explicit and direct among these candidates in characterizing Trump as the *unexceptional* president. Notably, in the second line of his campaign kickoff speech, Sanders called Trump "the most dangerous president in modern American history."[61] This was a line he would repeat over and over on the campaign trail and in tweets. He also referred to Trump as "the most racist, sexist, homophobic, bigoted president in history,"[62] "a pathological liar running the most corrupt administration in history,"[63] and "the worst candidate for president in the modern history of the United States."[64]

Sanders, however, was not alone in this line of attack. Former mayor Pete Buttigieg, for example, argued that Trump was "the most divisive president in modern American history."[65] Similarly, in her campaign kickoff speech, Senator, Elizabeth Warren, offered: "[T]he man in the White House is not the cause of what is broken, he is just the latest and most extreme symptom of what's gone wrong in America."[66] She then added: "We all know the Trump administration is the most corrupt in living memory." This emphasis on Trump's "exceptional" level of corruption was something that multiple candidates sought to highlight. Senator Kamala Harris, for instance, offered: "Donald Trump has been the most corrupt, unpatriotic president we've ever had."[67] To put it mildly, the Democratic candidates did not pull any punches in their attacks on Trump's claims that he and his presidency were exceptional. According to Democrats, Trump was exceptional, alright: exceptionally bad.

The candidates also often took aim at Trump's claims that the United States was better off than it had been before his presidency. Senators Amy Klobuchar, Kamala Harris, and Congressman Beto O'Rourke, for example, argued that Trump had weakened the security and reputation of the United States. In her campaign kickoff speech, where she launched her campaign slogan, "For the People," Harris argued: "Under this administration, America's position in the world has never been weaker."[68] At one of the Democratic presidential debates, she added: "[Y]ou asked before what is the greatest national security threat to the United States? It's Donald Trump."[69] Similarly, Klobuchar suggested that the United States was "less safe than we were when he [Trump] became president."[70] And O'Rourke offered this: "[U]nder this administration, President Trump has alienated our allies and our friends and our alliances. He's diminished our standing in the world and he's made us weaker as a country." These statements, of course, flew in the face of the various claims that Trump had offered throughout his presidency that America was more respected, more secure, and more powerful than ever before. Former Mayor, Mike Bloomberg, took this a step further, targeting something very dear to Trump when he pointed out: "Trump says he created the greatest economy of all time. Turns out, it ranks 6th out of the last 10 presidential terms. Either he's lying, or he doesn't know what he's talking about. Maybe it's both?"[71] Indeed, Democrats were arguing that Trump's record was the exact opposite of what he claimed: it was not exceptional in any way. Together, these examples are but a small sampling of the multitude of Democratic challenges to Trump, each designed to undermine his exceptional me strategy in the run up to the 2020 presidential election.

Former Vice President Joe Biden was no different than the others in his attacks on the exceptional me strategy. He too saw Trump as an aberration to the presidency, proclaiming that he was "the most erratic and incompetent commander in chief we've ever had."[72] Although Biden's attacks were varied, the central argument was always that Trump and his administration were exceptional in their flaws and failures. He referred to Trump as a "a serial liar and the most corrupt president in modern American history."[73] This line of attack was even more pronounced in an op-ed, Biden wrote in *Foreign Affairs* in early 2020:

> [W]hen the world's democracies look to the United States to stand for the values that unite the country—to truly lead the free world—Trump seems to be on the other team, taking the word of autocrats while showing disdain for democrats. By presiding over the most corrupt administration in modern American history, he has given license to kleptocrats everywhere.[74]

He also suggested that Trump had "abdicated American leadership" and "bankrupted the United States' word in the world." Beyond these attacks, Biden was keen to another aspect of Trump's exceptional me strategy. Specifically, he pointed out the weakness of Trump's penchant for focusing more on his supporters than all Americans, arguing: "Donald Trump is the only president who has decided not to represent the whole country. The president has his base. We need a president who works for all Americans."[75] According to Biden, Trump's populist, "Me the People," rhetorical tactic was not only an insult to many Americans, it was a losing political strategy for a sitting president.

There was one thing, however, that clearly set Biden apart from the pack of Democratic challengers: his absolute, unabashed embrace of American exceptionalism and his choice to make it *the* core principle of his presidential campaign. Indeed, more than any of his competitors, Biden sought to link his explicit challenges to Trump's exceptional me strategy to a much larger narrative, one that was anchored in American exceptionalism. Specifically, Biden's approach was not just to expose Trump's unexceptional traits and policies as president, he also sought to rehabilitate the idea within the minds of Americans. Perhaps this is why Biden so regularly talked about the need to "restore the soul of America." As Biden saw it, Trump posed a profound threat to America—its values, its institutions, and even its psyche—and the only way to overcome it was to revive and reclaim a version of American exceptionalism more in line with how every president before Trump had portrayed it to the American people. For Biden, American exceptionalism was not just about American superiority, as Trump had so vociferously portrayed it to be. Rather, it was a complex, multifaceted idea that lived in all aspects of American society. With that in mind, Biden was determined to convince the American people that he understood its many nuances—and that Trump, of course, did not.

This was on full display throughout Biden's presidential campaign. At one campaign event, for example, Biden spoke at length about American exceptionalism, invoking it in a number of different layers:

> America has been an idea. It's the most unique idea in all the world. Not a joke. The only thing that can defeat America is America. There is no army strong enough, no dictator powerful enough, no ocean wide enough that, in fact, can overcome what we are able to do. We can do whatever we want to do ... We are, we are the most unique idea. It's an idea we cannot abandon. And folks, we are better prepared to own the 21st century than any nation in the world by a long shot.[76]

Like so many presidents and presidential candidates before him, Biden seamlessly intermingled various notions of American exceptionalism—including singularity, superiority, and the role of the United States as a model for the world—into a single statement. Biden, unlike Trump, was also particularly fond of invoking the idea of American uniqueness in his speeches, regularly offering some variation of this statement: "We [America] started off as a unique idea. We are the unique idea in history. We the people in order to form a more perfect union. No country has ever been founded on a principle like that."[77] Biden was, in effect, taking a page from the 2016 Republican Party platform—the one that advocated for an unapologetic embrace of American exceptionalism—and he was owning it. He believed he could ride it to victory in 2020.

If there was one aspect of American exceptionalism that Biden emphasized the most, however, it was that America needed to reestablish its global leadership. At one campaign stop, for instance, he declared: "We own the world. And the world needs someone like the United States. They need a leader. I don't mean putting thousands of boots on the ground to do war. But leading the world in terms of being the one who moves the world forward across the spectrum. That's who we are." Biden's robust embrace of this facet of American exceptionalism was perhaps most evident when he said:

> [W]e have the most powerful military in the history of the world to be able to protect us. But that's not why the rest of the world responds to us. It's been the incredible example of our power. Not that. The power of our example. The reason the rest of the world responds to us, and we're able to form these great alliances, is because the rest of the world knows who we are. Our example. To quote a Republican, Ronald Reagan, "We're the shining city on a hill."

Biden then paused for a second before adding: "But the luster is coming off right now." In addition to restoring the more traditional form of American exceptionalism championed by presidents for decades before Trump, Biden was also resurrecting the modern jeremiad. In contrast to Trump's 2016 campaign strategy, Biden was fully dedicated to all aspects of American exceptionalism. Indeed, he wanted the American people to know that he believed in it with every fiber of his being, that he knew what it really meant, and that, most importantly, Trump posed an existential threat to it. As one scholar put it, Biden seemed determined to "Make American Exceptionalism Great Again."[78] This was the modern jeremiad in its purest and most effective form.

American Exceptionalism: Under New Management

And so it seemed, Democrats were answering the call to action that Michelle and Barack Obama had issued three years earlier in the immediate aftermath of the 2016 elections. They were taking up the mantle of American exceptionalism and, in effect, using it to convince the American people that Trump represented a unique and unprecedented threat to it. Such an embrace of this core American idea harkened back to an era before Trump had replaced "American exceptionalism" with "America First." Democrats had finally come together to establish a cohesive and unified rhetorical strategy that not only directly challenged Trump's exceptional me strategy but positioned their party to be the defenders of America's singular democracy. They had taken the baton of American exceptionalism from the likes of Ronald Reagan and John McCain, the same baton that Republicans in Congress had let fall to the dirt when they became the party of Trump, and they were running with it. They had put forth a clear and seemingly compelling argument to the American people that they were, in fact, the true party of American exceptionalism—at least the version of it that Trump seemed to neither fully understand nor care much about.

RIP American Exceptionalism?

Since Donald Trump took office, journalists, pundits, and scholars alike have grappled with the question of whether his ascendance to the American presidency meant that the time of American exceptionalism was officially over. On March 2, 2017, for example, just little over a month into the Trump presidency, Nick Bryant of the *BBC* posed the question: "Donald Trump and the end of American exceptionalism?"[79] Dozens of others across the media spectrum followed, all attempting to answer that same question from a number of different perspectives. By mid-2018, however, Historian Daniel Sargent decided that it was time to officially call it: "RIP American Exceptionalism, 1776–2018."[80] For those who professed that American exceptionalism had indeed ended, the reasons were varied, but the central theme was that with Trump at the helm, America had lost—or abandoned—its moral standing in the world. These perspectives, however, miss a very important point about this age-old national idea. In the minds of Americans across the political spectrum, American exceptionalism is not dead; it is very much alive—a reality that politicians like Trump know all too well. From this perspective, American exceptionalism is perhaps best understood not as a set of verifiable facts or specific foreign policies but as an idea, a belief that broadly resonates within the American electorate. To so many Americans, their country is exceptional regardless of any speculation or analyses pronouncing its demise. For them, it does not matter whether it is true or not. What matters most of all is that they believe it to be true. This is what makes the communication of American exceptionalism so particularly potent when wielded by politicians like Trump.

If there is one thing that Trump's exceptional me strategy has reaffirmed about American exceptionalism it is that it is not some fixed idea that is inflexible to the changing tides of time and political circumstance. If anything, it has reminded us that American exceptionalism is a concept that has, throughout its history, been redefined time and again by politicians of every era to fit their specific political moment. In fact, as we have documented, virtually every president since the country's inception has found creative ways to spin new narratives about American exceptionalism to help them define their vision for the country and to rally people to their cause. In this sense, Trump was not so exceptional. Every president has done it, to be sure, but few have done so in a way that fundamentally redefined the concept for generations. Only some presidents have had this power. In the modern political era, perhaps no one stands out in this regard more than Harry Truman. It was Truman who crafted a new language of American exceptionalism in the aftermath of the Second World War, which continues to be infused in how politicians speak of it to this day. It even shaped how Ronald Reagan spoke of it and it will continue to impact how the public understands American exceptionalism for generations to come.

This begs the question: Has Trump's exceptional me strategy redefined American exceptionalism in such a way that will shape how generations to come understand it? The answer is complicated and fitting for a complicated political time. What is likely the case is that the days when presidents of both parties aligned behind a singular vision of American exceptionalism are long gone. We argue, rather, that two camps, cut along partisan lines, have emerged with competing visions for the future of American exceptionalism and that this divergence is not likely to go away anytime soon. Trump, as we have shown, has defined one version; Obama, the other. As we discussed in Chapter 1, Obama came into office amidst a barrage of challenges to his patriotism and his belief in American exceptionalism. Instead of backing down or ignoring his challengers, Obama saw an opportunity. Unlike Bill Clinton, who had answered similar challenges by simply, albeit loudly, reaffirming his belief in American exceptionalism, Obama sought to redefine it. To be sure, Obama fully embraced the storied version of American exceptionalism that called on the United States to lead the world and to safeguard its singular democracy so that it could shine as beacon of excellence for the world to emulate. His argument, however, was that America would never be seen as exceptional if its democracy did not fully embrace the multicultural reality of its electorate. This was perhaps best evidenced in his second inaugural address when he offered:

> Each time we gather to inaugurate a President we bear witness to the enduring strength of our Constitution. We affirm the promise of our democracy. We recall that what binds this nation together is not the colors of our skin or the tenets of our faith or the origins of our names. What makes us exceptional—what makes us American—is our allegiance to an idea articulated in a declaration made more than two centuries ago: "We hold these truths to be self-evident, that all men are created equal; that they are endowed by their Creator with certain unalienable rights; that among these are life, liberty, and the pursuit of happiness."[81]

Obama's American exceptionalism, therefore, was about inclusion and making sure that no group of Americans was valued more than any other. That, according to Obama, was the example that the United States should set for the world. This became the rallying cry and a core identity piece for the Democratic Party. American exceptionalism meant a multicultural America.

There were many in the Republican Party, however, who saw this new vision for American exceptionalism as a direct threat to their power and to their own vision for the country. Many of them saw the ascent to power of a mixed-race man named Barack Hussain Obama as a national embarrassment and a stain on their vision of American exceptionalism. Trump did not start this movement. But he appropriated it, took the helm, and capitalized on it for his own political gain. As we have shown in this book, Trump seemed to want his American exceptionalism to be the antithesis of Obama's vision. In Trump's vision, there were clearly some Americans who should matter more than others. They were the true Americans and *they* should be the ones in charge and setting the example for the world. Perhaps this is part of the reason why Trump so actively sought to disentangle the notion of American exceptionalism from American democracy—almost never speaking about the values, traditions, and institutions that serve as the foundation of American democracy—and, instead, made it only about American superiority. Clearly, if Obama's redefined version of American exceptionalism were allowed to play out, minorities would start to take power from the white majority as they gained more equitable representation. Trump was standing ground for a waning demographic majority holding onto power by whatever means necessary, including undermining American democracy. Trump had fundamentally changed the Republican Party's notion of what American exceptionalism stood for, but because they needed to safeguard their claim to power, there were few voices within the party willing to object.

Trump's open disdain for democratic norms and checks on his presidency also profoundly changed what it meant for the country to be a "shining city upon a hill." With the president of the United States openly questioning the legitimacy of the country's democracy, the notion that America stood as a symbol of democratic excellence was damaged. The world was still watching, to be sure, but it was a new group of people that had started taking notes. It was no longer the nascent democracies around the world who were taking their cues from the American president, it was autocratic and authoritarian leaders who started to mimic Trump's attacks on his own democratic system and his characterization of the news media and the Democratic Party as "enemies of the people." It also seemed to flow both ways. Trump's self-exceptionalism and claims that American exceptionalism was doomed without him mirrored more the actions of an authoritarian leader than those of a democratically elected American president. His party's fervent support for him and his exceptional me strategy just worked to further legitimize the notion that he, Trump, and American exceptionalism were inextricably linked. At the end of the day, making American exceptionalism all about Trump meant that there would likely be a reckoning once he was gone. Trump or no Trump, his base is not going anywhere and, most importantly, they are now attuned to his vision of American exceptionalism.

Only time will tell whether either or both of these competing visions will take hold and impact the generations that follow. Of the two, Obama's vision appears more sustainable and reflective of the inevitable changes within the American electorate, but Trump's exclusionary vision has shown a resilience beyond what most political observers believed possible. Again, only time will tell. But one thing is clear: American exceptionalism is far from being dead. More prognostications of its demise are likely to come, but American exceptionalism is alive and well in the American psyche and it is not going anywhere, anytime soon. Politicians for generations to come will rely on the power of its ideas to inspire the American public and bring them into their fold. It will be redefined, of course, but its core will remain intact as long as there are people in America who believe in it. American exceptionalism will always be bigger than any one person. It is about the nation, not narcissism. It may be true that in modern Republican politics, Trump's version of American exceptionalism will continue to reign supreme, but on the long arc of history, he is likely but a blip on American exceptionalism's radar.

Epilogue

Trump walked off the stage after his 2020 State of the Union Address riding high. For three years, he had been spinning a fantastical narrative about how he was an exceptional, almost otherworldly, president who had achieved more than any other president in American history and that the country—thanks to him, of course—was doing better than ever before. Trump's exceptional me strategy was resonating with large swaths of the American electorate and the state of affairs within the country—in particular, the strength of the economy—seemed (to many) to be matching some of his over-the-top claims of presidential exceptionalism. Trump seemed to be peaking at just the right time and conventional wisdom suggested that he would likely win reelection in November. Indeed, that night, Kathleen Parker of the *Washington Post* went so far as to say: "Trump might be the luckiest president to ever hold office."[1] She then added: "For this all important week, the story is that Trump is still winning." Peter Bergen of CNN offered a similar analysis, suggesting that Trump's apparent success up to that point had been due almost entirely to luck. In addition to inheriting a growing economy, Bergen argued, Trump was lucky because he had never had to face a "major crisis on his watch of the type that has challenged every president in the half century before him."[2] Trump no doubt intended to ride this luck to his reelection, but Covid-19—Trump's first-ever major national crisis—was about to change everything.

Just days after Trump's State of the Union Address, it had become apparent to many that the tide had begun to turn. David Von Drehle of the *Washington Post*, for example, proclaimed that the emerging global pandemic meant that "Trump's luck is turning against him."[3] He argued that the coronavirus would inevitably and aggressively target Trump's best campaign asset, the thriving economy, and in so doing, would threaten to take down the image of his "exceptional" presidency like a house of cards. Trump's exceptional me strategy and his new slogan, "Keep America Great," were highly dependent on things staying the way they were before Covid-19 hit. With the virus spreading and a potential economic collapse on the horizon, it seemed likely that Trump's claims that the country was doing "better than ever before" would soon ring hollow, if not entirely insensitive, to many Americans. Von Drehle's conclusion was prescient: "Trump's going to need a new campaign script."

Trump and his campaign staff seemed to recognize this from the outset. Facing a public health crisis and a cratering economy, their need for new reelection messaging, strangely, seemed to be what they focused on the most. Their problem was exacerbated when they were forced to abruptly cancel all future MAGA rallies. It left Trump without his audiences to test his messages. By the end of May, without the help of his adoring crowds to help him know what worked and what didn't, Trump and his campaign thought that they had come up with a clever fix. They called a press conference and launched the new slogan "Transition to Greatness." It was an immediate flop. Nicholas Goldberg of the *LA Times* called it "the worst campaign slogan ever."[4] David Graham of *The Atlantic* took it a step further, calling it a "confession of failure"[5] because it was replacing "Keep America Great," which was based on the claim that Trump had already made the country great. It was abundantly clear that neither "Keep America Great" nor "Transition to Greatness" was going to work.

Trump had actually never fully committed to the "Keep America Great" slogan, commonly replacing it with "Make America Great Again" at rallies throughout his presidency. Even when he rolled out the new slogan at his reelection campaign announcement in June of 2019—which he referred to as "the greatest campaign announcement in the history of politics"[6]—Trump seemed uncommitted:

> So now I say, we've made America great again, but how do you give up the number one, call it theme, logo, statement, in the history of politics for a new one? But you know, there is a new one that really works. And that's called "Keep America Great." Right? *[Applause.]* Keep America Great. Right? Keep America Great. In other words, Make America Great Again, well, we've really done it.[7]

Furthermore, at many of his rallies throughout 2019 and early 2020 Trump routinely called upon his supporters to weigh in on which of these two slogans they preferred. More often than not, MAGA was the winner. And so, when "Keep America Great" and "Transition to Greatness" needed to be scrapped, the Trump campaign decided to go with an oldie but a goodie. But it was Mike Pence, not Trump, who would reintroduce it to the American people. During his speech at the Republican National Convention, Pence explained: "In our first three years, we built the greatest economy in the world. We made America great again. And then the coronavirus struck from China."[8] In other words, Trump had done it once already, so he could do it again, right? Pence finished his speech by saying: "[W]ith President Donald Trump in the White House for four more years, and God's help … we will make America great again, again." Clever.

Although the slogans changed with regularity, the claims, by and large, remained the same. Even though the national landscape had changed fundamentally with Covid-19, an economy in shambles, and the nationwide protests in response to the killings of George Floyd, Breonna Taylor, and others, Trump seemed unable to pivot. He was hellbent on sticking with the strategy that got him to the White House four years earlier. He turned up both versions of the exceptional me strategy to full volume and hit the campaign trail. In true 2016 mode, Trump regularly claimed "I'm not a politician. I'm embarrassed by the throne."[9] According to him, he was again the outsider candidate continuing to fight a "corrupt political class … desperate to regain their power by any means necessary." On American exceptionalism, Trump took full credit: "We made America into the single greatest nation in the history of the world, and the best is yet to come. Proud citizens like you help build this country and together we are taking back our country. We're returning power to you, the American people." Finally, in reaction to the downturn in the economy Trump's favorite 2020 election promise was: "Next year will be the greatest economic year in the history of our country."[10] Indeed, throughout the 2020 campaign, Trump seemed to swing effortlessly between claiming that he had indeed made the country great again, but that it was, yet again, in need of being made great again and that he was uniquely qualified to make America great again, again.

As Election Day approached, however, most doubted that Trump had made any headway with expanding his support beyond his very loyal base. The polls and pundits all seemed to predict that Trump would lose by a sizable margin and that the American people would deliver a clear rebuke of Trump, Trumpism, and his exceptional me strategy. Trump seemed to have a different idea. On November 3, 2020, Election Day, he settled in to watch the results roll in after a marathon of risky campaign rallies in the final days of the campaign. In his final tweets before the polls closed, Trump wanted to remind voters one last time: "Get out & VOTE! Under my Administration, our ECONOMY is growing at the fastest rate EVER at 33.1%. Next year will be the GREATEST ECONOMIC YEAR in American History!"[11] It was the exceptional me strategy on full display and a last-ditch effort to pull a come-from-behind win.

In true Trumpian terms, the 2020 election was, indeed, "historic," "one for the ages," and "nobody could believe it." At the end of the day, however, all of Trump's efforts were not enough. He was unsuccessful in convincing enough Americans to grant him another term as president. That said, even though Trump lost the election, his loss was nowhere close to the rebuke of Trump and Trumpism that so many had thought or hoped it would be. In fact, Trump had actually been successful in expanding his base of support, helping Republicans safeguard their standing in the Senate and close the gap in the House. And this occurred despite Trump's catastrophic mismanagement of the Covid-19 crisis. It was a testament, one could argue, to just how powerful and persuasive Trump and his exceptional me strategy had become—and would continue to be for the foreseeable future. Trump's presidency might be officially over, but Trump and Trumpism are likely to remain influential in American politics for years to come, especially if Trump has anything to do with crafting the narrative.

Indeed, the most important thing to Trump in the days after the election seemed to be his desire to, yet again, craft his own version of history. For Trump, it was easy to turn his loss into a win with a little PR elbow grease. If he simply focused on telling the story of only "real" and "true" Americans—those who voted for him, of course—then the story would continue to be the same one he had been spinning for the entirety of his political life. In the eyes of many of his devoted supporters, Donald Trump was like a superhero and he would continue to be exceptional no matter the circumstances. Trump could not have agreed more. Eight days after losing the election, for example, Trump offered this take: "With 72 MILLION votes, we received more votes than any sitting President in U.S. history."[12] Four days later, a full twelve days after losing the election by a sizeable margin to Joe Biden, Trump offered this head scratcher: "One thing has become clear these last few days [since the election], I am the American People's ALL-TIME favorite President."[13] It was the exceptional me strategy in a nutshell and it was taking on a new form yet again.

Although it was immediately clear that losing the 2020 election was the most difficult blow Trump's fragile ego had ever endured, one could argue that it may very well turn out to be the best-case scenario for him. If Trump made one thing clear throughout his presidency, it was that he much prefers campaigning to governing. Winning reelection, therefore, would have meant being stuck as a term-limited president with no reason to spend his time out on the campaign trail. By accepting his loss (at the time of this writing, he has yet to do so), he sets himself up to spend the next four years in the spotlight, using his exceptional me strategy to remain the ideological kingmaker of the Republican Party. More importantly, it would allow him to spend the next four years entirely on the campaign trail, speaking to adoring crowds as he gears up for another bid for the presidency in 2024. It would be, perhaps unsarcastically, "Make America Great Again, Again … Again." It could end up being the best thing that ever happened to Trump. Whether the same can be said about the country is another matter entirely.

Notes

Introduction

1   See Gilmore, J., & Rowling, C. M. (2019). Partisan patriotism in the American presidency: American exceptionalism, issue ownership, and the age of Trump. *Mass Communication and Society*, 22(3), 389–416; Edwards, J. A. (2011). Contemporary conservative constructions of American exceptionalism. *Journal of Contemporary Rhetoric*, 1, 40–54.

2   See Crawford, J. T., & Bhatia, A. (2012). Birther nation: Political conservatism is associated with explicit and implicit beliefs that president Barack Obama is foreign. *Analyses of Social Issues and Public Policy*, 12(1), 364–76. doi: 10.1111/j.1530-2415.2001.01279.x; Gingrich, N. (2011). *A nation like no other: Why American exceptionalism matters*. New York, NY: Simon and Schuster; and Romney, M. (2010). *No apology: The case for American greatness*. New York, NY: St. Martin's Press. Also see Gilmore, J., Sheets, P., & Rowling, C. M. (2016). Make no exception, save one: American exceptionalism and its culmination in the age of Obama. *Communication Monographs*, 83(4), 505–20; and Edwards, J. A. (2012). Review essay: An exceptional debate: The championing of and challenge to American exceptionalism. *Rhetoric and Public Affairs*, 15, 351–67.

3   Quote from Republican National Committee. (2016). *Republican platform: America resurgent*. Retrieved from http://www.gop.com/platform.

4   Quote in Corn, D. (2016, June 7). Donald Trump says he doesn't believe in "American exceptionalism." *Mother Jones*. Retrieved from http://www.motherjones.com/politics/2016/06/donald-trump-american-exceptionalism.

5   Quote from Trump, D. J. (2015). *Crippled America: How to make America great again*. New York, NY: Simon & Schuster. It is important to note that the harshness in tone of the title of the book was addressed eight months later when the book was re-released in paperback format under the title *Great Again: How to Fix Our Crippled America*. Although the title did some work to put more of the focus on Trump's campaign slogan, it still hinged the book on the idea that the United States was crippled and in ruins.

6   Donald and Ivanka Trump delivered these addresses on June 16, 2015, at Trump Tower in New York City. A transcript can be accessed at https://www.presidency.ucsb.edu.

7   Donald Trump delivered this address on July 21, 2016, at the Republican National Convention in Cleveland, Ohio. A transcript can be accessed at https://www.presidency.ucsb.edu.

8   Donald Trump delivered this inaugural address on January 20, 2017, in Washington, D.C. A transcript can be accessed at https://www.presidency.ucsb.edu.

9   Mike Pence and Donald Trump delivered these addresses on July 21, 2016, at the Republican National Convention in Cleveland, Ohio. A transcript can be accessed at https://www.presidency.ucsb.edu.

10 This slogan is the foundational slogan of the Trump 2020 campaign and can be found in various formats on his campaign website: http://www.donaldjtrump.com.

11 Donald Trump delivered these comments in his address on April 21, 2017, upon signing an executive order and memorandums on financial services industry regulatory policy. A transcript can be accessed at https://www.presidency.ucsb.edu.

12 Donald Trump regularly referenced "American carnage" in his speeches, but most notably in his inaugural address on January 20, 2017, in Washington, D.C. A transcript can be accessed at https://www.presidency.ucsb.edu.

13 Donald Trump delivered this address on February 16, 2017, in a press conference in Washington, D.C. A transcript can be accessed at https://www.presidency.ucsb.edu.

14 Donald Trump delivered this address on February 18, 2017, at a "Make America Great Again" Rally in Melbourne, Florida. A transcript can be accessed at https://www.presidency.ucsb.edu.

15 Quoted from Donald Trump's address on June 18, 2019, announcing his candidacy in 2020 in Orlando, Florida. A transcript can be accessed at https://www.presidency.ucsb.edu.

16 Donald Trump made these remarks in an interview with Margaret Brennan on CBS's *Face the Nation* on February 3, 2019. A transcript can be accessed at https://www.cbsnews.com/news/transcript-president-trump-on-face-the-nation-february-3-2019.

17 This slogan is the foundational slogan of the Sanders 2020 campaign and can be found in various formats on his campaign website: http://www.berniesanders.com.

18 Various presidents have invoked this idea throughout the post–Second World War era. For example, Barack Obama used this phrase in his first address before a joint session of Congress on February 24, 2009. A transcript can be accessed at https://www.presidency.ucsb.edu.

Chapter 1

1   Harry Truman delivered this State of the Union address on January 4, 1950, in Washington, D.C. A transcript can be accessed at https://www.presidency.ucsb.edu.

2   Madsen, D. L. (1998). *American exceptionalism*. Jackson, MS: University Press of
     Mississippi.
3   Quote in McCriskin, T. B. (2003). *American exceptionalism and the legacy
     of Vietnam: US foreign policy since 1974*. Basingstoke, Hampshire: Palgrave
     Macmillan.
4   Quote from Thomas Jefferson's inaugural address delivered on March 8, 1801, in
     Washington, D.C. A transcript can be accessed at https://www.presidency.ucsb.edu.
5   Gilmore, J., Sheets, P., & Rowling, C. M. (2016). Make no exception, save
     one: American exceptionalism and its culmination in the age of Obama.
     Communication Monographs, 83(4), 505–20.
6   Domke, D., & Coe, K. (2010). *The god strategy: How religion became a political
     weapon in America*. New York, NY: Oxford University Press.
7   Pease, D. E. (2009). *The new American exceptionalism*. Minneapolis, MN:
     University of Minnesota Press.
8   Hayden, C. (2011). Beyond the "Obama effect": Refining the instruments of
     engagement through U.S. public diplomacy. *American Behavioral Scientist*,
     55(6), 784–802; and Gilmore, J. (2014). Translating American exceptionalism:
     Presidential discourse about the United States in comparative perspective.
     International Journal of Communication, 9(22), 2416–37. Retrieved from
     http://ijoc.org; and Gilmore, J., & Rowling, C. M. (2018). Lighting the beacon:
     Presidential discourse, American exceptionalism, and public diplomacy in global
     contexts.
9   Bacevich, A. J. (2008). *The limits of power: The end of American exceptionalism*.
     New York, NY: Macmillan; McCriskin, T. B. (2003). *American exceptionalism
     and the legacy of Vietnam: US foreign policy since 1974*. Basingstoke, Hampshire:
     Palgrave Macmillan. McEvoy-Levy, S. (2001). *American exceptionalism and US
     foreign policy: Public diplomacy at the end of the cold war*. Basingstoke, Hampshire:
     Palgrave; Pease, D. E. (2009). *The new American exceptionalism*. Minneapolis, MN:
     University of Minnesota Press; Restad, H. E. (2014). *American exceptionalism: An
     idea that made a nation and remade the world*. New York, NY: Routledge.
10   Madsen, D. L. (1998). *American exceptionalism*. Jackson, MS: University Press of
     Mississippi.
11   Lipset, S. M. (1996). *American exceptionalism: A double-edged sword*. New York,
     NY: W. W. Norton; Lockhart, C. (2003). *The roots of American exceptionalism*. New
     York, NY: Palgrave Macmillan; McEvoy-Levy, S. (2001). *American exceptionalism
     and US foreign policy: Public diplomacy at the end of the Cold War*. Basingstoke,
     Hampshire: Palgrave; Restad, H. E. (2014). *American exceptionalism: An idea that
     made a nation and remade the world*. New York, NY: Routledge.
12   Saito, N. T. (2010). *Meeting the enemy: American exceptionalism and international
     law*. London: New York University Press.

13 Kohut, A., & Stokes, B. (2006). *America against the world: How we are different and why we are disliked*. New York, NY: Times Books. Restad, H. E. (2014). *American exceptionalism: An idea that made a nation and remade the world*. New York, NY: Routledge.

14 Cheney, D., Cheney, R. B., & Cheney, L. (2016). *Exceptional: Why the world needs a powerful America*. New York, NY: Simon and Schuster.

15 Lipset, S. M. (1996). *American exceptionalism: A double-edged sword*. New York, NY: W. W. Norton; Lockhart, C. (2003). *The roots of American exceptionalism*. New York, NY: Palgrave Macmillan; Pease, D. E. (2009). *The new American exceptionalism*. Minneapolis, MN: University of Minnesota Press.

16 Restad, H. (2017). American exceptionalism. In F. Moghaddam (Ed.) *The SAGE encyclopedia of political behavior* (pp. 25–7). Thousand Oaks, CA: SAGE Publications, Inc; Hodgson, G. (2009). *The myth of American exceptionalism*. New Haven, CT: Yale University Press.

17 Mason, D. S. (2009). *The end of the American century*. Lanham, MD: Rowman & Littlefield Publishers.

18 Zakaria, F. (2011). *The post-American world: Release 2.0*. New York, NY: W. W. Norton.

19 Gilmore, J. (2015). American exceptionalism in the American mind: Presidential discourse, national identity, and U.S. public opinion. *Communication Studies*, 66(3), 301–20. Gilmore, J., & Rowling, C. M. (2018) A post-American world? Assessing the cognitive and attitudinal impacts of challenges to American exceptionalism. *The Communication Review*, 21(1), 46–65; Gilmore, J., & Rowling, C. M. (2017). The United States in decline?: Assessing the impacts of international challenges to American exceptionalism. *International Journal of Communication*, 11(21), 137–57.

20 Edwards, J. A., & Weiss, D. (2011). *The rhetoric of American exceptionalism: Critical essays*. Jefferson, NC: McFarland & Company; Rojecki, A. (2008). Rhetorical alchemy: American exceptionalism and the war on terror. *Political Communication*, 25(1), 67–88. doi: 10.1080/10584600701807935; Söderlind, S., & Carson, J. T. (Eds.). (2011). *American exceptionalisms: From Winthrop to Winfrey*. New York, NY: SUNY Press.

21 Poll data from Gallup (2010). *USA Today/Gallup Poll: December Wave 1, December 2010, #10-12-022*. [Data set]. Gallup Inc. [Distributor]. Retrieved from https://news.gallup.com/poll/145358/americans-exceptional-doubt-obama.aspx.

22 Poll data from Public Religion Research Institute. (2010, November 17). *Old alignments, emerging fault lines: Religion in the 2010 elections and beyond*. Retrieved from http://publicreligion.org/research/2010/11/old-alignments-emerging-fault-lines-religion-in-the-2010-election-and-beyond.

23   Poll data from Rasmussen. (2017, February 8). *Voters still see America as a special place*. Retrieved from http://www.rasmussenreports.com/public_content/politics/ general_politics/february_2017/voters_still_see_america_as_a_special_place.

24   See Colbert, S. (2012). *America again: Re-becoming the greatness we never weren't*. New York, NY: Grand Central Publishing.

25   See Gilmore, J. (2014). Translating American exceptionalism: Presidential discourse about the United States in comparative perspective. *International Journal of Communication*, 9(22), 2416–37. Retrieved from http://ijoc.org; Gilmore, J., & Rowling, C. M. (2018). Lighting the beacon: Presidential discourse, American exceptionalism, and public diplomacy in global contexts. *Presidential Studies Quarterly*, 48(2), 271–91; Gilmore, J., Sheets, P., & Rowling, C. M. (2016). Make no exception, save one: American exceptionalism and its culmination in the age of Obama. *Communication Monographs*, 83(4), 505–20.

26   See Manheim, J. B. (1991). All of the people, all of the time: Strategic communication and American politics. Armonk, NY: M. E. Sharpe; Domke, D., & Coe, K. (2010). *The god strategy: How religion became a political weapon in America*. New York, NY: Oxford University Press; Tulis, J. K. (2017). *The rhetorical presidency: New edition* (Vol. 31). Princeton, NJ: Princeton University Press.

27   See Edwards, J. A. (2008). *Navigating the post-Cold War world: President Clinton's foreign policy rhetoric*. Lanham, MD: Lexington Studies in Political Communication.

28   Gilmore, J., Sheets, P., & Rowling, C. M. (2016). Make no exception, save one: American exceptionalism and its culmination in the age of Obama. *Communication Monographs*, 83(4), 505–20.

29   Gilmore, J., & Rowling, C. M. (2019). Partisan patriotism in the American presidency: American exceptionalism, issue ownership, and the age of Trump. *Mass Communication and Society*, 22(3), 389–416.

30   Harry Truman delivered this address on September 1, 1945, via radio from Washington D.C. A transcript can be accessed at https://www.presidency.ucsb.edu.

31   Quote from Abraham Lincoln's second annual address on December 1, 1862, in Washington, D.C. A transcript can be accessed at https://www.presidency.ucsb. edu.

32   Quote from Franklin Roosevelt's fourth inaugural address delivered on January 20, 1945, in Washington, D.C. A transcript can be accessed at https://www.presidency. ucsb.edu.

33   See Bacevich, A. J. (2008). *The limits of power: The end of American exceptionalism*. New York, NY: Macmillan; McCriskin, T. B. (2003). *American exceptionalism and the legacy of Vietnam: US foreign policy since 1974*. Basingstoke, Hampshire: Palgrave Macmillan; McEvoy-Levy, S. (2001). *American exceptionalism and US foreign policy: Public diplomacy at the end of the Cold War*. Basingstoke, Hampshire: Palgrave.

34   For a full analysis of American exceptionalism in presidential discourse since the
     end of the Second World War, see Gilmore, J., Sheets, P., & Rowling, C. M. (2016).
     Make no exception, save one: American exceptionalism and its culmination in
     the age of Obama. *Communication Monographs*, 83(4), 505–20; Gilmore, J., &
     Rowling, C. M. (2019). Partisan patriotism in the American presidency: American
     exceptionalism, issue ownership, and the age of Trump. *Mass Communication and
     Society*, 22(3), 389–416.

35   Quote from John Kennedy's second State of the Union address delivered on
     January 11, 1962, in Washington, D.C. A transcript can be accessed at https://www.
     presidency.ucsb.edu.

36   Quote from Richard Nixon's address to the nation on the war in Vietnam delivered
     on November 3, 1969, in Washington, D.C. A transcript can be accessed at https://
     www.presidency.ucsb.edu.

37   Quote from Ronald Reagan's first inaugural address delivered on January 21, 1981,
     in Washington, D.C. A transcript can be accessed at https://www.presidency.ucsb.
     edu.

38   See Krauthammer, C. (1990). The unipolar moment. *Foreign Affairs*, 70(1), 23–33.

39   Fukuyama, F. (1992). *The end of history and the last man*. New York, NY: Free
     Press.

40   The findings in this figure are an update to findings presented in Gilmore, J.,
     Sheets, P., & Rowling, C. M. (2016). Make no exception, save one: American
     exceptionalism and its culmination in the age of Obama. *Communication
     Monographs*, 83(4), 505–20.

41   Quote from Bill Clinton's remarks on international security delivered on August
     5, 1996, at George Washington University. A transcript can be accessed at https://
     www.presidency.ucsb.edu.

42   Quote from Madeleine Albright's interview with NBC's *The Today Show* on
     February 19, 1998, in Columbus, OH.

43   The findings in this figure are an updated version of data published in Gilmore,
     J., Sheets, P., & Rowling, C. M. (2016). Make no exception, save one: American
     exceptionalism and its culmination in the age of Obama. *Communication
     Monographs*, 83(4), 505–20.

44   Quote from George W. Bush's address to the nation on the attacks on 9/11
     delivered on September 12, 2001, in Washington, D.C. A transcript can be
     accessed at https://www.presidency.ucsb.edu.

45   See Gilmore, J. (2014). Translating American exceptionalism: Presidential
     discourse about the United States in comparative perspective. *International Journal
     of Communication*, 9(22), 2416–37. Retrieved from http://ijoc.org; Gilmore, J.,
     & Rowling, C. M. (2018). Lighting the beacon: Presidential discourse, American
     exceptionalism, and public diplomacy in global contexts. *Presidential Studies
     Quarterly*, 48(2), 271–91.

46 See Gilmore, J., Sheets, P., & Rowling, C. M. (2016). Make no exception, save one: American exceptionalism and its culmination in the age of Obama. *Communication Monographs*, 83(4), 505–20. See also Valenzano, J. M. III, & Edwards, J. A. (2014). Exceptionally distinctive: President Obama's complicated articulation of American exceptionalism. In. A. Bareto and R. O'Bryant (Eds) *American identity in the age of Obama* (pp. 175–97). New York, NY: Routledge; and Edwards, J. A. (2014). Resetting America's role in the world: Barack Obama's rhetoric of (re)conciliation and partnership. In J. Mercieca and J. Vaughn (Eds) *The rhetoric of heroic expectations: Establishing the Obama presidency* (pp. 130–50). College Station, TX: Texas A&M University Press.

47 Quote from Barack Obama's keynote address at the Democratic National Convention on July 27, 2004, in Boston, MA. A transcript can be accessed at https://www.presidency.ucsb.edu.

48 Quote from Barack Obama's remarks at the United States Military Academy commencement ceremony on May 28, 2014, in West Point, NY. A transcript can be accessed at https://www.presidency.ucsb.edu.

49 Ronald Reagan delivered this farewell address on January 12, 1980, from Washington, D.C. A transcript can be accessed at https://www.presidency.ucsb.edu.

50 See Edwards, J. A. (2011). Contemporary conservative constructions of American exceptionalism. *Journal of Contemporary Rhetoric*, 1, 40–54.

51 George H. W. Bush delivered this speech at the Republican National Convention on August 18, 1988, in New Orleans, LA. A transcript can be accessed at https://www.presidency.ucsb.edu.

52 Dillin, J. (1989, September 21). Why the flag, of all things, became an election issue. *Christian Science Monitor*. Retrieved September 1, 2019, from Nexis database.

53 Quote from George H. W. Bush during the first presidential debate of the 1988 presidential election on September 25, 1988, in Winston-Salem, NC. A transcript can be accessed at https://www.presidency.ucsb.edu.

54 Quote in Vobejda, B. (1988, September 5). Bennett Dukakis crowd has "disdain" for pledge. *The Washington Post*. Retrieved September 1, 2019, from Nexis database.

55 Quote from William Clinton during the first presidential debate of the 1992 presidential election on October 11, 1992, in St. Louis, MO. A transcript can be accessed at https://www.presidency.ucsb.edu.

56 Quote in Crockett, C. E. (2012). *A murder of crows: America's raucous right-wing*. Bloomington, IN: Xlibris Corporation.

57 Quote from John Kerry's candidacy announcement on September 2, 2003, in Mount Pleasant, SC. A transcript can be accessed at https://www.presidency.ucsb.edu.

58   Quote in Toner, R. (2004, June 4). Kerry presents himself as a patriot with a different view. *New York Times*. Retrieved September 1, 2019, from Nexis database.

59   Quote in Blumenthal, S. (2004, February 12). Kerry will win the patriot game: Bush is trying and failing to dent the Democratic front runner's war record—just as Nixon did before him. *The Guardian*. Retrieved September 1, 2019, from Nexis database.

60   Quote in Balz, D. (2004, April 17). Citing his Vietnam service, Kerry assails Cheney, Rove. *The Washington Post*. Retrieved September 1, 2019, from Nexis database.

61   Quote from John Kerry's remarks to the Arizona Democratic Leadership Council on May 7, 2004, in Phoenix, AZ. A transcript can be accessed at https://www.presidency.ucsb.edu.

62   Quote in Cluchey, J. (2004, September 20). North on questioning Kerry's patriotism: "I will do that. I've done that." *Media Matters*. Retrieved from https://www.mediamatters.org/legacy/north-questioning-kerrys-patriotism-i-will-do-ive-done.

63   See Cohen, R. (2004, April 3). The Republicans' barb: John Kerry "looks French." *New York Times*. Retrieved September 1, 2019, from Nexis database.

64   All Swift Boat Veterans for Truth advertisements can be found at the group's website http://www.swiftvets.com.

65   Quote in Blitzer, W., Dougherty, J., & Chance, M. (2004, August 22). Interview with Bob Dole. *CNN Late Edition with Wolf Blitzer*. Retrieved September 1, 2019, from Nexis database.

66   Quote from John Kerry's remarks at a campaign rally at the University of Pittsburgh on April 16, 2004, in Pittsburgh, PA. A transcript can be accessed at https://www.presidency.ucsb.edu.

67   Quote in Thomas, E. (2004, November 15). The vets attack. *Newsweek*. Retrieved September 1, 2019, from Nexis database.

68   For more on issue ownership theory, see Petrocik, J. R. (1996). Issue ownership in presidential elections, with a 1980 case study. *American Journal of Political Science*, 40(3), 825–50; Petrocik, J. R., Benoit, W. L., & Hansen, G. J. (2003). Issue ownership and presidential campaigning, 1952–2000. *Political Science Quarterly*, 118(4), 599–626; Hayes, D. (2005). Candidate qualities through a partisan lens: A theory of trait ownership. *American Journal of Political Science*, 49(4), 908–23; Banda, K. K. (2016). Issue ownership, issue positions, and candidate assessment. *Political Communication*, 33(4), 651–66; Benoit, W. L. (2007). Own party issue ownership emphasis in presidential television spots. *Communication Reports*, 20(1), 42–50.

69   See Kalmoe, N. P., & Gross, K. (2016). Cueing patriotism, prejudice, and partisanship in the age of Obama: Experimental tests of US flag imagery effects in presidential elections. *Political Psychology*, 37(6), 883–99; Hart, R. P. (2009).

Campaign talk: Why elections are good for us. Princeton, NJ: Princeton University Press.

70   See Gilmore, J., & Rowling, C. M. (2019). Partisan patriotism in the American presidency: American exceptionalism, issue ownership, and the age of Trump. *Mass Communication and Society, 22*(3), 389–416.

71   Poll data from Roper Center for Public Opinion Research. (2018). *Yankee doodle polling: Public opinion on patriotism.* Retrieved from https://ropercenter.cornell.edu/yankee-doodle-polling-public-opinion-on-patriotism.

72   See Geraghty, J. (2008, June 9). Obama could debunk some rumors by releasing his birth certificate. *National Review Online.* Retrieved September 1, 2019, from https://www.nationalreview.com/the-campaign-spot/obama-could-debunk-some-rumors-releasing-his-birth-certificate-jim-geraghty.

73   Quotes from Obama's speech "The America We Love" delivered on June 30, 2008, in Independence, MO. A transcript can be accessed at https://www.presidency.ucsb.edu.

74   Poll data from Roper Center for Public Opinion Research. (2018). *Yankee doodle polling: Public opinion on patriotism.* Retrieved from https://ropercenter.cornell.edu/yankee-doodle-polling-public-opinion-on-patriotism.

75   Quotes taken from transcript and video found at Segarra, L. M. (2017, July 20). Watch John McCain defend Barack Obama during the 2008 campaign. *Time Magazine.* Retrieved September 1, 2019, from Nexis database.

76   Quotes from Obama's press conference on April 4, 2009, in Strasbourg, France. A transcript can be accessed at https://www.presidency.ucsb.edu.

77   Quote in Hannity, S. (2009, April 6). Analysis with Dick Morris. *Fox News Network.* Retrieved September 1, 2019, from Nexis database.

78   Quote in Kirchick, J. (2009, April 28). Squanderer in chief. *The Los Angeles Times.* Retrieved September 1, 2019, from Nexis database.

79   Quote in Gingrich, N. (2011). *A nation like no other: Why American exceptionalism matters.* New York, NY: Simon and Schuster.

80   Poll data from Gallup (2010). *USA Today/gallup poll: December wave 1, December 2010,* #10-12-022. [Data set]. Gallup Inc. [Distributor]. Retrieved from https://news.gallup.com/poll/145358/americans-exceptional-doubt-obama.aspx.

81   A collection of Trump's birther claims can be found at Kreig, G. (2016, September 16). 14 of Trump's most outrageous "birther" claims—Half from after 2011. *CNN.* Retrieved from https://www.cnn.com/2016/09/09/politics/donald-trump-birther/index.html.

82   Quotes from Obama's address at the 2011 White House Correspondents Dinner on April 30, 2011, in Washington, D.C. A transcript can be accessed at https://www.presidency.ucsb.edu.

83   Poll data from Newport, F. (2011). Americans' beliefs about Obama's birth. *Gallup.* Retrieved from https://news.gallup.com/opinion/polling-matters/169724/americans-beliefs-obama-birth.aspx.

84   Poll data from Roper Center for Public Opinion Research. (2018). *Yankee doodle polling: Public opinion on patriotism*. Retrieved from https://ropercenter.cornell.edu/yankee-doodle-polling-public-opinion-on-patriotism.

85   Quotes from Mitt Romney's speech announcing his candidacy for the presidency on June 2, 2011, in Stratham, NH. A transcript can be accessed at https://www.presidency.ucsb.edu.

86   Quotes from Romney's speech on U.S. foreign policy on October 7, 2011, at The Citadel in Charleston, SC. A transcript can be accessed at https://www.presidency.ucsb.edu.

87   Quoted in Dwyer, D. (2012, April 2). Obama rebuffs Romney on "American exceptionalism." *ABC News.com*. Retrieved from http://abcnews.go.com/blogs/politics/2012/04/obama-rebuffs-romney-on-american-exceptionalism/.

88   Quote in Obama's news conference with the presidents of Mexico and Canada on April 2, 2012, in Washington, D.C. A transcript can be accessed at https://www.presidency.ucsb.edu.

89   Quote in Jindal, B. (2015, February 9). Jindal on why Obama refuses to acknowledge radical Islam. *Hannity. Fox News.com*. Retrieved from http://video.foxnews.com/v/4041687062001/jindal-on–why-obama-refuses-to-acknowledge-radical-islam/?playlist_id=2114913880001#sp=show-clips/primetime.

90   Quote in Bever, L. (2015, February 19). Report: Rudy Giuliani tells private dinner "I do not believe that the president loves America." *Washington Post*. Retrieved from http://www.washingtonpost.com/news/morning-mix/wp/2015/02/19/report-rudy-giuliani-tells-private-dinner-i-do-not-believe-that-the-president-loves-america/.

91   Kelly, M. (2015, February 20). Giuliani defends Obama's criticism, says president doesn't believe in American exceptionalism. *Fox News*. Retrieved from http://www.foxnews.com/politics/2015/02/20/giuliani-defends-obama-criticism-says-president-doesnt-believe-in-american/.

92   Quote in Hensch, M. (2015, September 2). Cheney: Obama rejects American exceptionalism. *The Hill*. Retrieved from http://thehill.com/blogs/blog-briefing-room/news/252551-cheney-obama-rejects-american-exceptionalism.

93   Quotes from Cheney, D., Cheney, R. B., & Cheney, L. (2016). *Exceptional: Why the world needs a powerful America*. New York, NY: Simon and Schuster.

94   Quote from Republican National Committee. (2016). *Republican platform: America resurgent*. Retrieved from http://www.gop.com/platform.

Chapter 2

1   Quote from Republican National Committee. (2016). *Republican platform: America resurgent*. Retrieved from http://www.gop.com/platform.

2   Quote in Trump, D. J. (2015). *Crippled America: How to make America great again.* New York, NY: Simon and Schuster.

3   Quotes from the fourth Republican Debate on November 10, 2015, in Milwaukee, WI. A transcript can be accessed at https://time.com/4107636/transcript-read-the-full-text-of-the-fourth-republican-debate-in-milwaukee/.

4   Johnson, J. (2016, July 21). Donald Trump's vision of doom and despair in America. *Washington Post.* Retrieved from https://www.washingtonpost.com/politics/donald-trumps-message-of-doom-and-despair-in-america/2016/07/21/8afe4cae-3f22-11e6-80bc-d06711fd2125_story.html.

5   Fisher, M. (2015, October 31). Seeking America's "lost" greatness and finding Trump most appealing. *Washington Post.* Retrieved from https://www.washingtonpost.com/politics/seeking-americas-lost-greatness-and-finding-trump-most-appealing/2015/10/31/2435e06e-7c12-11e5-b575-d8dcfedb4ea1_story.html.

6   Anholt, S. (2016, March 17). Is Trump tarnishing the American brand. *The Guardian.* Retrieved from https://www.theguardian.com/commentisfree/2016/mar/17/donald-trump-america-reputation.

7   Quotes in Corn, D. (2016, June 7). Donald Trump says he doesn't believe in "American exceptionalism." *Mother Jones.* Retrieved from http://www.motherjones.com/politics/2016/06/donald-trump-american-exceptionalism.

8   Jendrysik, M. S. (2002). The modern jeremiad: Bloom, Bennett, and Bork on American decline. *The Journal of Popular Culture,* 36(2), 361–83; Jendrysik, M. S. (2008). *Modern Jeremiahs: Contemporary visions of American decline.* Lanham, MD: Lexington Books.

9   Van Engen, A. C. (2020). *City on a hill: A history of American exceptionalism.* New Haven, CT: Yale University Press.

10 See Bercovitch, S. (2012). *The American jeremiad.* Madison, WI: University of Wisconsin Press; Bostdorff, D. M. (2003). George W. Bush's post-September 11 rhetoric of covenant renewal: Upholding the faith of the greatest generation. *Quarterly Journal of Speech,* 89(4), 293–319.

11 Johannesen, R. L. (1986). Ronald Reagan's economic jeremiad. *Communication Studies,* 37(2), 79–89; Murphy, J. M. (1990). "A time of shame and sorrow": Robert F. Kennedy and the American jeremiad. *Quarterly Journal of Speech,* 76(4), 401–14.

12 Quote from Jendrysik, M. S. (2008). *Modern Jeremiahs: Contemporary visions of American decline.* Lanham, MD: Lexington Books.

13 Ritter, K. W. (1980). American political rhetoric and the jeremiad tradition: Presidential nomination acceptance addresses, 1960–1976. *Communication Studies,* 31(3), 153–71.

14 Mitt Romney delivered these remarks on October 7, 2012, in Charleston, SC. A transcript can be accessed at https://www.presidency.ucsb.edu.

15 Donald Trump delivered these remarks on September 15, 2016, in New York, NY. A transcript can be accessed at https://www.presidency.ucsb.edu.

16 Barack Obama delivered these remarks on September 9, 2008, in Dayton, OH. A transcript can be accessed at https://www.presidency.ucsb.edu.

17 See Gilmore, J., Rowling, C. M., Edwards, J. A., & Allen, N. T. (2020). Exceptional "we" or exceptional "me"? Donald Trump, American exceptionalism and the remaking of the modern jeremiad. *Presidential Studies Quarterly*. Advance Online Publication. https://doi.org/10.1111/psq.12657.

18 See Gilmore, J. (2014). Translating American exceptionalism: Presidential discourse about the United States in comparative perspective. *International Journal of Communication*, 9(22), 2416–37. Also Gilmore, J., Sheets, P., & Rowling, C. M. (2016). Make no exception, save one: American exceptionalism and its culmination in the age of Obama. *Communication Monographs*, 83(4), 505–20; Gilmore, J., & Rowling, C. M. (2018). Lighting the Beacon: Presidential discourse, American exceptionalism, and public diplomacy in global contexts. *Presidential Studies Quarterly*, 48(2), 271–91; Gilmore, J., & Rowling, C. M. (2019). Partisan patriotism in the American presidency: American exceptionalism, issue ownership, and the age of Trump. *Mass Communication and Society*, 22(3), 389–416.

19 Although research has suggested that the two approaches to foreign policy associated with these themes are at odds with one another as they split along the interventionist (global leader) and the isolationist (exemplar) divide, US politicians routinely invoke both themes, often in tandem, in their political speeches, regardless of their foreign policy orientation. We are, therefore, interested in how these two themes manifest as rhetorical devices in presidential discourse, not as foreign policy outcomes.

20 To be specific, we analyzed all references to the United States as being singular, superior, a model for, or the leader of the rest of the world. First, one person identified all references to any of the four types of American exceptionalism in a 12 percent sampling of speeches. In order to check for accuracy, a second person independently analyzed those same speeches for the themes. Agreement between the readers was high, with a Krippendorff's alpha of 0.91 across the types of American exceptionalism. This exceeds the required sample level for reliable intercoder results. See Neuendorf, Kimberly A. (2016). *The content analysis guidebook*. Thousand Oaks, CA: Sage Publications. The same coding criteria were used for all speeches analyzed in this book.

21 In terms of breadth of invocations, a chi square test of independence found there to be significant differences between candidates (X^2 (3, $N = 332$) = 77.94, $p = 000$), with Trump invoking American exceptionalism significantly less than the average overall ($z = -7.36$, $p = .000$).

22 In terms of depth of invocation, an analysis of variance (ANOVA) found there to be significant differences between candidates in their average rates of invocations

of American exceptionalism per speech ($F(3, 328) = 21.24$, $p = .000$, $\eta_p^2 = .163$). Post-hoc Tukey tests showed that Trump invoked American exceptionalism ($M = .38$) significantly less than Kerry ($M = 2.17$, $p = .001$), Obama ($M = 2.18$, $p = .001$), and Romney ($M = 3.98$, $p = .000$).

23 Donald Trump delivered these remarks on August 18, 2016, in Charlotte, NC. A transcript can be accessed at https://www.presidency.ucsb.edu.

24 John Kerry delivered these remarks on May 7, 2004, in Washington, D.C. A transcript can be accessed at https://www.presidency.ucsb.edu.

25 Barack Obama delivered these remarks on July 26, 2007, in Columbia, SC. A transcript can be accessed at https://www.presidency.ucsb.edu.

26 Donald Trump delivered these remarks on August 15, 2016, in Youngstown, OH. A transcript can be accessed at https://www.presidency.ucsb.edu.

27 Mitt Romney delivered these remarks on February 10, 2012, in Washington, D.C. A transcript can be accessed at https://www.presidency.ucsb.edu.

28 For more on the debate on the effects of Trump's America First policy on American exceptionalism, see Edwards, J. A. (2018). Make America great again: Donald Trump and the redefining of the U.S. role in the world. *Communication Quarterly*, 66, 176–95; Restad, H. E. (2019). Whither the "city upon a hill"? Donald Trump, America first, and American exceptionalism. *Texas National Security Review*, 3(1), 62–92; Restad, H. E. (2020). What makes America great? Donald Trump, national identity, and U.S. foreign policy. *Global Affairs*, 6(1), 21–36; and Van Engen, A. C. (2020). *City on a hill: A history of American exceptionalism*. New Haven, CT: Yale University Press.

29 John Kerry delivered these remarks on May 7, 2004, in Washington, D.C. A transcript can be accessed at https://www.presidency.ucsb.edu.

30 Barack Obama delivered these remarks on June 19, 2007, in Washington, D.C. A transcript can be accessed at https://www.presidency.ucsb.edu.

31 Mitt Romney delivered these remarks on October 7, 2011, in Charleston, SC. A transcript can be accessed at https://www.presidency.ucsb.edu.

32 Donald Trump delivered these remarks on November 1, 2016, in Valley Forge, PA. A transcript can be accessed at https://www.presidency.ucsb.edu.

33 Donald Trump delivered these remarks on August 9, 2016, in Wilmington, NC. A transcript can be accessed at https://www.presidency.ucsb.edu.

34 See Gilmore, J., Rowling, C. M., Edwards, J. A., & Allen, N. T. (2020). Exceptional "we" or exceptional "me"? Donald Trump, American exceptionalism and the remaking of the modern jeremiad. *Presidential Studies Quarterly*. Advance Online Publication. https://doi.org/10.1111/psq.12657.

35 Agreement between the readers was again high, with a Krippendorff's alpha of 0.89 on all references to American *un*exceptionalism. The same coding criteria were used for all speeches analyzed in this book.

36 In terms of breadth of invocations, a chi square test of independence found there to be significant differences between candidates ($X^2 (3, N = 332) = 47.87$, $p = 000$),

with Trump invoking American unexceptionalism significantly more than the average overall ($z = 6.26, p = .000$).

37 In terms of depth of invocations, an analysis of variance (ANOVA) found there to be significant differences between candidates on their average rates of invocations per speech ($F(3, 328) = 19.89, p = .000, \eta_p^2 = .154$). Post-hoc Tukey tests showed that Trump invoked American unexceptionalism ($M = .76$) significantly more than Kerry ($M = .22, p = .000$), Obama ($M = .05, p = .000$), and Romney ($M = .19, p = .000$).

38 Barack Obama delivered these remarks on July 26, 2007, in Columbia, SC. A transcript can be accessed at https://www.presidency.ucsb.edu.

39 John Kerry delivered these remarks on March 28, 2004, in St. Louis, MO. A transcript can be accessed at https://www.presidency.ucsb.edu.

40 Mitt Romney delivered these remarks on September 27, 2012, in Springfield, VA. A transcript can be accessed at https://www.presidency.ucsb.edu.

41 Donald Trump delivered these remarks on September 15, 2016, in New York, NY. A transcript can be accessed at https://www.presidency.ucsb.edu.

42 Donald Trump delivered these remarks on August 31, 2016, in Phoenix, AZ. A transcript can be accessed at https://www.presidency.ucsb.edu.

43 Donald Trump delivered these remarks on June 16, 2015, in New York, NY. A transcript can be accessed at https://www.presidency.ucsb.edu.

44 Donald Trump delivered these remarks on September 9, 2016, in Washington, D.C. A transcript can be accessed at https://www.presidency.ucsb.edu.

45 Donald Trump delivered these remarks on June 16, 2015, in New York, NY. A transcript can be accessed at https://www.presidency.ucsb.edu.

46 Donald Trump delivered these remarks on August 12, 2016, in Erie, PA. A transcript can be accessed at https://www.presidency.ucsb.edu.

47 Donald Trump delivered these remarks on September 22, 2016, in Pittsburgh, PA. A transcript can be accessed at https://www.presidency.ucsb.edu.

48 Donald Trump delivered these remarks on October 27, 2016, in Springfield, OH. A transcript can be accessed at https://www.presidency.ucsb.edu.

49 Donald Trump delivered these remarks on June 16, 2015, in New York, NY. A transcript can be accessed at https://www.presidency.ucsb.edu.

50 Donald Trump delivered these remarks on November 7, 2016, in Raleigh, NC. A transcript can be accessed at https://www.presidency.ucsb.edu.

Chapter 3

1 Donald Trump delivered these remarks on June 16, 2015, in New York, NY. A transcript can be accessed at https://www.presidency.ucsb.edu.

2 Ivanka Trump delivered these remarks on July 21, 2016, in Cleveland, OH. A transcript can be accessed at https://www.presidency.ucsb.edu. https://time.com/4417579/.

3   Donald Trump delivered these remarks on July 21, 2016, in Cleveland, OH. A transcript can be accessed at https://www.presidency.ucsb.edu.

4   Johnson, J. (2016, July 21). Donald Trump's vision of Doom and Despair in America. *The Washington Post*. Retrieved from https://www.washingtonpost. com/politics/donald-trumps-message-of-doom-and-despair-in-america/2016/07/21/8afe4cae-3f22-11e6-80bc-d06711fd2125_story.html.

5   John Kerry delivered these remarks on September 2, 2003, in Patriot's Point, SC. A transcript can be accessed at https://www.presidency.ucsb.edu.

6   Barack Obama delivered these remarks on May 13, 2008, in Cape Girardeau, MO. A transcript can be accessed at https://www.presidency.ucsb.edu.

7   Mitt Romney delivered these remarks on June 2, 2011, in Charleston, SC. A transcript can be accessed at https://www.presidency.ucsb.edu.

8   Donald Trump delivered these remarks on June 22, 2016, in New York, NY. A transcript can be accessed at https://www.presidency.ucsb.edu.

9   Donald Trump delivered these remarks on August 5, 2016, in Green Bay, WI. A transcript can be accessed at https://www.presidency.ucsb.edu.

10   Donald Trump delivered these remarks on June 16, 2015, in New York, NY. A transcript can be accessed at https://www.presidency.ucsb.edu.

11   Quoted in Wheeler, L. (2015, August 9). Rand Paul: Trump a "fake conservative." *The Hill*. Retrieved from https://thehill.com/homenews/sunday-talk-shows/250679-rand-paul-trump-could-be-a-liberal

12   Quoted in Taylor, J. (2016, August 8). GOP Senator Susan Collins says she can't support Donald Trump. *NPR*. Retrieved from https://thehill.com/homenews/sunday-talk-shows/250679-rand-paul-trump-could-be-a-liberal.

13   Donald Trump delivered these remarks on September 9, 2016, in Pensacola, FL. A transcript can be accessed at https://www.presidency.ucsb.edu.

14   realDonaldTrump. (2016, May 9). I will win the election against Crooked Hillary despite the people in the republican party that are currently and selfishly opposed to me! [tweet] Retrieved from https://twitter.com/realdonaldtrump/status/729604 845716516864?lang=en.

15   Donald Trump delivered these remarks on June 16, 2015, in New York, NY. A transcript can be accessed at https://www.presidency.ucsb.edu.

16   Donald Trump delivered these remarks on August 18, 2016, in Charlotte, NC. A transcript can be accessed at https://www.presidency.ucsb.edu.

17   Quotes from the ninth GOP presidential debate in Greenville, SC. A transcript can be accessed at https://www.presidency.ucsb.edu.

18   CSPAN. (2016, July 18). Presidential candidate Donald Trump at the family leadership summit. (Full Video) [Video File]. Retrieved from https://www.c-span. org/video/?327045-5/presidential-candidate-donald-trump-family-leadership-summit.

19 Quoted in Schreckinger, B. (2015, July 18). Trump attacks McCain: "I like people Who weren't captured." *POLITICO*. Retrieved from https://www.politico.com/story/2015/07/trump-attacks-mccain-i-like-people-who-werent-captured-120317.

20 Quoted in Bradner, E. & Treyz, C. (2016, March 3). Romney implores: Bring down Trump. *CNN*. Retrieved from https://www.cnn.com/2016/03/03/politics/mitt-romney-presidential-race-speech/index.html

21 realDonaldTrump. (2016, March 3). Failed candidate Mitt Romney, who ran one of the worst races in presidential history, is working with the establishment to bury a big "R" win! [tweet] Retrieved from https://twitter.com/realDonaldTrump/status/705352657234481152

22 realDonaldTrump. (2016, March 3). I have brought millions of people into the republican party, while the dems are going down. Establishment wants to kill this movement! [tweet] Retrieved from https://twitter.com/realDonaldTrump/status/705354682886201348.

23 See, for example, Isenstadt, A. (2016, March 3). Welcome to the GOP civil war. *POLITICO*. Retrieved from https://www.politico.com/story/2016/03/gop-civil-war-2016-republicans-220209.

24 realDonaldTrump. (2016, October 10). Paul Ryan should spend more time on balancing the budget, jobs and illegal immigration and not waste his time on fighting republican nominee [tweet] Retrieved from https://twitter.com/realDonaldTrump/status/785530928256933888

25 realDonaldTrump. (2016, October 11). Despite winning the second debate in a landslide (every poll), it is hard to do when Paul Ryan and others give zero support! [tweet] Retrieved from https://twitter.com/realDonaldTrump/status/785816454042124288.

26 realDonaldTrump. (2016, October 11). Disloyal R's are far more difficult than Crooked Hillary. They come at you from all sides. They don't know how to win—I will teach them! [tweet] Retrieved from https://twitter.com/realDonaldTrump/status/785854588654092290

27 Waldman, P. (2016, May 26). Trump's attacks on other republicans matter. They show he is unfit for the presidency. *The Washington Post*. Retrieved from https://www.washingtonpost.com/blogs/plum-line/wp/2016/05/26/trumps-attacks-on-other-republicans-matter-they-show-he-is-unfit-for-the-presidency/.

28 To be specific, we ran a word search on all invocations in which a candidate iterated the word "politician" or "politicians" and then identified if the reference was innocuous or if it was used to place blame on them for the problems in the country.

29 Mitt Romney delivered these remarks on September 2, 2011, in Tampa, FL. A transcript can be accessed at https://www.presidency.ucsb.edu.

30 Mitt Romney delivered these remarks on February 10, 2012, in Washington, D.C. A transcript can be accessed at https://www.presidency.ucsb.edu.

31 Barack Obama delivered these remarks on February 13, 2008, in Janesville, WI. A transcript can be accessed at https://www.presidency.ucsb.edu.

32 Donald Trump delivered these remarks on June 22, 2016, in New York, NY. A transcript can be accessed at https://www.presidency.ucsb.edu.

33 Donald Trump delivered these remarks on October 22, 2016, in Gettysburg, PA. A transcript can be accessed at https://www.presidency.ucsb.edu.

34 Garcia, E. (2016, October 18). A history of "draining the swamp." *Roll Call*. Retrieved from https://www.rollcall.com/2016/10/18/a-history-of-draining-the-swamp/.

35 Garcia, E. (2016, October 18). A history of "draining the swamp." *Roll Call*. Retrieved from https://www.rollcall.com/2016/10/18/a-history-of-draining-the-swamp/.

36 Donald Trump delivered these remarks on October 17, 2016, in Newton, PA. A transcript can be accessed at https://www.presidency.ucsb.edu.

37 realDonaldTrump. (2016, October 18). I will make our government honest again—believe me. But first, I'm going to have to #DrainTheSwamp in DC. [tweet] Retrieved from https://twitter.com/realDonaldTrump/status/788402585816276992.

38 Donald Trump delivered these remarks on November 7, 2016, in Raleigh, NC. A transcript can be accessed at https://www.presidency.ucsb.edu.

39 Donald Trump delivered these remarks on October 22, 2016, in Gettysburg, PA. A transcript can be accessed at https://www.presidency.ucsb.edu.

40 Donald Trump delivered these remarks on April 27, 2016, in Green Bay, WI. A transcript can be accessed at https://www.presidency.ucsb.edu.

41 Donald Trump delivered these remarks on August 30, 2016, in Everett, WA. A transcript can be accessed at https://www.presidency.ucsb.edu.

42 Donald Trump delivered these remarks on June 22, 2016, in New York, NY. A transcript can be accessed at https://www.presidency.ucsb.edu.

43 Donald Trump delivered these remarks on November 9, 2016, in New York, NY. A transcript can be accessed at https://www.presidency.ucsb.edu.

44 Donald Trump delivered these remarks on June 16, 2015, in New York, NY. A transcript can be accessed at https://www.presidency.ucsb.edu.

45 Donald Trump delivered these remarks on June 22, 2016, in New York, NY. A transcript can be accessed at https://www.presidency.ucsb.edu.

46 See Benoit, P. J. (1997). *Telling the success story: Acclaiming and disclaiming discourse*. Albany, NY: SUNY Press; Benoit, W. L., Blaney, J. R., & Pier, P. M. (2000). Acclaiming, attacking, and defending: A functional analysis of US nominating convention keynote speeches. *Political Communication*, 17(1), 61–84;

and Benoit, W. L. (2001). The functional approach to presidential television spots: Acclaiming, attacking, defending 1952–2000. *Communication Studies*, 52(2), 109–26. doi: 10.1080/10510970109388546.

47 See Gilmore, J., Rowling, C. M., Edwards, J. A., & Allen, N. T. (2020). Exceptional "we" or exceptional "me"? Donald Trump, American exceptionalism and the remaking of the modern jeremiad. *Presidential Studies Quarterly*. Advance Online Publication. https://doi.org/10.1111/psq.12657.

48 Agreement between the readers was again high, with a Krippendorff's alpha of 0.87 on all references to American *un*exceptionalism. The same coding criteria were used for all speeches analyzed in this book.

49 Trump invoked self-exceptionalism significantly and overwhelmingly more than the other opposition candidates in both breadth (X^2 (3, N = 332) = 47.87, p = .000) and depth (F(3, 328) = 19.89, p = .000, η_p^2 = .307) of invocations.

50 Mitt Romney delivered these remarks on September 26, 2012, in Washington, D.C. A transcript can be accessed at https://www.presidency.ucsb.edu.

51 Donald Trump delivered these remarks on June 16, 2015, in New York, NY. A transcript can be accessed at https://www.presidency.ucsb.edu.

52 Trump, again, was by and large alone in this tactic. Notably, John Kerry never referred to himself in the third person. Mitt Romney did it once saying, "I told you I'm going to do five things and I want you to know what they are so when your friends ask you why are you voting for Mitt Romney you can say, look, the things that he's going to do that are going to get this economy going." Among Trump's predecessors, Barack Obama referred to himself in the third person the most. Specifically, on five separate occasions, he invoked his name as a way of building the story that it was "unlikely" that a person with a "funny name" like Barack Obama could be running for president. Specifically, he offered: "I would not be on this stage if generations of Americans had not fought before me so that the American dream could be extended to a man named Barack Obama." These examples, however, pale in comparison to how often Trump used this tactic.

53 Donald Trump delivered these remarks on June 16, 2015, in New York, NY. A transcript can be accessed at https://www.presidency.ucsb.edu.

54 Donald Trump delivered these remarks on June 16, 2015, in New York, NY. A transcript can be accessed at https://www.presidency.ucsb.edu.

55 Donald Trump delivered these remarks on December 30, 2015, in Hilton Head, SC. A transcript can be accessed at https://www.presidency.ucsb.edu.

56 Donald Trump delivered these remarks on March 22, 2016, in Washington, D.C. A transcript can be accessed at https://www.presidency.ucsb.edu.

57 Donald Trump delivered these remarks on June 13, 2016, in Manchester, NH. A transcript can be accessed at https://www.presidency.ucsb.edu.

58   Donald Trump delivered these remarks on June 16, 2015, in New York, NY. A transcript can be accessed at https://www.presidency.ucsb.edu.

59   Donald Trump delivered these remarks on August 5, 2015, in Green Bay, WI. A transcript can be accessed at https://www.presidency.ucsb.edu.

60   Donald Trump delivered these remarks on July 21, 2016, in Cleveland, OH. A transcript can be accessed at https://www.presidency.ucsb.edu.

61   Donald Trump delivered these remarks on October 3, 2016, in Pueblo, CO. A transcript can be accessed at https://www.presidency.ucsb.edu.

62   Donald Trump delivered these remarks on October 3, 2016, in Pueblo, CO. A transcript can be accessed at https://www.presidency.ucsb.edu.

63   Donald Trump delivered these remarks on October 12, 2016, in Ocala, FL. A transcript can be accessed at https://www.presidency.ucsb.edu.

64   Quoted in Neuman, S. (2018, May 2). Doctor: Trump dictated letter attesting to his "extraordinary" health. *NPR*. Retrieved from https://www.npr.org/sections/thetwo-way/2018/05/02/607638733/doctor-trump-dictated-letter-attesting-to-his-extraordinary-health.

65   Donald Trump delivered these remarks on July 27, 2016, in Doral, FL. A transcript can be accessed at https://www.presidency.ucsb.edu.

66   Donald Trump delivered these remarks on March 21, 2016, in Washington, D.C. A transcript can be accessed at https://www.presidency.ucsb.edu..

67   Donald Trump delivered these remarks on July 16, 2016, in New York, NY. A transcript can be accessed at https://www.presidency.ucsb.edu.

68   Donald Trump delivered these remarks on November 7, 2016, in Raleigh, NC. A transcript can be accessed at https://www.presidency.ucsb.edu.

69   Donald Trump delivered these remarks on August 5, 2016, in Green Bay, WI. A transcript can be accessed at https://www.presidency.ucsb.edu.

70   Donald Trump delivered these remarks on October 18, 2016, in Colorado Springs, CO. A transcript can be accessed at https://www.presidency.ucsb.edu.

71   Donald Trump delivered these remarks on August 30, 2016, in Everett, WA. A transcript can be accessed at https://www.presidency.ucsb.edu.

72   Donald Trump delivered these remarks on September 9, 2016, in Washington, D.C. A transcript can be accessed at https://www.presidency.ucsb.edu.

73   Donald Trump delivered these remarks on September 22, 2016, in Pittsburgh, PA. A transcript can be accessed at https://www.presidency.ucsb.edu.

74   Donald Trump delivered these remarks on September 15, 2016, in New York, NY. A transcript can be accessed at https://www.presidency.ucsb.edu.

75   Donald Trump delivered these remarks on August 30, 2016, in Everett, WA. A transcript can be accessed at https://www.presidency.ucsb.edu.

76   Donald Trump delivered these remarks on August 24, 2016, in Jackson, MS. A transcript can be accessed at https://www.presidency.ucsb.edu.

77   Donald Trump delivered these remarks on August 9, 2016, in Wilmington, NC. A transcript can be accessed at https://www.presidency.ucsb.edu.

78   Donald Trump delivered these remarks on June 16, 2015, in New York, NY. A transcript can be accessed at https://www.presidency.ucsb.edu.

79   Donald Trump delivered these remarks on November 7, 2016, in Raleigh, NC. A transcript can be accessed at https://www.presidency.ucsb.edu.

80   Donald Trump delivered these remarks on November 2, 2016, in Miami, FL. A transcript can be accessed at https://www.presidency.ucsb.edu.

81   Donald Trump delivered these remarks on October 27, 2016, in Springfield, OH. A transcript can be accessed at https://www.presidency.ucsb.edu.

82   Donald Trump delivered these remarks on October 23, 2016, in Naples, FL. A transcript can be accessed at https://www.presidency.ucsb.edu.

83   Donald Trump delivered these remarks on November 7, 2016, in Raleigh, NC. A transcript can be accessed at https://www.presidency.ucsb.edu.

84   Trump did not limit his exceptional praise to himself and his movement. He regularly praised those in his campaign as being exceptional as well. In reference to his vice presidential candidate, Mike Pence, he offered: "Governor Pence enacted the largest income tax cut in the state's history" and "Mike had the single most decisive victory in the history of Vice-Presidential Debates."

85   Donald Trump delivered these remarks on July 27, 2016, in Doral, FL. A transcript can be accessed at https://www.presidency.ucsb.edu.

86   Donald Trump delivered these remarks on July 21, 2016, in Cleveland, OH. A transcript can be accessed at https://www.presidency.ucsb.edu.

87   Donald Trump delivered these remarks on July 27, 2016, in Doral, FL. A transcript can be accessed at https://www.presidency.ucsb.edu.

88   Donald Trump delivered these remarks on October 18, 2016, in Colorado Springs, CO. A transcript can be accessed at https://www.presidency.ucsb.edu.

89   Donald Trump delivered these remarks on August 19, 2016, in Dimondale, MI. A transcript can be accessed at https://www.presidency.ucsb.edu.

90   Donald Trump delivered these remarks on October 31, 2016, in Warren, MI. A transcript can be accessed at https://www.presidency.ucsb.edu.

91   Donald Trump delivered these remarks on October 18, 2016, in Colorado Springs, CO. A transcript can be accessed at https://www.presidency.ucsb.edu.

92   Donald Trump delivered these remarks on September 14, 2016, in Canton, OH. A transcript can be accessed at https://www.presidency.ucsb.edu.

93   Donald Trump delivered these remarks on October 12, 2016, in Ocala, FL. A transcript can be accessed at https://www.presidency.ucsb.edu.

94   Donald Trump delivered these remarks on August 12, 2016, in Erie, PA. A transcript can be accessed at https://www.presidency.ucsb.edu.

95 Donald Trump delivered these remarks on November 7, 2016, in Raleigh, NC. A transcript can be accessed at https://www.presidency.ucsb.edu.

96 Donald Trump delivered these remarks on November 2, 2016, in Miami, FL. A transcript can be accessed at https://www.presidency.ucsb.edu.

97 Quote in Trump, D. J. (2015). *Crippled America: How to make America great again.* New York, NY: Simon and Schuster.

98 Jendrysik, M. S. (2002). The modern jeremiad: Bloom, Bennett, and Bork on American decline. *The Journal of Popular Culture*, 36(2), 361–83; Jendrysik, M. S. (2008). *Modern jeremiahs: Contemporary visions of American decline.* Lanham, MD: Lexington Books; Ritter, K. W. (1980). American Political rhetoric and the jeremiad tradition: Presidential nomination acceptance addresses, 1960–1976. *Communication Studies*, 31(3), 153–71.

99 Quote in Trump, D. J. (2015). *Crippled America: How to make America great again.* New York, NY: Simon and Schuster.

100 Donald Trump delivered these remarks on October 13, 2016, in Palm Beach, FL. A transcript can be accessed at https://www.presidency.ucsb.edu.

Chapter 4

1 Donald Trump delivered these remarks on January 9, 2020, in Toldedo, Ohio. A transcript can be accessed at https://www.presidency.ucsb.edu.

2 See Weprin, A. (2017, January 24). Trump campaign applies to trademark "keep America great!." *POLITICO*. Retrieved from https://www.politico.com/blogs/on-media/2017/01/trump-trademark-keep-america-great-234110

3 Donald Trump delivered these remarks on January 20, 2017, in Washington, D.C. A transcript can be accessed at https://www.presidency.ucsb.edu.

4 Donald Trump delivered these remarks on February 28, 2017, in Washington, D.C. A transcript can be accessed at https://www.presidency.ucsb.edu.

5 Donald Trump delivered these remarks on February 18, 2017, in Melbourne, FL. A transcript can be accessed at https://www.presidency.ucsb.edu.

6 Donald Trump delivered these remarks on April 29, 2017, in Harrisburg, PA. A transcript can be accessed at https://www.presidency.ucsb.edu.

7 Donald Trump delivered these remarks on February 16, 2017, in Washington, D.C. A transcript can be accessed at https://www.presidency.ucsb.edu.

8 realDonaldTrump. (2019, December 10). To impeach a president who has proven through results, including producing perhaps the strongest economy in our country's history, to have one of the most successful presidencies ever, and most importantly, who has done NOTHING wrong, is sheer political madness! #2020Election [tweet]. Retrieved from https://twitter.com/realdonaldtrump/status/1204379706235203586?lang=en.

9   Donald Trump delivered these remarks on December 10, 2019, in Hershey, PA. A transcript can be accessed at https://www.presidency.ucsb.edu.

10   Quote in Domke, D. and Coe, K. (2010). *The god strategy: How religion became a weapon in America*. Oxford, UK: Oxford University Press. P. 53.

11   Ronald Reagan delivered these remarks on January 20, 1981, in Washington, D.C. A transcript can be accessed at https://www.presidency.ucsb.edu.

12   Barrack Obama delivered these remarks on January 20, 2009, in Washington, D.C. A transcript can be accessed at https://www.presidency.ucsb.edu.

13   Donald Trump delivered these remarks on January 20, 2017 in Washington, D.C. A transcript can be accessed at https://www.presidency.ucsb.edu.

14   Donald Trump delivered these remarks on February 18, 2017, in Melbourne, FL. A transcript can be accessed at https://www.presidency.ucsb.edu.

15   Donald Trump delivered these remarks on August 15, 2019, in Manchester, NH. A transcript can be accessed at https://www.presidency.ucsb.edu.

16   Donald Trump delivered these remarks on November 1, 2018, in Columbia, MO. A transcript can be accessed at https://www.presidency.ucsb.edu.

17   Donald Trump delivered these remarks on November 5, 2018, in Cape Girardeau, MO. A transcript can be accessed at https://www.presidency.ucsb.edu.

18   Donald Trump delivered these remarks on July 17, 2019, in Greenville, NC. A transcript can be accessed at https://www.presidency.ucsb.edu.

19   Donald Trump delivered these remarks on January 14, 2020, in Milwaukee, WI. A transcript can be accessed at https://www.presidency.ucsb.edu.

20   Bill Clinton delivered these remarks on January 20, 1993, in Washington, D.C. A transcript can be accessed at https://www.presidency.ucsb.edu.

21   Bill Clinton delivered these remarks on January 20, 1997, in Washington, D.C. A transcript can be accessed at https://www.presidency.ucsb.edu.

22   George W. Bush delivered these remarks on September 11, 2002, in Washington, D.C. A transcript can be accessed at https://www.presidency.ucsb.edu.

23   George W. Bush delivered these remarks on September 2, 2004, in New York, NY. A transcript can be accessed at https://www.presidency.ucsb.edu.

24   Ronald Reagan delivered these remarks on November 22, 1982, in Washington, D.C. A transcript can be accessed at https://www.presidency.ucsb.edu.

25   Ronald Reagan delivered these remarks on January 25, 1984, in Washington, D.C. A transcript can be accessed at https://www.presidency.ucsb.edu.

26   Donald Trump delivered these remarks on January April 13, 2018, in Washington, D.C. A transcript can be accessed at https://www.presidency.ucsb.edu.

27   Donald Trump delivered these remarks on July 17, 2019, in Greenville, NC. A transcript can be accessed at https://www.presidency.ucsb.edu.

28   Barrack Obama delivered these remarks on January 27, 2010, in Washington, D.C. A transcript can be accessed at https://www.presidency.ucsb.edu.

29 Harry Truman delivered these remarks on January 7, 1948, in Washington, D.C. A transcript can be accessed at https://www.presidency.ucsb.edu.

30 Lyndon Johnson delivered these remarks on January 8, 1964, in Washington, D.C. A transcript can be accessed at https://www.presidency.ucsb.edu.

31 Lyndon Johnson delivered these remarks on January 4, 1965, in Washington, D.C. A transcript can be accessed at https://www.presidency.ucsb.edu.

32 Donald Trump delivered these remarks on November 1, 2018, in Washington, D.C. A transcript can be accessed at https://www.presidency.ucsb.edu.

33 realDonaldTrump. (2019, June 28). The stock market went up massively from the day after I won the election, all the way up to the day that i took office, because of the enthusiasm for the fact that I was going to be president. That big stock market increase must be credited to me. If Hillary won—a big crash! [tweet] Retrieved from https://twitter.com/realdonaldtrump/status/1144533973428842496?lang=en.

34 realDonaldTrump. (2018, January 24). Will soon be heading to Davos, Switzerland, to tell the world how great America is and is doing. Our economy is now booming and with all I am doing, will only get better... Our country is finally WINNING again! [tweet] Retrieved from https://twitter.com/realdonaldtrump/status/956322473955545089?lang=en.

35 Schmidt, M. S., & Haberman, M. (2018, January 25). Trump ordered Mueller fired, but backed off when white house counsel threated to quit. *New York Times.* Retrieved from https://www.nytimes.com/2018/01/25/us/politics/trump-mueller-special-counsel-russia.html.

36 realDonaldTrump. (2018, January 28). Somebody please inform Jay-Z that because of my policies, black unemployment has just been reported to be at the LOWEST RATE EVER RECORDED! [tweet] Retrieved from https://twitter.com/realdonaldtrump/status/957603800579297280?lang=en.

37 Donald Trump delivered these remarks on January 30, 2018, in Washington, D.C. A transcript can be accessed at https://www.presidency.ucsb.edu.

38 realDonaldTrump. (2019, January 1). Happy new year to everyone, including the haters and the fake news media! 2019 will be a fantastic year for those not suffering from Trump derangement syndrome. Just calm down and enjoy the ride, great things are happening for our country! [tweet] Retrieved from https://twitter.com/realdonaldtrump/status/1080088373451206656?lang=en.

39 Pace, J., & Miller, Z. (2018, December 23). Analysis: One by one, Trump's "axis of adults" leaving. *The Associated Press.* Retrieved from https://apnews.com/b3e12e162abd46f2bb4ac9b4f3a81109.

40 Wright, T. (2019, November 5). The yes-men have taken over the Trump administration. *Brookings.* Retrieved from https://www.brookings.edu/blog/order-from-chaos/2019/11/05/the-yes-men-have-taken-over-the-trump-administration/

41 Donald Trump delivered these remarks on February 5, 2019, in Washington, D.C. A transcript can be accessed at https://www.presidency.ucsb.edu.

42 Donald Trump delivered these remarks on March 28, 2019, in Grand Rapids, MI. A transcript can be accessed at https://www.presidency.ucsb.edu.

43 Donald Trump delivered these remarks on October 6, 2018, in Topeka, KS. A transcript can be accessed at https://www.presidency.ucsb.edu.

44 Donald Trump delivered these remarks on July 31, 2018, in Tampa, FL. A transcript can be accessed at https://www.presidency.ucsb.edu.

45 Donald Trump delivered these remarks on October 11, 2019, in Lake Charles, LA. A transcript can be accessed at https://www.presidency.ucsb.edu.

Chapter 5

1 Quote from Guarnieri, G. (2018, February 1). Trump says he was called the "greatest president ever" by Republican Orrin Hatch. *Newsweek*. Retrieved from https://www.newsweek.com/greatest-president-trump-orrin-hatch-797615.

2 Donald Trump delivered these remarks on February 4, 2020, in Washington, D.C. A transcript can be accessed at https://www.presidency.ucsb.edu.

3 Schear, M. (2020, February 5). Trump claims end of "American decline" while avoiding mention of impeachment. *New York Times*. Retrieved from https://www.nytimes.com/2020/02/05/us/politics/trump-state-of-the-union.html.

4 CNN Opinion. (2020, February 5). We've never seen a state of the union like this. *CNN*. Retrieved from https://www.cnn.com/2020/02/04/opinions/twitter-commentary-state-of-the-union/index.html.

5 Harris, J. F. (2020, February 5). The strangest state of the union ever. *Politico*. Retrieved from https://www.politico.com/news/2020/02/05/trump-sotu-analysis–110803.

6 This is an example of Trump's use of the rhetorical tool of *argumentum ad nauseam*, which is fallacious argument where the speaker repeats something over and over to signal to his or her audience that it is true. Research on the illusory truth effect suggests that repeating the same claims over and over again, regardless of their basis in truth, can be incredibly effective in shaping the public's understanding of issues. In other words, repeating an argument (ad nauseam) that what you want the public to believe will influence many people to believe that it is true. See Hasher, L., Goldstein, D., & Toppino, T. (1977). Frequency and the conference of referential validity. *Journal of Verbal Learning And Verbal Behavior*, 16(1), 107–112;
Pennycook, G., Cannon, T. D., & Rand, D. G. (2018). Prior exposure increases perceived accuracy of fake news. *Journal of Experimental Psychology: General*, 147(12), 1865; Colley, D. F. (2018). Of Twit-storms and Demagogues: Trump, illusory truths of patriotism, and the language of the twittersphere. In M. Lockhart (Ed.) *President Donald Trump and his political discourse* (pp. 33–51). New York, NY: Routledge;

Murray, S., Stanley, M., McPhetres, J., Pennycook, G., & Seli, P. (2020, January 15). "I've said it before and I will say it again": Repeating statements made by Donald Trump increases perceived truthfulness for individuals across the political spectrum, *PsyArxiv Preprint*. These perspectives further help to answer the questions about how and why people are persuaded by Trump's hyperbolic, and oftentimes false, claims.

7   Trump, D. J., & Schwartz, T. (2009). *Trump: The art of the deal*. New York, NY: Ballantine Books.

8   The Beard. *Seinfeld*. NBC. February 9, 1995. Television.

9   secupp. (2020, February 4). This #SOTU speech is winning. I mean, let's be clear—it's full of lies and half-truths. But for millions of Americans the stuff he's saying tonight sounds really, really good. Like, four more years good. Democrats ignore this at their peril. [tweet] Retrieved from https://twitter.com/secupp/status/122488 9949431980042?lang=en

10 Guarnieri, G. (2018, February 1). Trump says he was called the "greatest president ever" by republican Orrin Hatch. *Newsweek*. Retrieved from https://www. newsweek.com/greatest-president-trump-orrin-hatch-797615.

11 Harry Truman delivered these remarks on January 20, 1949, in Washington, D.C. A transcript can be accessed at https://www.presidency.ucsb.edu.

12 Lyndon Johnson delivered these remarks on November 27, 1963, in Washington, D.C. A transcript can be accessed at https://www.presidency.ucsb.edu.

13 Donald Trump delivered these remarks on August 2, 2018, in Wilkes-Barre, PA. A transcript can be accessed at https://www.presidency.ucsb.edu.

14 Bush, G. W. (2014, November 13). An hour with George W. Bush. *Hannity*. Fox News.

15 Lyndon Johnson delivered these remarks on January 8, 1964, in Washington, D.C. A transcript can be accessed at https://www.presidency.ucsb.edu.

16 Richard Nixon delivered these remarks on August 23, 1972, in Miami, FL. A transcript can be accessed at https://www.presidency.ucsb.edu.

17 Bill Clinton delivered these remarks on January 25, 1994, in Washington, D.C. A transcript can be accessed at https://www.presidency.ucsb.edu.

18 Donald Trump delivered these remarks on January 30, 2018, in Washington, D.C. A transcript can be accessed at https://www.presidency.ucsb.edu.

19 Donald Trump delivered these remarks on February 28, 2017, in Washington, D.C. A transcript can be accessed at https://www.presidency.ucsb.edu.

20 Donald Trump delivered these remarks on June 1, 2017, in Washington, D.C. A transcript can be accessed at https://www.presidency.ucsb.edu.

21 Donald Trump delivered these remarks on August 14, 2017, in Washington, D.C. A transcript can be accessed at https://www.presidency.ucsb.edu.

22 Donald Trump delivered these remarks on February 5, 2019, in Washington, D.C. A transcript can be accessed at https://www.presidency.ucsb.edu.

23 This number represents only Trump's invocations of exceptional presidency in MAGA rallies. This number skyrockets to over 3,500 when we take into account all of the references from major addresses to the nation and tweets between January 20, 2017, and February 4, 2020.

24 Donald Trump delivered these remarks on October 10, 2018, in Erie, PA. A transcript can be accessed at https://www.presidency.ucsb.edu.

25 Donald Trump delivered these remarks on June 27, 2018, in Fargo, ND. A transcript can be accessed at https://www.presidency.ucsb.edu.

26 Donald Trump delivered these remarks on January 30, 2020, in Des Moines, IA. A transcript can be accessed at https://www.presidency.ucsb.edu.

27 realDonaldTrump. (2019, January 19). @newtgingrich just stated that there has been no president since Abraham Lincoln, who has been treated worse or more unfairly by the media than your favorite president, me! At the same time there has been no president who has accomplished more in his first two years in office! [tweet] Retrieved from https://twitter.com/realdonaldtrump/status/108659704722 9300737?lang=en.

28 realDonaldTrump. (2019, February 24). HOLD THE DATE. We will be having one of the biggest gatherings in the history of Washington, D.C., on July 4th. It will be called "A salute to America" and will be held at the Lincoln memorial. Major fireworks display, entertainment and an address by your favorite president, me! [tweet] Retrieved from https://twitter.com/realdonaldtrump/status/109965112108 8466946?lang=en.

29 Trump, D. (2020, March 4). *Hannity*. Fox News. Retrieved from foxnews.com.

30 realDonaldTrump. (2019, July 31). CNN's Don Lemon, the dumbest man on television, insinuated last night while asking a debate "question" that I was a racist, when in fact I am "the least racist person in the world." Perhaps someone should explain to Don that he is supposed to be neutral, unbiased & fair, …. [tweet] Retrieved from https://twitter.com/realdonaldtrump/status/1156588090456256512 ?lang=en

31 Not surprisingly, crowd sizes at his rallies were also a crucial talking point for Trump. He routinely opened each speech with a five-to-ten--minute riff about how he had broken an attendance record, that thousands of other supporters were waiting outside unable to get in, and that other politicians—from rivals to former presidents—would have only attracted hundreds, not thousands of supporters, at such an event. He boasted, for example, that "we set records at every arena" and, on one occasion, stated: "There have never been crowds like this, just so you understand, in the history of politics."

32 Donald Trump delivered these remarks on July 17, 2019, in Greenville, NC. A transcript can be accessed at https://www.presidency.ucsb.edu.

33 Donald Trump delivered these remarks on September 21, 2019, in Springfield, MO. A transcript can be accessed at https://www.presidency.ucsb.edu.

34   Donald Trump delivered these remarks on October 10, 2018, in Erie, PA.
     A transcript can be accessed at https://www.presidency.ucsb.edu.
35   Donald Trump delivered these remarks on September 21, 2019, in Springfield,
     MO. A transcript can be accessed at https://www.presidency.ucsb.edu.
36   Donald Trump delivered these remarks on January 28, 2020, in Wildwood, NJ.
     A transcript can be accessed at https://www.presidency.ucsb.edu.
37   Donald Trump delivered these remarks on October 10, 2018, in Erie, PA.
     A transcript can be accessed at https://www.presidency.ucsb.edu.
38   Donald Trump delivered these remarks on October 31, 2018, in Fort Myers, FL.
     A transcript can be accessed at https://www.presidency.ucsb.edu.
39   At a rally in Pennsylvania, after cycling through a list of his "greatest hits" about
     why his presidency was so exceptional, Trump paused and then proclaimed: "You
     are so lucky I became your president." This was yet another way that Trump sought
     to portray himself and his presidency as exceptional.
40   Donald Trump delivered these remarks on March 15, 2017, in Nashville, TN.
     A transcript can be accessed at https://www.presidency.ucsb.edu.
41   Donald Trump delivered these remarks on July 26, 2017, in Youngstown, OH.
     A transcript can be accessed at https://www.presidency.ucsb.edu.
42   Donald Trump delivered these remarks on August 23, 2017, in Phoenix, AZ.
     A transcript can be accessed at https://www.presidency.ucsb.edu.
43   Donald Trump delivered these remarks on November 26, 2019, in Sunrise, FL.
     A transcript can be accessed at https://www.presidency.ucsb.edu.
44   Donald Trump delivered these remarks on March 10, 2018, in Moon Township,
     PA. A transcript can be accessed at https://www.presidency.ucsb.edu.
45   It should also be noted that Trump routinely specified how he had done more
     than any previous president on a host of other issues, from taxes to regulations
     to jobs to military spending to countless others. Trump took credit for passing
     "the biggest tax cuts and reform in American history" and suggested that his
     administration had cut "more regulations than any President in the history of our
     country." On jobs, Trump proclaimed: "Since the election, we have created seven
     million new jobs. The average unemployment rate, under my administration,
     listen to this, is lower than any previous administration in the history of our
     country." And on the military, Trump emphasized over and over throughout his
     first term in office that he had rebuilt the military by achieving "record funding"
     for it. In addition, Trump stated that his administration had been "taking care of
     health care like nobody's been able to do," "undertaken an unprecedented effort to
     secure the southern border of the United States," delivered "a policy of American
     energy independence like you've never seen before," and taken "historic steps to
     protect religious liberty." Regarding judicial appointments, he often reminded
     his audiences: "We confirmed more circuit judges than any administration" and

"We have confirmed 191 federal judges, a record" (of note, this number appeared as 84, 100, 160, 182, 187, and 191 over the course of his presidency, always with the same mention of it being a "record"). Trump even went so far as to suggest that "there has never been, ever before, an administration that's been so open and transparent" as his.

46 Donald Trump delivered these remarks on July 31, 2018, in Tampa, FL. A transcript can be accessed at https://www.presidency.ucsb.edu.

47 Donald Trump delivered these remarks on January 9, 2020, in Toledo, OH. A transcript can be accessed at https://www.presidency.ucsb.edu.

48 Donald Trump delivered these remarks on November 4, 2019, in Lexington, KY. A transcript can be accessed at https://www.presidency.ucsb.edu.

49 Donald Trump delivered these remarks on June 27, 2018, in Fargo, ND. A transcript can be accessed at https://www.presidency.ucsb.edu.

50 Donald Trump delivered these remarks on March 10, 2018, in Moon Township, PA. A transcript can be accessed at https://www.presidency.ucsb.edu.

51 Donald Trump delivered these remarks on June 27, 2018, in Fargo, ND. A transcript can be accessed at https://www.presidency.ucsb.edu.

52 Elsewhere, Trump mentioned the fact that Reagan had lost the state of Wisconsin when running for president, allowing him to then say: "I won Wisconsin." And, in reference to his Make America Great Again slogan, Trump at one point stated: "It may be the greatest slogan ever. Ronald Reagan had one, 'Let's Make America Great.' I like it, but ours is better."

53 Donald Trump delivered these remarks on July 26, 2017, in Youngstown, OH. A transcript can be accessed at https://www.presidency.ucsb.edu.

54 realDonaldTrump. (2019, April 21). Can you believe that I had to go through the worst and most corrupt political Witch Hunt in the history of the United States (No Collusion) when it was the "other side" that illegally created the diversionary & criminal event and even spied on my campaign? Disgraceful! [tweet] Retrieved from https://twitter.com/realdonaldtrump/status/1119969946002440198?lang=en.

55 Donald Trump delivered these remarks on January 14, 2020, in Milwaukee, WI. A transcript can be accessed at https://www.presidency.ucsb.edu.

56 realDonaldTrump. (2020, January 13). "We demand fairness" shouts Pelosi and the do nothing democrats, yet the Dems in the house wouldn't let us have 1 witness, no lawyers or even ask questions. It was the most unfair witch-hunt in the history of congress! [tweet] Retrieved from https://twitter.com/realdonaldtrump/status/1216774903036334080?lang=en.

57 realDonaldTrump. (2019, September 25). There has been no president in the history of our country who has been treated so badly as I have. The democrats are frozen with hatred and fear. They get nothing done. This should never be allowed to happen to another president. Witch Hunt! [tweet] Retrieved from https://twitter.com/realdonaldtrump/status/1176819645699043328?lang=en.

58   At various times, Trump alluded to the fact that several people, including Rush
     Limbaugh, Sean Hannity, and Lou Dobbs, had said that there is "no other man
     that we've ever met that could have taken" this mistreatment.

59   Donald Trump delivered these remarks on December 10, 2019, in Hershey, PA.
     A transcript can be accessed at https://www.presidency.ucsb.edu. It should be
     noted that, elsewhere, Trump did a slightly modified version of this, saying: "Who
     the hell else could they take in this stuff? Right? Can I get some credit for that?
     Most guys would have been in a corner with their thumb in their mouth saying,
     'Mommy, Mommy, take me home.'"

60   Donald Trump delivered these remarks on December 1, 2016, Cincinnati, OH.
     A transcript can be accessed at https://www.presidency.ucsb.edu.

61   Donald Trump delivered these remarks on December 6, 2019, in Fayetteville, NC.
     A transcript can be accessed at https://www.presidency.ucsb.edu.

62   Donald Trump delivered these remarks on December 6, 2019, in Fayetteville, NC.
     A transcript can be accessed at https://www.presidency.ucsb.edu.

63   Donald Trump delivered these remarks on January 30, 2020, in Des Moines, IA.
     A transcript can be accessed at https://www.presidency.ucsb.edu.

64   Donald Trump delivered these remarks on January 14, 2020, in Milwaukee, WI.
     A transcript can be accessed at https://www.presidency.ucsb.edu.

65   Donald Trump delivered these remarks on November 3, 2018, in Belgrade, MT.
     A transcript can be accessed at https://www.presidency.ucsb.edu.

66   realDonaldTrump. (2019, September 2) …and watched. NAFTA is the worst trade
     deal ever made—terrible for labor—and Richard let it stand. No wonder unions
     are losing so much. The workers will vote for me in 2020 (lowest unemployment,
     most jobs ever), and should stop paying exorbitant $Dues, not worth it! [tweet]
     Retrieved from https://twitter.com/realdonaldtrump/status/1168490496857128960
     ?lang=en.

67   Here is a perfect illustration of how Trump sought to appeal to different
     demographic groups by citing "record" economic numbers: "You have the best
     economy you've ever had. You have your best unemployment numbers…You have
     your best Black unemployment numbers, best Hispanic unemployment numbers,
     best women unemployment numbers, best Asian unemployment numbers."
     On numerous occasions, it should be noted, Trump rattled off these claims
     consecutively. He would also occasionally include other groups, such as veterans,
     those without a college education, youth, those who are disabled, and even former
     prisoners. In sum, essentially every demographic, according to Trump, was living
     better than ever before. And it was all thanks to him.

68   Donald Trump delivered these remarks on June 27, 2018, in Fargo, ND.
     A transcript can be accessed at https://www.presidency.ucsb.edu.

69   This same expression was also often used by Trump in reference to Latino voters,
     followed by the claimed that Latinos have been employed at record numbers.

70   Donald Trump delivered these remarks on October 9, 2018, in Council Bluffs, IA. A transcript can be accessed at https://www.presidency.ucsb.edu.

71   Donald Trump delivered these remarks on February 5, 2019, in Washington, D.C. A transcript can be accessed at https://www.presidency.ucsb.edu.

72   Donald Trump delivered these remarks on May 10, 2018, in Belgrade, MT. A transcript can be accessed at https://www.presidency.ucsb.edu.

73   Donald Trump delivered these remarks on November 3, 2018, in Washington, D.C. A transcript can be accessed at https://www.presidency.ucsb.edu.

74   realDonaldTrump. (2019, October 15). Just out: MEDIAN HOUSEHOLD INCOME IS AT THE HIGHEST POINT EVER, EVER, EVER! How about saying it this way, IN THE HISTORY OF OUR COUNTRY! Also, MORE PEOPLE WORKING TODAY IN THE USA THAN AT ANY TIME IN HISTORY! Tough numbers for the Radical Left Democrats to beat! Impeach the Pres. [tweet] Retrieved from https://twitter.com/realdonaldtrump/status/1184129825231069184?lang=en.

75   Donald Trump delivered these remarks on July 26, 2017, in Youngstown, OH. A transcript can be accessed at https://www.presidency.ucsb.edu.

76   Donald Trump delivered these remarks on January 28, 2020, in Wildwood, NJ. A transcript can be accessed at https://www.presidency.ucsb.edu.

77   realDonaldTrump. (2019, October 15). We now have the greatest economy in history! [tweet] Retrieved from https://twitter.com/realdonaldtrump/status/1184308485237948416?lang=en.

78   Donald Trump delivered these remarks on March 15, 2017, in Nashville, TN. A transcript can be accessed at https://www.presidency.ucsb.edu.

79   Donald Trump delivered these remarks on November 23, 2017, in Riviera, FL. A transcript can be accessed at https://www.presidency.ucsb.edu.

80   Donald Trump delivered these remarks on November 4, 2018, in Chattanooga, TN. A transcript can be accessed at https://www.presidency.ucsb.edu.

81   Donald Trump delivered these remarks on May 20, 2019, in Montoursville, PA. A transcript can be accessed at https://www.presidency.ucsb.edu.

82   Donald Trump delivered these remarks on August 15, 2019, in Manchester, NH. A transcript can be accessed at https://www.presidency.ucsb.edu.

83   Donald Trump delivered these remarks on January 9, 2020, in Toledo, OH. A transcript can be accessed at https://www.presidency.ucsb.edu.

84   Donald Trump delivered these remarks on January 14, 2020, in Milwaukee, WI. A transcript can be accessed at https://www.presidency.ucsb.edu.

85   Donald Trump delivered these remarks on August 15, 2019, in Manchester, NH. A transcript can be accessed at https://www.presidency.ucsb.edu.

86   Donald Trump delivered these remarks on January 9, 2020, in Toledo, OH. A transcript can be accessed at https://www.presidency.ucsb.edu.

87 Donald Trump delivered these remarks on August 15, 2019, in Manchester, NH. A transcript can be accessed at https://www.presidency.ucsb.edu.

88 Donald Trump delivered these remarks on July 31, 2018, in Tampa, FL. A transcript can be accessed at https://www.presidency.ucsb.edu.

89 Donald Trump delivered these remarks on June 18, 2019, in Orlando, FL. A transcript can be accessed at https://www.presidency.ucsb.edu.

90 Donald Trump delivered these remarks on February 18, 2017, in Melbourne, FL. A transcript can be accessed at https://www.presidency.ucsb.edu.

91 Donald Trump delivered these remarks on January 28, 2020, in Wildwood, NJ. A transcript can be accessed at https://www.presidency.ucsb.edu.

92 Donald Trump delivered these remarks on November 5, 2018, in Cape Girardeau, MO. A transcript can be accessed at https://www.presidency.ucsb.edu.

93 Donald Trump delivered these remarks on January 30, 2020, in Des Moines, IA. A transcript can be accessed at https://www.presidency.ucsb.edu.

94 Donald Trump delivered these remarks on August 15, 2019, in Manchester, NH. A transcript can be accessed at https://www.presidency.ucsb.edu.

95 Donald Trump delivered these remarks on June 27, 2018, in Fargo, ND. A transcript can be accessed at https://www.presidency.ucsb.edu.

96 Donald Trump delivered these remarks on February 10, 2020, in Manchester, NH. A transcript can be accessed at https://www.presidency.ucsb.edu.

97 Donald Trump delivered these remarks on April 29, 2017, in Harrisburg, PA. A transcript can be accessed at https://www.presidency.ucsb.edu.

98 Donald Trump delivered these remarks on November 26, 2019, in Sunrise, FL. A transcript can be accessed at https://www.presidency.ucsb.edu.

99 Donald Trump delivered these remarks on January 30, 2020, in Des Moines, IA. A transcript can be accessed at https://www.presidency.ucsb.edu.

100 Donald Trump delivered these remarks on October 11, 2019, in Lake Charles, LA. A transcript can be accessed at https://www.presidency.ucsb.edu.

101 Donald Trump delivered these remarks on January 14, 2020, in Milwaukee, WI. A transcript can be accessed at https://www.presidency.ucsb.edu.

102 Donald Trump delivered these remarks on November 26, 2019, in Sunrise, FL. A transcript can be accessed at https://www.presidency.ucsb.edu.

103 Donald Trump delivered these remarks on September 16, 2019, in Rio Rancho, NM. A transcript can be accessed at https://www.presidency.ucsb.edu.

104 Donald Trump delivered these remarks on December 18, 2019, in Battle Creek, MI. A transcript can be accessed at https://www.presidency.ucsb.edu.

105 Donald Trump delivered these remarks on November 1, 2019, in Tupelo, MS. A transcript can be accessed at https://www.presidency.ucsb.edu.

106 Donald Trump delivered these remarks on October 17, 2019, in Dallas, TX. A transcript can be accessed at https://www.presidency.ucsb.edu.

107 Donald Trump delivered these remarks on October 1, 2018, in Johnson City, TN. A transcript can be accessed at https://www.presidency.ucsb.edu.

108 Donald Trump delivered these remarks on October 18, 2018, in Missoula, MT. A transcript can be accessed at https://www.presidency.ucsb.edu.

109 Donald Trump delivered these remarks on February 11, 2019, in El Paso, TX. A transcript can be accessed at https://www.presidency.ucsb.edu.

110 There was one occasion where Trump's claim that men and women were crying behind him was able to be fact-checked. In a June 2019 speech at a Renewable Energy Summit in Council Bluffs, Iowa, Trump recounted the story of an executive order he signed in early 2017 cutting environmental regulations, saying: "And I signed that and behind me I had homebuilders and farmers, mostly, and ranchers and many of them never cried in their life including when they were born and they were crying. It's true though. They were crying behind me." In this case, however, news organizations reported on the fact that Trump's claims were false, citing a White House video of the signing. The video clearly showed that no one was crying. See Brice-Sadler, M. (2019, June 13). Trump claims farmers wept behind him when he signed an executive order. Video shows otherwise. *The Washington Post.* Retrieved from https://www.washingtonpost.com/politics/2019/06/14/trump-claims-farmers-wept-behind-him-when-he-signed-an-executive-order-video-shows-otherwise/.

111 Donald Trump delivered these remarks on August 15, 2019, in Manchester, NH. A transcript can be accessed at https://www.presidency.ucsb.edu.

112 Donald Trump delivered these remarks on January 9, 2020, in Toledo, OH. A transcript can be accessed at https://www.presidency.ucsb.edu.

113 Donald Trump delivered these remarks on January 30, 2020, in Des Moines, IA. A transcript can be accessed at https://www.presidency.ucsb.edu.

114 Donald Trump delivered these remarks on May 10, 2018, in Elkhart, IN. A transcript can be accessed at https://www.presidency.ucsb.edu.

115 Donald Trump delivered these remarks on July 17, 2019, in Greenville, NC. A transcript can be accessed at https://www.presidency.ucsb.edu.

Chapter 6

1 Donald Trump delivered these remarks on August 23, 2016, in Austin, TX. A transcript can be accessed at https://www.presidency.ucsb.edu.

2 Donald Trump delivered these remarks on January 20, 2017, in Washington, D.C. A transcript can be accessed at https://www.presidency.ucsb.edu.

3 See Domke, D., & Coe, K. (2010). *The god strategy: How religion became a weapon in America.* Oxford, UK: Oxford University Press.

4   Ronald Reagan delivered these remarks on January 20, 1981, in Washington, D.C.
     A transcript can be accessed at https://www.presidency.ucsb.edu.

5   Quote from Müller, J. W. (2016). *What is populism?* Philadelphia, PA: University
     of Pennsylvania Press. Also see Mudde, C., & Kaltwasser, C. R. (2017). *Populism:
     A very short introduction.* Oxford University Press and Rowland, R. C. (2019).
     The populist and nationalist roots of Trump's rhetoric. *Rhetoric and Public Affairs,*
     22(3), 343–88.

6   Donald Trump delivered these remarks on July 21, 2016, in Cleveland, OH.
     A transcript can be accessed at https://www.presidency.ucsb.edu.

7   Donald Trump delivered these remarks on October 22, 2016, in Gettysburg, PA.
     A transcript can be accessed at https://www.presidency.ucsb.edu.

8   realDonaldTrump. (2016, August 17). We are going to make this a government of
     the people once again! #MakeAmericaGreatAgain #ImWithYou. [tweet] Retrieved
     from https://twitter.com/realDonaldTrump/status/766028026987491328.

9   Donald Trump delivered these remarks on September 9, 2016, in Pensacola, FL.
     A transcript can be accessed at https://www.presidency.ucsb.edu.

10   Donald Trump delivered these remarks on October 21, 2016, in Newton, PA.
     A transcript can be accessed at https://www.presidency.ucsb.edu.

11   Donald Trump delivered these remarks on September 28, 2016, in Council Bluffs,
     IA. A transcript can be accessed at https://www.presidency.ucsb.edu.

12   Donald Trump delivered these remarks on November 7, 2016, in Raleigh, NC.
     A transcript can be accessed at https://www.presidency.ucsb.edu.

13   realDonaldTrump. (2018, December 17). When the American people speak, ALL
     OF US should listen. Just over a year ago, you spoke loud and clear. On November
     8, 2016, you voted to MAKE AMERICA GREAT AGAIN! [tweet] Retrieved from
     http://www.trumptwitterarchive.com/archive.

14   realDonaldTrump. (2017, September 27). Facebook was always anti-Trump. The
     networks were always anti-Trump hence, Fake News, @nytimes (apologized) & @
     WaPo were anti-Trump. Collusion? [tweet] Retrieved from https://twitter.com/
     realDonaldTrump/status/913034591879024640.

15   realDonaldTrump. (2017, September 27). *But the people were Pro-Trump!*
     Virtually no president has accomplished what we have accomplished in the first
     9 months-and economy roaring! [tweet] Retrieved from https://twitter.com/
     realDonaldTrump/status/913035855509491712.

16   Donald Trump delivered these remarks on September 29, 2018, in Wheeling, WV.
     A transcript can be accessed at https://www.presidency.ucsb.edu.

17   realDonaldTrump. (2018, August 8). As long as I campaign and/or support
     Senate and House candidates (within reason), they will win! I LOVE the people,
     & they certainly seem to like the job I'm doing. If I find the time, in between
     China, Iran, the economy and much more, which I must, we will have a giant

red wave! [tweet] Retrieved from https://twitter.com/realDonaldTrump/status/1027214330503352320.

18 Donald Trump delivered these remarks on October 10, 2018, in Erie, PA. A transcript can be accessed at https://www.presidency.ucsb.edu.

19 Donald Trump delivered these remarks on July 26, 2017, in Youngstown, OH. A transcript can be accessed at https://www.presidency.ucsb.edu.

20 Donald Trump delivered these remarks on February 4, 2019, in Washington, D.C. A transcript can be accessed at https://www.presidency.ucsb.edu.

21 realDonaldTrump. (2019, February 11). We are fighting for all Americans, from all backgrounds, of every age, race, religion, birthplace, color & creed. Our agenda is NOT a partisan agenda—it is the mainstream, common sense agenda of the American people. Thank you El Paso, Texas—I love you! [tweet] Retrieved from https://twitter.com/realDonaldTrump/status/1095168756374921227.

22 realDonaldTrump. (2016, January 22). A wonderful article by a writer who truly gets it. I am for the people and the people are for me. #Trump2016. [tweet] Retrieved from https://twitter.com/realDonaldTrump/status/690732776920743937.

23 Quote from Müller, J. W. (2016). *What is populism?* Philadelphia, PA: University of Pennsylvania Press.

24 Donald Trump delivered these remarks on August 18, 2016, in Charlotte, NC. A transcript can be accessed at https://www.presidency.ucsb.edu.

25 Donald Trump delivered these remarks on July 11, 2015, in Phoenix, AZ. A transcript can be accessed at https://www.presidency.ucsb.edu.

26 Donald Trump delivered these remarks on December 15, 2016, in Hershey, PA. A transcript can be accessed at https://www.presidency.ucsb.edu.

27 Donald Trump delivered these remarks on April 27, 2019, in Green Bay, WI. A transcript can be accessed at https://www.presidency.ucsb.edu.

28 Donald Trump delivered these remarks on August 4, 2018, in Lewis Center, OH. A transcript can be accessed at https://www.presidency.ucsb.edu.

29 realDonaldTrump. (2017, September 30). ......#FakeNews critics are working overtime, but we're getting great marks from the people that truly matter! #PRStrong [tweet] Retrieved from https://twitter.com/realDonaldTrump/status/914217477495717889.

30 realDonaldTrump. (2019, July 9) ...to your favorite president, me! These people are vicious and totally crazed, but remember, there are far more great people ("Deplorables") in this country, than bad. Do to them what they do to you. Fight for Bernie Marcus and Home Depot! [tweet] Retrieved from https://twitter.com/realDonaldTrump/status/1148766319640227841.

31 Donald Trump delivered these remarks on October 9, 2018, in Council Bluffs, IA. A transcript can be accessed at https://www.presidency.ucsb.edu.

32   Donald Trump delivered these remarks on November 5, 2018, in Cape Girardeau, MO. A transcript can be accessed at https://www.presidency.ucsb.edu.

33   Donald Trump delivered these remarks on June 25, 2018, in West Columbia, SC. A transcript can be accessed at https://www.presidency.ucsb.edu.

34   Quote from Cillizza, C. (2020, February 11). The thirty-five most eye-popping lines from Donald Trump's new Hampshire rally. *CNN*. Retrieved from https://www.cnn.com/2020/02/11/politics/trump-new-hampshire-rally/index.html.

35   Donald Trump delivered these remarks on December 8, 2017, in Pensacola, FL. A transcript can be accessed at https://www.presidency.ucsb.edu.

36   Donald Trump delivered these remarks on September 21, 2018, in Springfield, MO. A transcript can be accessed at https://www.presidency.ucsb.edu.

37   Donald Trump delivered these remarks on October 22, 2016, in Gettysburg, PA. A transcript can be accessed at https://www.presidency.ucsb.edu.

38   Donald Trump delivered these remarks on October 13, 2016, in West Palm Beach, FL. A transcript can be accessed at https://www.presidency.ucsb.edu.

39   realDonaldTrump. (2019, June 14). The radical left Dems are working hard, but THE PEOPLE are much smarter. Working hard, thank you! [tweet] Retrieved from https://twitter.com/realDonaldTrump/status/1139606178680463367.

40   Donald Trump delivered these remarks on August 30, 2018, in Evansville, IN. A transcript can be accessed at https://www.presidency.ucsb.edu.

41   Donald Trump delivered these remarks on October 10, 2019, in Minneapolis, MN. A transcript can be accessed at https://www.presidency.ucsb.edu.

42   realDonaldTrump. (2016, June 15). The press is so totally biased that we have no choice but to take our tough but fair and smart message directly to the people! [tweet] Retrieved from https://twitter.com/realDonaldTrump/status/743076652662431744.

43   realDonaldTrump. (2017, July 16). With all of its phony unnamed sources & highly slanted & even fraudulent reporting, #Fake News is DISTORTING DEMOCRACY in our country! [tweet] Retrieved from https://twitter.com/realDonaldTrump/status/886544734788997125.

44   realDonaldTrump. (2018, January 2). The failing New York Times has a new publisher, A.G. Sulzberger. Congratulations! Here is a last chance for the times to fulfill the vision of its founder, Adolph Ochs, "to give the news impartially, without fear or FAVOR, regardless of party, sect, or interests involved." Get… [tweet] Retrieved from https://twitter.com/realDonaldTrump/status/948202173049049088.

45   realDonaldTrump. (2018, January 2). Impartial journalists of a much higher standard, lose all of your phony and non-existent "sources," and treat the president of the United States FAIRLY, so that the next time I (and the people) win, you won't have to write an apology to your readers for a job poorly done! [tweet] Retrieved from https://twitter.com/realDonaldTrump/status/948205689683562496.

46 realDonaldTrump. (2018, August 16). The fake news media is the opposition party. It is very bad for our great country... BUT WE ARE WINNING! [tweet] Retrieved from https://twitter.com/realDonaldTrump/status/1030074380397752320.

47 realDonaldTrump. (2017, February 17). The FAKE NEWS media (failing @nytimes, @CNN, @NBCNews and many more) is not my enemy, it is the enemy of the American people. SICK! [tweet] Retrieved from http://www.trumptwitterarchive.com/archive.

48 Donald Trump delivered these remarks on October 31, 2018, in Fort Myers, FL. A transcript can be accessed at https://www.presidency.ucsb.edu.

49 realDonaldTrump. (2019, March 19). The fake news media has NEVER been more dishonest or corrupt than it is right now. There has never been a time like this in American history. Very exciting but also, very sad! Fake News is the absolute enemy of the people and of our country itself! [tweet] Retrieved from https://twitter.com/realDonaldTrump/status/1107981131012628481.

50 realDonaldTrump. (2018, October 29). CNN and others in the fake news business keep purposely and inaccurately reporting that I said the "media is the enemy of the people." Wrong! I said that the "fake news (media) is the enemy of the people," a very big difference. When you give out false information— not good. [tweet] Retrieved from https://twitter.com/realDonaldTrump/status/1057059603605831680.

51 realDonaldTrump. (2018, August 2). They asked my daughter Ivanka whether or not the media is the enemy of the people. She correctly said no. It is the FAKE NEWS, which is a large percentage of the media, that is the enemy of the people! [tweet] Retrieved from https://twitter.com/realDonaldTrump/status/1025115155632455680.

52 realDonaldTrump. (2017, May 18). This is the single greatest witch hunt of a politician in American history! [tweet] Retrieved from https://twitter.com/realDonaldTrump/status/865173176854204416.

53 Donald Trump delivered these remarks on June 18, 2019, in Orlando, FL. A transcript can be accessed at https://www.presidency.ucsb.edu.

54 Donald Trump delivered these remarks on May 17, 2017, in New London, CT. A transcript can be accessed at https://www.presidency.ucsb.edu.

55 realDonaldTrump. (2018, September 15). While my (our) poll numbers are good, with the economy being the best ever, if it weren't for the rigged Russian Witch Hunt, they would be 25 points higher! Highly conflicted Bob Mueller & the 17 angry democrats are using phony issue to hurt us in the midterms. No collusion! [tweet] Retrieved from https://twitter.com/realDonaldTrump/status/1041086383505465345.

56 realDonaldTrump. (2019, May 5). Despite the tremendous success that I have had as president, including perhaps the greatest ECONOMY and most successful first two years of any president in history, they have stollen two years of my (our) presidency (collusion delusion) that we will never be able

to get back… [tweet] Retrieved from https://twitter.com/realDonaldTrump/status/1125235130002489345.

57 realDonaldTrump. (2019, May 5). … The Witch Hunt is over but we will never forget. MAKE AMERICA GREAT AGAIN! [tweet] Retrieved from https://twitter.com/realDonaldTrump/status/1125235131759960064.

58 Donald Trump delivered these remarks on April 27, 2019, in Green Bay, WI. A transcript can be accessed at https://www.presidency.ucsb.edu.

59 realDonaldTrump. (2019, March 26). The mainstream media is under fire and being scorned all over the world as being corrupt and FAKE. For two years they pushed the Russian Collusion delusion when they always knew there was no collusion. They truly are the enemy of the people and the real opposition party! [tweet] Retrieved from https://twitter.com/realDonaldTrump/status/1110495339369377793.

60 Donald Trump delivered these remarks on March 28, 2019, in Grand Rapids, MI. A transcript can be accessed at https://www.presidency.ucsb.edu.

61 realDonaldTrump. (2019, October 1). As I learn more and more each day, I am coming to the conclusion that what is taking place is not an impeachment, it is a COUP, intended to take away the power of the… [tweet] Retrieved from https://twitter.com/realDonaldTrump/status/1179179573541511176.

62 realDonaldTrump. (2019, October 1). … People, their VOTE, their freedoms, their second amendment, religion, military, border wall, and their God-given rights as a citizen of The United States of America! [tweet response] Retrieved from https://twitter.com/realDonaldTrump/status/1179179575059927040.

63 Donald Trump delivered these remarks on October 15, 2019, in Minneapolis, MN. A transcript can be accessed at https://www.presidency.ucsb.edu.

64 Quote from "Letter from President Donald J. Trump to the Speaker of the House of Representatives" sent on December 17, 2019. A transcript can be accessed at https://www.whitehouse.gov/briefings-statements/letter-president-donald-j-trump-speaker-house-representatives/

65 Donald Trump delivered these remarks on December 18, 2019, in Battle Creek, MI. A transcript can be accessed at https://www.presidency.ucsb.edu.

66 See Bump, P. (2020, January 29). Trump's impeachment team argues that anything he does to win reelection isn't impeachable. *The Washington Post.* https://www.washingtonpost.com/politics/2020/01/29/trumps-impeachment-team-offers-trumpiest-possible-argument-his-defense/

67 Campaign email sent to supporters on February 4, 2020.

68 realDonaldTrump. (2020, February 5). I will be making a public statement at 12:00pm from the @WhiteHouse to discuss our country's VICTORY on the impeachment Hoax! [tweet] Retrieved from https://twitter.com/realDonaldTrump/status/1225179058000089090.

69   Donald Trump delivered these remarks on February 5, 2020, in Washington, D.C. A transcript can be accessed at https://www.presidency.ucsb.edu.

70   Donald Trump delivered these remarks on October 10, 2019, in Minneapolis, MN. A transcript can be accessed at https://www.presidency.ucsb.edu.

Chapter 7

1   Bowden, J. (2019, April 27). Trump praises Lou Dobbs in WaPo profile: "He really gets the word out." *The Hill*. Retrieved from https://thehill.com/homenews/media/440963-trump-praises-lou-dobbs-in-wapo-profile-he-really-gets-the-word-out.

2   Kamala Harris. (2019, November 7). Donald Trump has been the most corrupt, unpatriotic president we've ever had, so it's sad to see the level of desperation congressional republicans will stoop to to protect him. [tweet] Retrieved from https://twitter.com/kamalaharris/status/1192482210672189440.

3   See Thrush, G. (2016, July 26). 5 takeaways from Day 1 of the DNC. *POLITICO*. Retrieved from https://www.politico.com/story/2016/07/democratic-national-convention-sanders-clinton-226194.

4   Michelle Obama delivered these remarks on July 25, 2016, in Philadelphia, PA. A transcript can be accessed at https://www.presidency.ucsb.edu.

5   Quote from Appelbaum, Y. (2016, July 25). Michelle Obama's speech for the ages. *The Atlantic*. Retrieved from https://www.theatlantic.com/politics/archive/2016/07/a-speech-for-the-ages/493010/.

6   Quote from Hohmann, J. (2016, July 26). The daily 202: Michelle Obama is the Democrats' best weapon against Donald Trump. *The Washington Post*. Retrieved from https://www.washingtonpost.com/news/powerpost/paloma/daily-202/2016/07/26/daily-202-michelle-obama-is-the-democrats-best-weapon-against-donald-trump/5796b38e4acce20505161e31/.

7   Barack Obama delivered these remarks on January 10, 2017, in Chicago, IL. A transcript can be accessed at https://www.presidency.ucsb.edu.

8   Excerpts from Obama's thank-you note to the nation released on January 19, 2017. Retrieved from https://obamawhitehouse.archives.gov/blog/2017/01/19/thank-you.

9   See, for example, Wallace, T., Yourish, K., & Griggs, T. (2017, January 20). Trump's inauguration vs. Obama's: comparing the crowds. *The New York Times*. Retrieved from https://www.nytimes.com/interactive/2017/01/20/us/politics/trump-inauguration-crowd.html?mtrref=www.google.com&gwh=17B52ECE52A4460D470622527A6D9BB5&gwt=pay&assetType=REGIWALL.

10   Sean Spicer delivered these remarks on January 21, 2017, in Washington, D.C.
     A transcript can be accessed at https://www.politico.com/story/2017/01/transcript-
     press-secretary-sean-spicer-media-233979.

11   See Gibbs, N. (2017, January 24). A note to our readers. *Time Magazine*. Retrieved
     from https://time.com/4645541/donald-trump-white-house-oval-office/.

12   Mike Pence delivered these remarks on September 17, 2019, in Washington, D.C.
     A transcript can be accessed at https://www.heritage.org/trade/commentary/full-
     transcript-vice-president-mike-pence-speaks-heritage-trade-policy.

13   Mike Pence delivered these remarks on January 22, 2018, in Jerusalem, Israel.
     A transcript can be accessed at https://www.jpost.com/Israel-News/Full-transcript-
     of-Pences-Knesset-speech-539476.

14   Donald Trump's full interview with Bill O'Reilly on Fox News' *O'Reilly Factor* was
     accessed from https://video.foxnews.com/v/5311416183001#sp=show-clips.

15   John Kasich. (2017, February 5). America has been a beacon of light and freedom.
     There is no equivalency with the brutal regime of Vladimir Putin. [tweet]
     Retrieved from https://twitter.com/JohnKasich/status/828323662591832064.

16   Quote in Rogin, A. (2017, February 5). GOP Sen. Sasse doesn't "understand"
     Trump's statements on Putin or on "so-called judges." *ABC News*. Retrieved from
     https://abcnews.go.com/Politics/gop-sen-sasse-understand-trumps-statements-
     putin-called/story?id=45278912.

17   Quote from Boot, M. (2017, February 6). Trump's American is as deadly as Putin's
     Russia. *USA Today*. Retrieved from the Lexis Nexis Academic Universe database at
     http://nexisuni.com.

18   See Carney, J. (2017, February 7). McCain: "No moral equivalence" between
     Russia and US. *The Hill*. Retrieved from https://thehill.com/blogs/floor-action/
     senate/318378-mccain-no-moral-equivalence-between-russia-us.

19   Rush Limbaugh delivered these remarks on November 5, 2018, in Cape Girardeau,
     MO. A video of this event can be accessed at https://www.realclearpolitics.com/
     video/2018/11/05/rush_limbaugh_at_trump_maga_rally_in_cape_girardeau_
     democrats_havent_accepted_they_lost_in_2016.html.

20   Sean Hannity later deleted this tweet, but it was captured by various news
     organizations. For example, see Burke, M. (2018, November 5). Hannity clarifies
     appearance at Trump rally: 'I will not be on stage campaigning.' *The Hill*. Retrieved
     from https://thehill.com/homenews/campaign/414925-hannity-clarifies-
     appearance-at-trump-rally-i-will-not-be-on-stage

21   Sean Hannity and Jeanine Pirro delivered these remarks on November 5, 2018, in
     Cape Girardeau, MO. A transcript can be accessed at https://factba.se/transcript/
     donald-trump-speech-maga-rally-cape-girardeau-mo-november-5-2018.

22   Bowden, J. (2019, April 27). Trump praises Lou Dobbs in WaPo profile: "He
     really gets the word out." *The Hill*. Retrieved from https://thehill.com/homenews/

media/440963-trump-praises-lou-dobbs-in-wapo-profile-he-really-gets-the-word-out.

23   Bennett, A. (2019, December 24). President Trump Tweetstorm—Christmas Eve Edition. *Deadline*. Retrieved from https://deadline.com/2019/12/trump-tweetstorm-christmas-eve-edition–1202816862/.

24   realDonaldTrump. (2019, December 19). Jesse (Watters), this is the best year any President has ever had, plus we get an impeachment. @greggutfeld The Five @ FoxNews [tweet] Retrieved from https://twitter.com/realdonaldtrump/status/1207 808421275275264?lang=en.

25   realDonaldTrump. (2019, January 5). Jobs up big, plus 312,000. Record number working. Manufacturing best in 20 years (Previous administration said this could not happen). Hispanic unemployment lowest ever. Dow plus 747 (for day). @DRUDGE_REPORT [tweet] Retrieved from https://twitter.com/ realDonaldTrump/status/1081717108176752640.

26   realDonaldTrump. (2019, January 5). The last three years of Trump policy have finally brought real hope and real change. Unemployment this year hit a 50 year low. With President Trump we've seen the lowest EVER African American and Hispanic unemployment. The booming Trump Economy has pushed up workers wages.... [tweet] Retrieved from https://twitter.com/realdonaldtrump/status/1168 493185758355456?lang=en.

27   realDonaldTrump. (2019, January 5). No President in modern times has kept more promises than Donald Trump! Thank you Bill Bennett @ SteveHiltonx [tweet] Retrieved from https://twitter.com/realDonaldTrump/ status/1087213958950465536.

28   Gingrich, N. (2017). *Understanding Trump*. New York City, NY: Center Street.

29   Pleat, Z. (2019, March 8). Trump misquoted Fox host Stuart Varney—and Varney thanked him for it. *Media Matters*. Retrieved from https://www.mediamatters.org/ fox-friends/trump-misquoted-fox-host-stuart-varney-and-varney-thanked-him-it.

30   GovChristie. (2017, November 29). @POTUS has done more to combat the addiction crisis than any other President. [tweet] Retrieved from https://twitter. com/govchristie/status/935955740103249922.

31   Staff. (2018, February 6). Fox & Friends guest: The Trump administration has been "three of the greatest years since maybe Jesus walked the Earth with his ministry." *Media Matters*. Retrieved from https://www.mediamatters.org/fox-friends/fox-friends-guest-trump-administration-has-been-three-greatest-years-maybe-jesus-walked.

32   realDonaldTrump. (2019, August 31). Has anyone noticed that the top shows on @foxnews and cable ratings are those that are Fair (or great) to your favorite President, me! Congratulations to @seanhannity for being the number one show on Cable Television! [tweet] https://twitter.com/realdonaldtrump/status/11678052 41926066176?lang=en.

33 McCarthy, T. (2020, January 21). Lindsey Graham: Senator Who Became Trump's Loudest Impeachment Bulldog. *The Guardian*. Retrieved from https://www. theguardian.com/us-news/2020/jan/21/lindsey-graham-senator-trump-bulldog-impeachment-trial.

34 Kwong, J. (2019, July 19). Lindsey Graham says Donald Trump's not Racist. But called him a "Race-Baiting Bigot" in 2015. Retrieved from https://www.newsweek. com/lindsey-graham-trump-not-racist-tweets–1450060.

35 McCaskill, N. (2016, March 17). Graham: We should have kicked Trump out of the party. *Politico*. Retrieved from https://www.politico.com/blogs/2016-gop-primary-live-updates-and-results/2016/03/lindsey-graham-donald-trump-kicked-out–220402.

36 Lindsey Graham delivered these remarks on February 28, 2020, in North Charleston, SC. A transcript can be accessed at https://www.presidency.ucsb.edu.

37 Givas, N. (2019, October 27). Trump determined to destroy ISIS "unlike anybody I've ever met," Lindsey Graham says. *Fox News*. Retrieved from https://www. foxnews.com/media/lindsey-graham-trump-destroy-isis-determination.

38 Graham, L. (2020, February 4). Republican lawmakers praise President Trump's State of the Union. *Hannity*. Fox News. Retrieved from https://www.foxnews.com/ transcript/republican-lawmakers-praise-president-trumps-state-of-the-union.

39 Sutton, K. (2017, April 19). Lindsey Graham heaps praise on Trump: "I am all in." *Politico*. Retrieved from https://www.politico.com/story/2017/04/lindsey-graham-praises-trump–237361.

40 McCarthy, K. (2020, February 4). House Minority Leader McCarthy: Thanks to Trump, America is winning like never before. *Fox News*. Retrieved from https:// www.foxnews.com/opinion/trump-america-winning-leader-kevin-mccarthy.

41 Perdue, D. (2019, February 5). Interview with Sen. David Perdue. *The Ingraham Angle*. *Fox News*. Retrieved from https://votesmart.org/public-statement/1322069/ fox-news-the-ingraham-angle-transcript-interview-with-sen-david-perdue#. XnVVlohKg2w.

42 Ted Cruz delivered these remarks on October 22, 2018, in Houston, TX. A transcript can be accessed at https://www.presidency.ucsb.edu.

43 SenJohnBarrasso (2020, January 24). Since @realDonaldTrump took office, we've added 7 million new jobs, consumer confidence & the stock market are at all-time highs, & wages have gone up. The president has been doing an excellent job for America & will continue to do so. @NBCNews [tweet] Retrieved from https:// twitter.com/senjohnbarrasso/status/1220816613055901698?lang=en.

44 RepGregWalden (2020, February 28). As I have said before, no president has leaned farther forward to lower the cost of prescription drugs than @ realDonaldTrump! It's time to get a bill to POTUS's desk that lowers drug costs without stifling innovation, H.R. 19 does that. Let's get it done. [tweet] Retrieved from https://twitter.com/repgregwalden/status/1233500995164016641.

45   Ron DeSantis delivered these remarks on October 31, 2018, in Fort Myers, FL. A transcript can be accessed at https://www.presidency.ucsb.edu.

46   Pete Stauber delivered these remarks on June 20, 2018, in Duluth, MN. A transcript can be accessed at https://www.presidency.ucsb.edu.

47   Lou Barletta delivered these remarks on August 2, 2018, in Wilkes-Barre, PA. A transcript can be accessed at https://www.presidency.ucsb.edu.

48   Greg Pence delivered these remarks on January 9, 2020, in Washington, D.C. A transcript can be accessed at www.congress.gov.

49   Mike Kelley delivered these remarks on October 10, 2018, in Erie, PA. A transcript can be accessed at https://www.presidency.ucsb.edu.

50   Cindy Hyde-Smith delivered these remarks at a Trump rally on October 2, 2018, in Southaven, MI. A transcript can be accessed at https://www.presidency.ucsb.edu.

51   Videos of these remarks were captured by CSPAN and are available at https://www.youtube.com/watch?v=qK9Ft80SMmc.

52   Schumer, C. (2020, January 14). ABC. *The View*. Retrieved from https://abcnews.go.com/Politics/pelosi-announces-resolution-vote-send-impeachment-articles-senate/story?id=68260357&cid=social_twitter_abcn.

53   Littleton, C. (2020, March 3). How Nancy Pelosi Emerged as a Media Star and Trump's Most Formidable Foe. *Vanity Fair*. Retrieved from https://variety.com/2020/politics/features/nancy-pelosi-trump-election-2020-democrats-hollywood–1203521090/.

54   RepMaxineWaters. (2019, March 4). Lying Trump said he believes killer Kim Jong-un, that he didn't know what happened to #ottowarmbier. Now he wants to flip the script. No one can believe this unworthy president. He is the most prolific, consistent, good for nothing liar this country has ever experienced. [tweet] Retrieved from https://twitter.com/repmaxinewaters/status/1102771758279606272.

55   RepMaxineWaters. This is the most unpatriotic president that has ever occupied the Oval Office. He doesn't care abt anybody but himself. He's earning money on his golf clubs, hotels, & Trump Org deals while skimming Americans' money, & overusing SecretService to protect him on his many golf trips. [tweet] Retrieved from https://twitter.com/repmaxinewaters/status/1156385210323410945.

56   Impeachment was something that was on the minds of many Americans from the minute President Trump took office. On inauguration day, for example, one headline from the *Washington Post* read: "The Campaign to Impeach President has Begun." Democrats, however, seemed to lack a compelling narrative to take that final step and make the case against Trump. That was until it was revealed that Trump had threatened to withhold military aid to Ukraine in order to coerce Ukrainian president, Volodymyr Zelensky, to announce an investigation into Joe Biden.

57   Nancy Pelosi delivered these remarks on December 18, 2019, in Washington, D.C. A transcript can be accessed at www.congress.gov.

58   Ayanna Pressley delivered these remarks on December 18, 2019, in Washington, D.C. A transcript can be accessed at www.congress.gov

59   Adam Schiff delivered these remarks on November 21, 2019, in Washington, D.C. A transcript can be accessed at www.congress.gov.

60   Adam Schiff delivered these remarks on January 22, 2020, in Washington, D.C. A transcript can be accessed at www.congress.gov

61   Bernie Sanders delivered these remarks on March 2, 2019, in Brooklyn, NY. Retrieved from https://vtdigger.org/2019/03/02/full-text-sen-bernie-sanders-2020-presidential-campaign-kickoff-speech/.

62   Bernie Sanders delivered these remarks on October 31, 2018, in College Park, MDC. Retrieved from https://thehill.com/homenews/campaign/414133-bernie-sanders-calls-trump-most-racist-sexist-homophobic-bigoted-president.

63   BernieSanders. (2019, December 19). Donald Trump is: A pathological liar running the most corrupt administration in history a fraud We will defeat him. #DemDebate. [tweet] Retrieved from https://twitter.com/berniesanders/status/1207830684846428165?lang=en.

64   BernieSanders. (2016, October 4). Our job is to defeat, and defeat badly, the worst candidate for president in the modern history of the United States. [tweet] Retrieved from https://twitter.com/berniesanders/status/783449908003176449?lang=en.

65   PeteButtigieg. (2020, February 12). We won't defeat the most divisive president in modern American history by tearing down anybody who doesn't agree with us 100%. "My way or the highway" politics is the road to reelecting Donald Trump. [tweet] Retrieved from https://twitter.com/petebuttigieg/status/1227764567947849728.

66   Elizabeth Warren delivered these remarks on February 9, 2019, in Lawrence, MA. A transcript can be accessed at https://www.masslive.com/politics/2019/02/read-elizabeth-warrens-2020-announcement-speech.html.

67   KamalaHarris. (2019, November 7). Donald Trump has been the most corrupt, unpatriotic president we've ever had, so it's sad to see the level of desperation congressional Republicans will stoop to to protect him. [tweet] Retrieved from https://twitter.com/kamalaharris/status/1192482210672189440.

68   Kamala Harris delivered these remarks on January 27, 2019, in Oakland, CA. A transcript can be accessed at https://www.ktvu.com/news/transcript-kamala-harris-kicks-off-presidential-campaign-in-oakland.

69   Kimelman, J. (2019, June 27). Full transcript: 2019 Democratic debate Night Two, sortable by topic. *NBC News*. Retrieved from https://www.nbcnews.com/politics/2020-election/full-transcript-2019-democratic-debate-night-two-sortable-topic-n1023601.

70 Kimelman, J. (2019, June 26). Full transcript: 2019 Democratic debate Night One, sortable by topic. *NBC News*. Retrieved from https://www.nbcnews.com/politics/2020-election/full-transcript-first-democratic-primary-debate–2019–n1022816.

71 MikeBloomberg. (2020, February 17). Trump says he created the greatest economy of all time. Turns out, it ranks 6th out of the last 10 presidential terms. Either he's lying, or he doesn't know what he's talking about. Maybe it's both? [tweet] Retrieved from https://twitter.com/mikebloomberg/status/1229524256511471617?lang=en.

72 JoeBiden. (2020, January 5). This is a crisis of Donald Trump's own making. He claimed pulling out of the Iran deal would deter Iranian aggression and result in a better deal. He has failed on both counts. He is the most erratic and incompetent commander in chief we've ever had. [tweet] Retrieved from https://twitter.com/joebiden/status/1213955345372065792?lang=en.

73 JoeBiden. (2019, November 25). @realDonaldTrump, you're a serial liar and the most corrupt president in modern American history. I can hardly wait to take you on. [tweet] Retrieved from https://twitter.com/joebiden/status/1199037535827030023.

74 Biden, J. (2020). Why America Must Lead Again. *Foreign Affairs* (March/April).

75 Joe Biden delivered these remarks on April 29, 2019, in Pittsburgh, PA. A transcript can be accessed at https://www.c-span.org/video/?c4794842/user-clip-joe-biden-campaign-kickoff-speech.

76 Joe Biden delivered these remarks on August 8, 2019, in Des Moines, IA. A transcript can be accessed at https://www.c-span.org/video/?463114-3/vice-president-joe-biden-speaks-iowa-state-fair.

77 Joe Biden delivered these remarks on January 4, 2020, in Vinton, IA. A transcript can be accessed at https://www.c-span.org/video/?467789-1/joe-biden-holds-town-hall-vinton-iowa.

78 Ashford, E. and Kroenig, M. (2020, March 7). What Does Super Tuesday Mean for U.S. Foreign Policy? *Foreign Policy*. Retrieved from https://foreignpolicy.com/2020/03/07/sanders-biden-super-tuesday-2020-election-democrats-its-debatable/.

79 Bryant, N. (2017, March 2). Donald Trump and the end of American exceptionalism? *BBC*. Retrieved from https://www.bbc.com/news/world-us-canada–39133677

80 Sargent, D. (2018, July 23). RIP American exceptionalism, 1776–2018. *Foreign Policy*. Retrieved from Nexis database.

81 Barack Obama delivered these remarks on January 21, 2013, in Washington, D.C. A transcript can be accessed at https://www.presidencoy.ucsb.edu.

Epilogue

1 Quote from Parker, K. (2020, February 4). Trump might be the luckiest president to ever hold office. *Washington Post*. Retrieved from https://www.washingtonpost.com/opinions/trump-won-the-iowa-caucuses-and-impeachment/2020/02/04/327c45c4-47a0-11ea-ab15-b5df3261b710_story.html

2 Quote from Bergen, P. (2020, March 2). Coronavirus crisis underlines eight of Trump's failings as a leader. *CNN*. Retrieved from https://www.cnn.com/2020/03/02/opinions/trump-failings-coronavirus-opinions-bergen/index.html

3 Quote from Von Drehle, D. (2020, March 6). Trump's luck is turning against him. *Washington Post*. Retrieved from https://www.washingtonpost.com/opinions/trumps-luck-is-turning-against-him/2020/03/06/f365b982-5fdd-11ea-b29b-9db42f7803a7_story.html

4 Quote from Goldberg, N. (2020, May 14). Trump has come up with the worst campaign slogan ever. *LA Times*. Retrieved from https://www.latimes.com/opinion/story/2020-05-14/trump-transition-to-greatness-worst-slogan

5 Quote from Graham, D. A. (2020, May 26). Trump's new campaign slogan is a confession of failure. *The Atlantic*. Retrieved from https://www.theatlantic.com/ideas/archive/2020/05/transition-to-greatness-is-a-confession-of-failure/612073

6 Campaign email sent to supporters on June 18, 2019.

7 Donald Trump delivered these remarks on June 18, 2019 in Orlando, FL. A transcript can be accessed at https://www.presidency.ucsb.edu.

8 Mike Pence delivered these remarks on August 26, 2020 at the Republican National Convention in Washington, DC. A transcript can be accessed at https://www.cnn.com/2020/08/26/politics/mike-pence-speech-transcript/index.html

9 Donald Trump delivered these remarks on October 12, 2020 in Orlando, FL. A transcript can be accessed at https://www.presidency.ucsb.edu.

10 Donald Trump delivered these remarks on November 1, 2020 in Rome, GA. A transcript can be accessed at https://www.presidency.ucsb.edu.

11 realDonaldTrump. (2020, November 3). Get out & VOTE! Under my Administration, our ECONOMY is growing at the fastest rate EVER at 33.1%. Next year will be the GREATEST ECONOMIC YEAR in American History! [tweet] Retrieved from https://twitter.com/realDonaldTrump/status/1323725991148167171

12 realDonaldTrump. (2020, November 11). I am pleased to announce that I have given my full support and endorsement to Ronna McDaniel to continue heading the Republican National Committee (RNC). With 72 MILLION votes, we received more votes than any sitting President in U.S. history – and we will win! Retrieved from https://twitter.com/realDonaldTrump/status/1326673766915641345

13 Campaign email sent to supporters on November 15, 2020.

Selected Bibliography

Bacevich, A. J. (2008). *The limits of power: The end of American exceptionalism*. New York, NY: Macmillan.

Banda, K. K. (2016). Issue ownership, issue positions, and candidate assessment. *Political Communication*, 33(4), 651–66.

Benoit, P. J. (1997). *Telling the success story: Acclaiming and disclaiming discourse*. Albany, NY: SUNY Press.

Benoit, W. L. (2001). The functional approach to presidential television spots: Acclaiming, attacking, defending 1952–2000. *Communication Studies*, 52(2), 109–26. doi: 10.1080/10510970109388546.

Benoit, W. L. (2007). Own party issue ownership emphasis in presidential television spots. *Communication Reports*, 20(1), 42–50.

Benoit, W. L., Blaney, J. R., & Pier, P. M. (2000). Acclaiming, attacking, and defending: A functional analysis of US nominating convention keynote speeches. *Political Communication*, 17(1), 61–84.

Bercovitch, S. (2012). *The American jeremiad*. Madison, WI: University of Wisconsin Press.

Bostdorff, D. M. (2003). George W. Bush's post-September 11 rhetoric of covenant renewal: Upholding the faith of the greatest generation. *Quarterly Journal of Speech*, 89(4), 293–319.

Cheney, D., Cheney, R. B., & Cheney, L. (2016). *Exceptional: Why the world needs a powerful America*. New York, NY: Simon and Schuster.

Colbert, S. (2012). *America again: Re-becoming the greatness we never weren't*. New York, NY: Grand Central Publishing.

Colley, D. F. (2018). Of twit-storms and demagogues: Trump, illusory truths of patriotism, and the language of the twittersphere. In M. Lockhart (Ed.) *President Donald Trump and his political discourse* (pp. 33–51). New York, NY: Routledge.

Crawford, J. T., & Bhatia, A. (2012). Birther Nation: Political conservatism is associated with explicit and implicit beliefs that President Barack Obama is foreign. *Analyses of Social Issues and Public Policy*, 12(1), 364–76. doi: 10.1111/j.1530-2415.2001.01279.x.

Crockett, C. E. (2012). *A murder of crows: America's raucous right-wing*. Bloomington, IN: Xlibris Corporation.

Domke, D., & Coe, K. (2010). *The god strategy: How religion became a weapon in America* (p. 53). Oxford, UK: Oxford University Press.

Edwards, J. A. (2008). *Navigating the post-Cold War world: President Clinton's foreign policy rhetoric.* Lanham, MD: Lexington Studies in Political Communication.

Edwards, J. A. (2011). Contemporary conservative constructions of American exceptionalism. *Journal of Contemporary Rhetoric,* 1, 40–54.

Edwards, J. A. (2012). Review essay: An exceptional debate: The championing of and challenge to American exceptionalism. *Rhetoric and Public Affairs,* 15, 351–67.

Edwards, J. A. (2014). Resetting America's role in the world: Barack Obama's rhetoric of (re)conciliation and partnership. In J. Mercieca and J. Vaughn (Eds) *The rhetoric of heroic expectations: Establishing the Obama presidency* (pp. 130–50). College Station, TX: Texas A&M University Press.

Edwards, J. A. (2018). Make America great again: Donald Trump and the redefining of the U.S. role in the world. *Communication Quarterly,* 66, 176–95.

Edwards, J. A., & Weiss, D. (2011). *The rhetoric of American exceptionalism: Critical essays.* Jefferson, NC: McFarland & Company.

Fukuyama, F. (1992). *The end of history and the last man.* New York, NY: Free Press.

Gilmore, J. (2014). Translating American exceptionalism: Presidential discourse about the United States in comparative perspective. *International Journal of Communication,* 9(22), 2416–37. Retrieved from http://ijoc.org.

Gilmore, J. (2015). American exceptionalism in the American mind: Presidential discourse, national identity, and U.S. public opinion. *Communication Studies,* 66(3), 301–20.

Gilmore, J., & Rowling, C. M. (2017). The United States in decline?: Assessing the impacts of international challenges to American exceptionalism. *International Journal of Communication,* 11(21), 137–57.

Gilmore, J., & Rowling, C. M. (2018a). Lighting the beacon: Presidential discourse, American exceptionalism, and public diplomacy in global contexts. *Presidential Studies Quarterly,* 48(2), 271–91.

Gilmore, J., & Rowling, C. M. (2018b). A post-American world? Assessing the cognitive and attitudinal impacts of challenges to American exceptionalism. *The Communication Review,* 21(1), 46–65.

Gilmore, J., & Rowling, C. M. (2019). Partisan patriotism in the American presidency: American exceptionalism, issue ownership, and the age of Trump. *Mass Communication and Society,* 22(3), 389–416.

Gilmore, J., Sheets, P., & Rowling, C. (2016). Make no exception, save one: American exceptionalism, the American presidency, and the age of Obama. *Communication Monographs,* 83(4), 505–20.

Gilmore, J., Rowling, C. M., Edwards, J. A., & Allen, N. T. (2020). Exceptional "we" or exceptional "me"? Donald Trump, American exceptionalism and the remaking of the modern jeremiad. *Presidential Studies Quarterly.* Advance Online Publication. https://doi.org/10.1111/psq.12657

Gingrich, N. (2011). *A nation like no other: Why American exceptionalism matters.* New York, NY: Simon and Schuster.

Gingrich, N. (2017). *Understanding Trump.* New York City, NY: Center Street.

Hart, R. P. (2009). *Campaign talk: Why elections are good for us.* Princeton, New Jersey: Princeton University Press.

Hasher, L., Goldstein, D., & Toppino, T. (1977). Frequency and the conference of referential validity. *Journal of Verbal Learning and Verbal Behavior,* 16(1), 107–12.

Hayden, C. (2011). Beyond the "Obama effect": Refining the instruments of engagement through U.S. public diplomacy. *American Behavioral Scientist,* 55(6), 784–802.

Hayes, D. (2005). Candidate qualities through a partisan lens: A theory of trait ownership. *American Journal of Political Science,* 49(4), 908–23.

Hodgson, G. (2009). *The myth of American exceptionalism.* New Haven, CT: Yale University Press.

Jendrysik, M. S. (2002). The modern jeremiad: Bloom, Bennett, and Bork on American decline. *The Journal of Popular Culture,* 36(2), 361–83.

Jendrysik, M. S. (2008). *Modern Jeremiahs: Contemporary visions of American decline.* Lanham, MD: Lexington Books.

Johannesen, R. L. (1986). Ronald Reagan's economic jeremiad. *Communication Studies,* 37(2), 79–89.

Kalmoe, N. P., & Gross, K. (2016). Cueing patriotism, prejudice, and partisanship in the age of Obama: Experimental tests of US flag imagery effects in presidential elections. *Political Psychology,* 37(6), 883–99.

Kohut, A., & Stokes, B. (2006). *America against the world: How we are different and why we are disliked.* New York, NY: Times Books.

Krauthammer, C. (1990). The unipolar moment. *Foreign Affairs,* 70(1), 23–33.

Lipset, S. M. (1996). *American exceptionalism: A double-edged sword.* New York, NY: W. W. Norton.

Lockhart, C. (2003). *The roots of American exceptionalism.* New York, NY: Palgrave Macmillan.

Madsen, D. L. (1998). *American exceptionalism.* Jackson, MS: University Press of Mississippi.

Manheim, J. B. (1991). *All of the people, all of the time: Strategic communication and American politics.* Armonk, NY: M. E. Sharpe.

Mason, D. S. (2009). *The end of the American century.* Lanham, MD: Rowman & Littlefield Publishers.

McCriskin, T. B. (2003). *American exceptionalism and the legacy of Vietnam: US foreign policy since 1974.* Basingstoke, Hampshire: Palgrave Macmillan.

McEvoy-Levy, S. (2001). *American exceptionalism and US foreign policy: Public diplomacy at the end of the cold war.* Basingstoke, Hampshire: Palgrave.

Mudde, C., & Kaltwasser, C. R. (2017). *Populism: A very short introduction.* Oxford, UK: Oxford University Press.

Müller, J. W. (2016). *What is populism?* Philadelphia, PA: University of Pennsylvania Press.

Murphy, J. M. (1990). "A time of shame and sorrow": Robert F. Kennedy and the American jeremiad. *Quarterly Journal of Speech*, 76(4), 401–14.

Murray, S., Stanley, M., McPhetres, J., Pennycook, G., & Seli, P. (2020, January 15). "I've said it before and I will say it again": Repeating statements made by Donald Trump increases perceived truthfulness for individuals across the political spectrum. *PsyArxiv Preprint*. https://doi.org/10.31234/osf.io/9evzc.

Pease, D. E. (2009). *The new American exceptionalism*. Minneapolis, MN: University of Minnesota Press.

Pennycook, G., Cannon, T. D., & Rand, D. G. (2018). Prior exposure increases perceived accuracy of fake news. *Journal of Experimental Psychology: General*, 147(12), 1865.

Petrocik, J. R. (1996). Issue ownership in presidential elections, with a 1980 case study. *American Journal of Political Science*, 40(3), 825–50.

Petrocik, J. R., Benoit, W. L., & Hansen, G. J. (2003). Issue ownership and presidential campaigning, 1952–2000. *Political Science Quarterly*, 118(4), 599–626.

Restad, H. (2017). American exceptionalism. In F. Moghaddam (Ed.) *The SAGE encyclopedia of political behavior* (pp. 25–7). Thousand Oaks, CA: SAGE Publications, Inc.

Restad, H. E. (2014). *American exceptionalism: An idea that made a nation and remade the world*. New York, NY: Routledge.

Restad, H. E. (2019). Whither the "City upon a Hill"? Donald Trump, America first, and American exceptionalism. *Texas National Security Review*, 3(1), 62–92.

Restad, H. E. (2020). What makes America great? Donald Trump, National identity, and U.S. foreign policy. *Global Affairs*, 6(1), 21–36.

Ritter, K. W. (1980). American political rhetoric and the jeremiad tradition: Presidential nomination acceptance addresses, 1960–1976. *Communication Studies*, 31(3), 153–71.

Rojecki, A. (2008). Rhetorical alchemy: American exceptionalism and the war on terror. *Political Communication*, 25(1), 67–88. doi: 10.1080/10584600701807935.

Romney, M. (2010). *No apology: The case for American greatness*. New York, NY: St. Martin's Press.

Rowland, R. C. (2019). The populist and nationalist roots of Trump's rhetoric. *Rhetoric and Public Affairs*, 22(3), 343–88.

Saito, N. T. (2010). *Meeting the enemy: American exceptionalism and international law*. London: New York University Press.

Söderlind, S., & Carson, J. T. (Eds) (2011). *American exceptionalisms: From Winthrop to Winfrey*. New York, NY: SUNY Press.

Trump, D. J. (2015). *Crippled America: How to make America great again*. New York, NY: Simon and Schuster.

Trump, D. J., & Schwartz, T. (2009). *Trump: The art of the deal*. New York, NY: Ballantine Books.

Tulis, J. K. (2017). *The rhetorical presidency New Edition* (Vol. 31). Princeton, NJ: Princeton University Press.

Valenzano, J. M., & Edwards, J. A. (2014). Exceptionally distinctive: President Obama's complicated articulation of American exceptionalism. In A. Bareto and R. O'Bryant (Eds) *American identity in the age of Obama* (pp. 175–97). New York, NY: Routledge.

Van Engen, A. C. (2020). *City on a hill: A history of American exceptionalism.* New Haven, CT: Yale University Press.

Zakaria, F. (2011). *The post-American world: Release 2.0.* New York, NY: W. W. Norton.

Index